THE UNIVERSITY OF CHICAGO PUBLICATIONS
IN RELIGIOUS EDUCATION

Edited by

SHAILER MATHEWS   THEODORE G. SOARES
W. C. BOWER

HANDBOOKS OF ETHICS AND RELIGION

This series of Handbooks is intended to set forth in a readable form the results of the scientific study of religion and ethics. The various authors do not undertake to embody in any detail the processes which lie back of their conclusions. Such technical treatment is more appropriate for works of a strictly scientific character than for those intended not only to be used as textbooks and collateral reading in colleges and theological seminaries, but also to be of help to general readers. The volumes all seek to conserve the values of past religious experience. While each author is free to present his own conclusions, the entire series has the common characteristic of historical method. The editors have not prescribed any rigorous uniformity of treatment, but believe that the individuality of treatment will serve to stimulate thought and discussion. It is hoped that the series will help to show that the method of experiment and criticism contributes to stronger religious faith and moral idealism.—THE EDITORS.

A Bibliographical Guide to
the History of Christianity

A Bibliographical Guide to the History of Christianity

COMPILED BY S. J. CASE, J. T. McNEILL, W. W. SWEET
W. PAUCK, M. SPINKA

EDITED BY S. J. CASE

Εἰ ξένος κόσμου ὁ μὴ γνωρίζων τὰ ἐν αὐτῷ ὄντα οὐχ ἧττον
ξένος καὶ ὁ μὴ γνωρίζων τὰ γινόμενα.

⸙ ⸙ ⸙

Ἐρχόμενος φέρε καὶ τὰ βιβλία μάλιστα
τὰς μεμβράνας.

NEW YORK
PETER SMITH
1951

PREFACE

This *Guide* offers a careful selection of representative titles rather than an exhaustive bibliographical compilation. It is prepared for the use of students or teachers who desire suggestions as to the chief topics for study and the fundamental literature to use either in obtaining a general and well-proportioned survey of Christian history or in conducting more intensive research within any area chosen for detailed investigation. The divisional grouping of books and the brief explanatory introductions to topics will, it is hoped, serve to indicate the outstanding phases of church history especially deserving of attention, while the appended comments to certain titles will enable the reader to estimate the type and significance of different books within the several divisions. By reference to the more extensive bibliographies in certain volumes mentioned, it ought to be comparatively easy for one using the *Guide* to enlarge almost indefinitely his acquaintance with any single topic that he may select for further research. Thus this handbook may be used to supplement any textbook or outline. Or, if one desires to stimulate greater initiative on the part of the student than is possible by the use of any standard summary of historical information, the *Guide* itself may be made the basal text for a course of study and discussion either in elementary classes or in the early stages of research.

The subject matter has been treated comprehensively. In surveying so large a field as the entire history of Christianity it is not easy to preserve a just proportion

among the several parts. Many books, even when pro-
fessing to cover the whole subject, give chief attention
to the church within the Roman Empire and among the
peoples of Western Europe, while its development in
other parts of the world receives only incidental treatment.
An effort has been made to correct this defect by including, as integral parts of the present work, the history of
Christianity in the Western Hemisphere, its career in
Eastern Europe and Western Asia, and its growth in the
newer fields of Africa, Asia, and the islands of the Pacific.

Five persons have collaborated in assembling and ar-
ranging the titles presented. Although each contributor
is immediately responsible for his particular section, an
effort has been made, by frequent conferences and personal intercourse, to carry on the work in such fashion
as to preserve a unity of design and purpose throughout
the book. Chapters i, ii, iii, and ix have been prepared
by S. J. Case, Professor of the History of Early Christianity and Chairman of the Department of Church History
in the Divinity School of the University of Chicago;
chapters iv and vi have been prepared by J. T. McNeill,
Professor of the History of European Christianity in the
same school; and W. W. Sweet, Professor of the History
of American Christianity, also in the Divinity School, has
prepared chapter viii. Chapter v is by W. Pauck, Professor of Church History in the Chicago Theological
Seminary (affiliated with the Divinity School); and
chapter vii is by M. Spinka, Librarian and Assistant
Professor of the History of Eastern Christianity in the
Chicago Theological Seminary.

THE EDITOR

CHICAGO, ILLINOIS
April 1, 1931

CONTENTS

ABBREVIATIONS

References are to marginal numbers

CHAPTER I

INTRODUCTION

In modern times the study of history has become a rigorous scientific procedure. The search for documents and other sources of information, the critical examination of the records, and the problem of reconstructing from them the life-story of the movements and persons whom they represent, impose upon the historian today a very exacting task. At the outset he seriously considers questions of method in his study, he uses and evaluates the work of predecessors in the field, he seeks the largest possible acquaintance with the source materials, and he equips himself with every available aid for the evaluation and interpretation of data.

The history of Christianity is a particular phase of general history. Consequently the methods pursued by modern research in an effort to make historical inquiry more scientific and efficient are of very immediate concern to one who studies the history of the Christian movement, which has been closely associated with the political, social, cultural, and spiritual interests of Western civilization for many centuries.

HISTORICAL METHOD
GENERAL

1. **Bernheim, E.** *Lehrbuch der historischen Methode und der Geschichtsphilosophie mit Nachweis der wichtigsten Quellen und Hilfsmittel zum Studium der Geschichte.* Leipzig: Duncker & Humblot, 1889; 5th ed., 1908. x+842 pages. (This is the classic work on historical methodology.)

1

2. **Bleich, E.** "Neuere Schriften zur Methodologie und Philosophie der Geschichte so wie zur Historiographie," *MHL* (Item 144), N.S., XVIII (1930), 25–37.

3. **Feder, A.** *Lehrbuch der geschichtlichen Methode.* 3d ed. Regensburg: Kösel & Pustet, 1924. xvi+372 pages. (The work of a Jesuit scholar with a genius for detail; virtually Bernheim brought down to date.)

4. **George, H. B.** *Historical Evidence.* Oxford: Clarendon Press, 1909. 223 pages. (Aims to "sum up shortly the different sources of information and the principles that should guide the inquirer in estimating their evidential value.")

5. **Johnson, A.** *The Historian and Historical Evidence.* New York: Scribner's, 1926. 179 pages. (A popular presentation suitable for students and general readers.)

6. **Jusserand, J. J., and Others.** *The Writing of History.* New York: Scribner's, 1926. xiii+143 pages.

7. **Langlois, C. V., and Seignobos, C.** *Introduction to the Study of History.* Translated from French. New York: Holt, 1898. xv +350 pages. (Follows the lines of Bernheim but in a more popular form and with somewhat less concern for the "philosophy" of history.)

8. **Robinson, J. H.** *The New History: Essays Illustrating the Modern Historical Outlook.* New York: Macmillan, 1912. 266 pages. (Separate essays several of which deal in a stimulating manner with the methods, aims, and problems of a historian.)

9. **Vincent, J. M.** *Historical Research: An Outline of Theory and Practice.* New York: Holt, 1911. 350 pages. (A systematic presentation with a "Selected Bibliography of Historical Research" on pages 327–39.)

Types of Interpretation
Economic

10. **Sée, H.** *The Economic Interpretation of History.* Translated from French. New York: Adelphi Co., 1930. 154 pages.

11. **Seligman, E. R. A.** *The Economic Interpretation of History.* New York: Macmillan, 1902. ix+166 pages. (A Marxian interpretation; economic interests are thought fundamental.)

GEOGRAPHICAL AND CLIMATIC

12. **Febvre, L.** *A Geographical Introduction to History.* Translated from French. New York: Knopf, 1925. xxv+388 pages. (A standard work.)
13. **George, H. B.** *The Relations of Geography and History.* 4th ed. Oxford: Clarendon Press, 1910. vi+309 pages.
14. **Huntington, E.** *Civilization and Climate.* 3d ed. New Haven: Yale University Press, 1924. xix+453 pages.

SOCIO-PSYCHOLOGICAL

15. **Aubrey, E. E.** "Social Psychology as Liaison between History and Sociology," *AHR* (Item 23), XXXIII (1928), 257-77.
16. **Barnes, H. E.** *The New History and the Social Studies.* New York: Century, 1925. xix+605 pages. (An exponent of "synthetic" history.)

PHILOSOPHICAL

17. **Cheyney, E. P.** *Law in History, and Other Essays.* New York: Knopf, 1927. viii+174 pages. (A group of interpretative essays written over a period of twenty years.)
18. **Croce, B.** *Theory and History of Historiography* (London, 1921) translated from the Italian, is entitled by the American publishers *History: Its Theory and Practice.* New York: Harcourt Brace, 1920. 317 pages. (The philosopher reflects on the nature of history and remarks that thought must start "from the principle that spirit itself is history, maker of history at every moment of its existence, and also the result of all anterior history.")
19. **Sée, H.** *Science et philosophie de l'histoire.* Paris: Alcan, 1928. 513 pages. (Describes and evaluates the chief attempts to formulate a philosophy of history.)
20. **Troeltsch, E.** *Der Historismus und seine Probleme.* Tübingen: Mohr, 1922. xi+777 pages. (A detailed criticism of different philosophies of history in the light of the author's conception of the logic of history.)

RELIGIOUS

21. **McLaughlin, R. W.** *The Spiritual Element in History.* New York: Abingdon Press, 1926. 312 pages.

22. **Mathews, S.** *The Spiritual Interpretation of History.* Cambridge: Harvard University Press, 1916. xiv+227 pages. (Both Mathews and McLaughlin, though in somewhat different ways, stress the religious significance of history.)

The foregoing list of books may be enlarged, and new publications in the field added, by consulting the review sections of standard historical periodicals, e.g.,

23. *American Historical Review,* New York: Macmillan, 1912——. (*AHR*)

24. *English Historical Review,* London: Longmans, 1886——. (*EHR*)

25. *Historische Zeitschrift,* München: Oldenburg, 1859——. (*HZ*)

26. *Revue historique,* Paris: Alcan, 1876——. (*RH*)

STUDY OF CHURCH HISTORY

The newer phases of historical research, particularly the appraisal of psychological, social, cultural, and physical factors in the shaping of a historical movement, and the recognition of these interests as a key to the criticism and interpretation of documents, have not as yet been widely discussed by church historians. Many older general histories of the church in their opening section treat briefly certain questions of definition, procedure, aim, and value, e.g. Alzog, I, 1-24 (Item 43); Schaff, I, 1-27 (Item 101); Kirsch, pp. 1-48 and 766 f. (Item 54).

INTRODUCTIONS

27. **Benigni, U.** *Historiae ecclesiasticae propaedeutica: I. Introductio in historiae ecclesiasticae scientiam.* Rome: Pustet, 1905. xv+145 pages. (Written to advance historical study among the Italian clergy.)

28. **Collins, W. E.** *The Study of Ecclesiastical History.* London: Longmans, 1903. xv+166 pages. (Along the lines of Bernheim, or Langlois and Seignobos; good selected bibliographies.)

29. **Guilday, P.** *An Introduction to Church History: A Book for Beginners.* St. Louis, Missouri: Herder, 1925. vii+350 pages. (Prepared primarily for Roman Catholics, but generally useful.)

30. **Smedt, C. de.** *Introductio generalis ad historiam ecclesiasticam.* Louvain: Fonteyn; Paris: Palmé, 1876. xiii+533 pages. (The work of a Jesuit scholar who attempted to furnish a complete bibliographical guide.)

METHOD OF TREATMENT

31. **Case, S. J.** *Evolution of Early Christianity* (Item 361), chaps. i and ii; *Social Origins of Christianity* (Item 362), chap. i; also "Historical Study of Religion," *JR* (Item 150), I (1921), 1–17; "Rehabilitation of Church History in Ministerial Education" and "Religious Meaning of the Past," *ibid.*, IV (1924), 225–42 and 576–91. (Stresses the social approach in the study of history and the importance of viewing and estimating the past in terms of the situations, interests, and activities of real people.)

32. **Emerton, E.** "Definition of Church History," *ASCH* (Item 348) 2d Ser., VII (1925), 55–68. ("Church History is nothing more nor less than one chapter in that continuous record of human affairs to which we give the name of history in general.")

33. **Nichols, R. H.** "Aims and Methods of Teaching Church History," *ASCH* (Item 348) 2d Ser., VII (1925), 37–51.

34. **Schubert, H. v.** *Die heutige Auffassung und Behandlung der Kirchengeschichte.* Tübingen: Mohr, 1902. iv+33 pages. (Would go beyond the usual interest in institutions and dogma, and treat Christianity as a phase of the history of civilization.)

PERIODIZING

35. **Below, G. v.** *Die historischen Periodisierungen mit besonderem Blick auf die Grenze zwischen Mittelalter und Neuzeit.* Berlin: Deutsche Verlagsgesellschaft für Politik und Geschichte, 1925. 108 pages.

36. **Heussi, K.** *Altertum, Mittelalter und Neuzeit in der Kirchengeschichte.* Ein Beitrag zum Problem der historischen Periodisierung. Tübingen: Mohr, 1921. 68 pages.

37. **Seeberg, E.** *Über Bewegungsgesetze der Welt- und Kirchengeschichte,* 1, 4. Berlin: Deutsche Verlagsgesellschaft für Politik und Geschichte, 1924. iv+25 pages. (Would make two periods, one the Hellenizing, when Christianity was subject to a fundamentally primitive tendency to sublimate sacramental religion,

and, second, the reforming and intellectualizing period with an interest in returning to the prophetic, personal, and ethical type of early Christian spirituality.)

EVALUATION

38. "Christianity and History," *Modern Churchman* (Item 152), XVIII (1928), 281–514. (Papers read at the Fifteenth Conference of Modern Churchmen.)

39. **Dibelius, M.** *Geschichte und übergeschichtliche Religion im Christentum.* Göttingen: Vandenhoeck & Ruprecht, 1925. iv +173 pages. (An effort to distinguish the transitory from the permanent in Christianity; republished in 1929 under the title *Evangelium und Welt.*)

40. **Faulkner, J. A.** *On the Value of Church History.* New York: Methodist Book Concern, 1920. 50 pages. (An edifying pamphlet.)

41. **Köhler, W.** *Idee und Persönlichkeit in der Kirchengeschichte.* Tübingen: Mohr, 1910. 103 pages. (Motto is "Back to Hegel.")

42. **Schaff, P.** *What Is Church History? Vindication of the Idea of Historical Development.* Philadelphia: Lippincott, 1846. 128 pages. (Still a very suggestive little book along the lines of the Hegelian philosophy of history. Christianity is "in its inmost nature a genesis, movement, process, development . . . . the evolution of God's plan of redemption, proceeding according to rational and necessary laws.")

CHAPTER II

HISTORY OF CHRISTIANITY IN GENERAL

The student's introduction to the history of Christianity is, perhaps, most conveniently effected by the use of one of the numerous outlines or more comprehensive manuals available in various languages. But one who seeks thorough knowledge will early cultivate an acquaintance with standard comprehensive works. A helpful perspective will be acquired by surveying the older writings on the history of Christianity. Dictionaries and encyclopedias are frequently of great value in furnishing detailed information on a wide range of subjects. Also, bibliographical collections are very helpful tools of research, while periodicals are necessary as a means of keeping in touch with new investigation and current literature. A desire for greater specialization will lead one to read books that deal with specific phases of Christianity, such as missionary activities, organization, and the like. The real specialist will, of course, study original sources and concentrate his efforts on some limited area or chosen topic of investigation, suggestions for which are provided in subsequent chapters of this *Guide*.

OUTLINES AND MANUALS

43. **Alzog, J.** *Manual of Universal Church History.* 4 vols. Translated from German. Dublin: Gill, 1874. (Often reprinted and much used; a substantial product of Roman Catholic scholarship.)

44. **Bartlet, J. V., and Carlyle, A. J.** *Christianity and History: A Study of Religious Development.* London: Macmillan, 1917.

7

xix+613 pages. (An interpretation rather than a syllabus, but substantial in content.)

45. **Clarke, C. P. S.** *A Short History of the Christian Church.* London: Longmans, 1929. xiii+532 pages. (A conservative Anglican survey popularly presented.)

46. **Funk, F. X.** *A Manual of Church History.* 2 vols. Translated from German. New York: Benziger, 1914. (Much detail, with abundant references to original sources and to modern Catholic authorities.)

47. **Guggenberger, A.** *A General History of the Christian Era.* 3 vols. 15th ed. St. Louis, Missouri: Herder, 1925. (Designed for use in Catholic Colleges and for the general reader.)

48. **Guignebert, C.** *Christianity, Past and Present.* Translated from French. New York: Macmillan, 1927. xxvi+507 pages. (A spirited review of the course of Christianity's history; mainly a criticism of Roman Catholicism.)

49. **Hase, K. A.** *Kirchengeschichte: Lehrbuch zunächst für akademische Vorlesungen.* 10th edition. Leipzig: Breitkopf & Härtel, 1877. xxii+774 pages. (English translation from the 7th German edition: *A History of the Christian Church.* New York: Appleton, 1855. xxxvii+720 pages.) (Reliable and comprehensive.)

50. **Hergenröther, J.** *Handbuch der allgemeinen Kirchengeschichte.* 4 vols. Freiburg: Herder, 1925. (This is a 6th edition with bibliographical supplements by J. P. Kirsch; see Item 54.)

51. **Heussi, K.** *Kompendium der Kirchengeschichte.* 6th ed. Tübingen: Mohr, 1928. xxxii+482 pages. (An outline that has been much used.)

52. *History of Christianity in the Light of Modern Knowledge.* A collective work. New York: Harcourt, Brace, 1929. xxii+780 pages. (Twenty-two writers; the various sections are uneven in quality and lacking in proportion; some excellent parts for the earlier period.)

53. **Jacobs, C. M.** *The Story of the Church.* Philadelphia: United Lutheran Publication House, 1925. 422 pages. (An outline from end of first to close of nineteenth century.)

54. **Kirsch, J. P., and Others.** *Kirchengeschichte.* 4 vols. (in progress). Freiburg: Herder, 1930———. (Vol. I, *Die Kirche*

in der antiken griechisch-römischen Kulturwelt, and Vol. IV, 1, *Die Kirche im Zeitalter des Individualismus 1648 bis zur Gegenwart, 1648 bis 1800*, appeared late in 1930. For detailed information, comprehensive grasp of the subject, and wide acquaintance with its literature, this product of Roman Catholic scholarship is especially valuable. Essentially a new edition of No. 50.)

55. **Krüger, G., and Others.** *Handbuch der Kirchengeschichte für Studierende.* 2 (4) vols., with a Register. Tübingen: Mohr, 1912–13. (A very compact summary of data and literature; a new edition of the first two parts appeared in 1923–29.)

56. **Kurtz, J. H.** *Lehrbuch der Kirchengeschichte für Studierende.* 14th ed. 2 vols. Leipzig: Neumann, 1906. English translation from the 7th German edition: *Text-Book of Church History.* 2 (1) vols. Philadelphia: Nelson S. Quiney, 1881. (Once widely used; still valuable.)

57. **Loofs, F.** *Grundlinien der Kirchengeschichte in der Form von Dispositionen für seine Vorlesungen.* 2d ed. Halle a. S.: Niemeyer, 1910. xxvi+430 pages. (Especially useful for teachers.)

58. **Marion, L.** *Histoire de l'église.* 8th ed., revised by V. Lacombe. 4 vols. Paris: Roger & Chernoviz, 1922. (A popular Roman Catholic manual.)

59. **Moeller, W.** *History of the Christian Church.* 3 vols. Translated from German. London: Swan Sonnenschein, 1892–1900. (Encyclopedic information; carries the history down to 1648.)

60. **Müller, K.** *Kirchengeschichte.* 2 (3) vols. Tübingen: Mohr, 1892–1902. (Presents a readable account with a modicum of bibliography. A new edition of the first half of Volume I was completed in 1929.)

61. **Nagler, A. W.** *The Church in History.* New York: Abingdon Press, 1929. (A rapid sketch of the outward history of the church is followed by a more elaborate treatment of "institutions and movements.")

62. **Newman, A. H.** *A Manual of Church History.* 2 vols. Philadelphia: American Baptist Publication Society, 1900–1903. (A compact body of information.)

63. **Schubert, H. v.** *Outlines of Church History.* Translated from German. London: Williams & Norgate, 1907. x+399 pages. (Brief but reliable account unencumbered by notes and bibliographies. There is a 9th edition in German: *Grundzüge der Kirchengeschichte.* Tübingen: Mohr, 1928.)

64. **Sohm, R.** *Outlines of Church History.* Translated from German. London: Macmillan, 1895. xii+260 pages. (A vigorous presentation by one who saw in the church a development from a sacramental to a corporate consciousness.)

65. **Walker, W.** *History of the Christian Church.* New York: Scribner's, 1918. 630 pages. (Compressed information about dates, persons, events, doctrines, and practices.)

66. **Wellhausen, J.; Jülicher, A.; Harnack, A.; and Others.** *Geschichte der christlichen Religion. Mit Einleitung: Die israelitischjüdische Religion.* 2d ed. Leipzig: Tuebner, 1909. x+792 pages. (Accurate, comprehensive interpretation, with bibliographical summaries. The work constitutes Teil I, Abteilung IV. i, of "Die Kultur der Gegenwart" edited by P. Hinneberg.)

HISTORY OF CHURCH HISTORIOGRAPHY
GENERAL SURVEYS

67. **Baur, F. C.** *Die Epochen der kirchlichen Geschichtschreibung.* Tübingen: Fues, 1852. xii+269 pages. (A survey of the history of church historiography interpreted from the Hegelian postulates of thesis, antithesis and synthesis.)

68. **Fueter, E.** *Geschichte der neueren Historiographie.* Munich: Oldenbourg, 1911. xx+626 pages. (General, but suggestive for study of church history.)

69. **Gooch, G. P.** *History and Historians in the Nineteenth Century.* 3d impression. London: Longmans, 1920. iv+604 pages. (Includes writers on Christianity.)

70. **Guilday, P.** (editor). *Church Historians.* New York: P. J. Kenedy, 1926. vii+430 pages. (Essays and brief bibliographies by various Roman Catholic writers on Eusebius, Orosius, Bede, Odericus, Vitalis, Las Casas, Baronius, Bollandus, Muratori, Möhler, Lingrad, Hergenröther, Janssen, Denifle, Ludwig von Pastor.)

71. **Kirsch, J. P.** "History, Ecclesiastical," (*CE* Item 112), VII, 372–80. (Roman Catholic, but includes Protestant writers.)

72. **Koehler, W.** "Kirchengeschichte: I. Kirchengeschichtsschreibung," *RGG* (Item 136), Vol. III, cols. 886–96. (A summary Protestant account, with bibliography.)

73. **Leclercq, H.** "Historiens du christianisme," *DACL* (Item 124), Vol. VI, cols. 2533–2735. (Full statistical account with literature to the year 1920; Roman Catholic.)

74. **Plummer, A.** "Historians, Ecclesiastical," *DCB* (Item 115), III, 107–12. (Careful survey to about 800, by an Anglican scholar.)

75. **Shotwell, J. T.** *Introduction to the History of History.* New York: Columbia University Press, 1922. xii+339 pages. (Has sections on "Jewish History" and "Christianity and History.")

76. **Stäudlin, C. F.** *Geschichte und Literatur der Kirchengeschichte.* xii+376 pages. Hannover: Hahn, 1827. (Still the most complete account of writing on church history up to the beginning of the nineteenth century; posthumously edited by J. T. Hemsen.)

77. **Völker, K.** *Die Kirchengeschichtsschreibung der Aufklärung.* Tübingen: Mohr, 1921. vii+92 pages.

Pre-Reformation Historians of Christianity
Eastern Writers

The earliest attempt to record the story of Christianity as a movement in history is the two-volume work, Luke-Acts. But the oldest extant treatise specifically known as a "church history" is that of Eusebius of Caesarea, who died about 340 A.D., and this interest was perpetuated by a succession of church historians in the East who continued to write Greek.

78. **Cadbury, H. J.** *The Making of Luke-Acts.* New York: Macmillan, 1927. x+385 pages.

79. **Laqueur, R.** *Eusebius als Historiker seiner Zeit.* Berlin: De Gruyter, 1929. x+227 pages.

80. **Lawlor, H. J.** *Eusebiana: Essays on the Ecclesiastical History of Eusebius.* London: Frowde, 1912. 316 pages.

81. Articles "Eusebius," "Evagrius," "Philostorgius," "Socrates," "Sozomen," "Theodoret," etc., in dictionaries and encyclopedias (Items 111–37).

82.   Latin Christians had relatively slight interest in the past of Christianity and were content with translations made from Greek originals. These they sometimes condensed and extended by adding later chronicles. But aside from Augustine's *City of God* and Orosius' history of the world to the year 430 (A.D.), the Latin church showed little taste for either the interpretation or the study of history in general. In this field one should consult the articles "Cassiodorus," "Orosius," "Rufinus," "Sulpicius Severus," in the dictionaries and encyclopedias (Items 111–37).

83.   Prior to the Reformation new historical writing in Western Christendom was mainly local and annalistic. An idea of the extent and content of this type of work may be obtained by consulting the encyclopedias for representative names like Gregory of Tours, Jordanes, Bede, the "Anglo-Saxon Chronicle," Isidore of Seville, Paul the Deacon, Adam of Bremen, Oderic Vital, Otto of Freising, Matthew of Paris, William of Tyre—to mention only representative chroniclers, annalists, biographers, and local historians of the time.

PROTESTANT CHURCH HISTORIANS

The Reformation movement produced a lively interest in the study of Christianity's past. In the main the reformers were concerned to show that the Catholic church as an institution, and particularly the alleged supremacy of the papacy, represented a perversion of true Christianity; while Catholic scholars were equally ready to defend the historical validity of their institution. In surveying the writers of this period, a chronological, rather than an alphabetical, order is followed.

84. **Flacius, Matthias Illyricus, and Others.** *Ecclesiastica historia, etc.* Basel: Oporinus, 1559–1574. (Thirteen volumes, each covering a century of Christian history. This work, commonly called the "Magdeburg Centuries," is bitterly anti-papal; also strongly pro-Lutheran and antagonistic toward both Melanchthon and Calvin.)

85. **Hottinger, J. H.** *Historia ecclesiastica Novi Testamenti.* 9 vols. Zurich: Hamberger, 1561–1667. (The Reformed equivalent of the "Magdeburg Centuries.")

86. **Arnold, G.** *Unpartheiische Kirchen- und Ketzerhistorie.* 4 vols. Frankfurt: Fritsch, 1699–1715. (The first church history written in German; the work of a pietist and mystic, who looked with disfavor on ecclesiastical authority, whether Catholic or Protestant. See further, E. Seeberg, *Gottfried Arnold, die Wissenschaft und die Mystik seiner Zeit.* Meerane i. Sa.: E. R. Herzog, 1923. 611 pages.)

87. **Mosheim, J. L. v.** *Institutiones historiae ecclesiasticae antiquae et recentioris.* Helmstädt: Weygand, 1764. (English translation by A. Maclaine: *An Ecclesiastical History, Ancient and Modern, etc.* 6 vols. Philadelphia: S. C. Ustick, 1797–98. A better translation by J. Murdock, *Institutes of Ecclesiastical History.* 3 vols. New York: Stanford & Swords, 1832; 5th ed., 1854.) (Follows the century plan but is less polemical than earlier Protestant works.)

88. **Schröckh, J. M.** *Christliche Kirchengeschichte.* 45 vols. Leipzig: Schwickert, 1768–1812. (Treats the subject by natural periods of division rather than by centuries; marks an advance in scientific method.)

89. **Henke, H. P. C.** *Allgemeine Geschichte der christlichen Kirche.* 9 vols. Braunschweig: Verlag der Schulbuchhandlung, 1788–1820. (Well documented, critical, representing the rationalistic school of the early nineteenth century.)

90. **Gibbon, E.** *History of the Decline and Fall of the Roman Empire.* Edited in 7 vols. by J. B. Bury. London: Methuen, 1896. (This work, the first instalment of which appeared in 1775, is virtually a history of Christianity for the first fifteen centuries. The ecclesiastical historians lamented the neglect of the supernatural in Gibbon's interpretation, but his diligence in using the literary sources has made his work a classic.)

91. **Milner, J.** *History of the Church of Christ, with Additions and Corrections by Isaac Milner.* Revised and continued to the close of the Reformation by George Stokes. 6 vols. London: Religious Tract Society, 1895. (Represents evangelical

Anglican scholarship at the beginning of the nineteenth century. The first edition of 4 volumes was published in 1794–1812; "genuine piety" said the author, "is the only thing I intend to celebrate.")

92. **Haweis, T.** *An Impartial and Succinct History of the Rise, Declension and Revival of the Church of Christ from the Birth of our Saviour to the Present Time.* 3 vols. London: Mawman, 1800. (A leader in the interdenominational movement to found the London Missionary Society wrote "to soften down all asperities of controversy.")

93. **Neander, A.** *Allegemeine Geschichte der christlichen Religion und Kirche.* 6 vols. in 11 parts. Hamburg: Perthes, 1825–52. (English translation by J. Torrey: *General History of the Christian Religion and Church.* 5 vols. and Index. Boston: Houghton Mifflin, 1871–81.) (Knowledge and piety were combined in an effort "to exhibit the history of the Church of Christ as a living witness to the divine power of Christianity.")

94. **Priestley, J.** *A General History of the Christian Church.* 6 vols. Northumberland, Pennsylvania: Andrew Kennedy, 1802–3. (A popular exposition by a learned Nonconformist minister who also gained fame as a chemist; he explains that he is the first "unitarian" church historian; also this appears to have been the first general history of Christianity to be written and published in America.*

95. *NOTE.—After suffering severely for both his religious and his political liberalism, Priestley migrated to America in 1794, and the last decade of his life was spent at Northumberland, Pennsylvania, where the author devoted himself to completing his church history, the first two volumes of which had been published in 1790. This earlier work was revised and four more volumes were composed, and the work was dedicated to Thomas Jefferson, president of the United States, who is praised as the champion of religious as well as civil liberty. On such matters as early church government and the "essence" of Christianity, the author presented views not unlike those of Hatch and Harnack, advanced nearly a century later. He had a high regard for the learning of Fleury (Item 106),

whom he used extensively, and for Mosheim (Item 87); but he
sharply criticized the latter for following the "artificial and
unnatural" division by centuries, and he deplored the "artful
insinuations" of Gibbon (Item 90). Mosheim, translated by
a Scotch minister in Holland, had just been brought out in
America and was adjudged by Priestley to be the book "most
read by Protestants" and to possess many merits in spite of
some serious defects which Priestley aimed to correct. But
one can readily understand that this new work would not
appeal to that age as a proper substitute for the more traditional type of church history. Mosheim continued to be
popular in America, especially in the new translation of Murdock. The history of Milner, imported from England, was in
use especially in the 744-page abridgment of J. Townsend
published at Utica in 1816. Another English book made available for American readers during this period was G. Gregory's
History of the Christian Church, revised by M. Ruter. (Cincinnati: Roff & Young, 1832, iv+637 pages). Then came the
first translation of Gieseler, made by F. Cunningham: *Text-
Book of Ecclesiastical History.* (3 vols.; Philadelphia: Carey,
Lea & Blanchard, 1836), superseded by H. B. Smith's translation twenty years later (Item 98).

96. **Matter, J.** *Histoire universelle de l'église chrétienne.* 4 vols.
Strasbourg: Silbermann, 1829–35. (The work of a professor
at Strasbourg; significant for French Protestantism.)

97. **Baur, F. C.** *Geschichte der christlichen Kirche.* 5 vols. Tübing-
en: Fues, 1853–63. (This work, the later volumes of which
were written by the author's son, and E. Zeller, marks the
beginning of a new period of criticism and method in the
study of church history.)

98. **Gieseler, J. C. L.** *Lehrbuch der Kirchengeschichte.* 5 vols.
Bonn: Marcus, 1824–56. (American translation by H. B.
Smith: *Text-Book of Church History.* 4 vols. New York:
Harper, 1857–61.) (Well documented; objective treatment of
subject.)

99. **Hagenbach, K. R.** *Kirchengeschichte von der ältesten Zeit bis
zum 19. Jahrhundert.* 7 vols. Leipzig: Hirzel, 1869–72. (An
exponent of evangelical theology at Basel.)

100. **Chastel, E. L.** *Histoire du christianisme depuis son origine jusqu'à nos jours.* 5 vols. Paris: Fischbacher, 1881–83. (A Reformed theologian and professor at Geneva, stressed the advantages of separation between church and state.)

101. **Schaff, P.** *History of the Christian Church.* 7 (8) vols. Vol. V by D. S. Schaff. New York: Scribner's, 1882–1910. (The author is thoroughly acquainted with sources and modern literature, and interprets the history in much the same temper as Neander [Item 93].)

Post-Reformation Roman Catholic Historians

The work of Flaccius and his helpers aroused Roman Catholic scholars to defend their ecclesiastical institution by an appeal to history. Several refutations of the Protestant attack appeared (see *DACL* [Item 124], Vol. VI, cols. 2614 f.) before Cardinal Baronius (Item 102) began the publication of his new history of the church conceived on the same broad program as that of the "Centuries" and written on the basis of much sound historical learning. The study of general church history among Roman Catholics now received a new impetus and underwent a rapid development. The following writers are listed chronologically.

102. **Baronius, C.** *Annales ecclesiastici.* 12 vols. Rome: Vatican, 1588–93. (Helpers and successors continued the work. By 1759 it had grown into 34 volumes, to which were added 1 volume of apparatus and 2 volumes of tables.)

103. **Godeau, A.** *Histoire de l'église, depuis la naissance de Jésus-Christ jusqu'au fin du IX siècle.* 5 vols. Paris, 1653–78. (A French popularization of Baronius.)

104. **Bossuet, J. B.** *Discours sur l'histoire universelle.* Paris: Le-doux, 1681. (While not so much a church history as a philosophy of history, this treatise and other writings of Bossuet are so important for understanding the historical problems of that day, such as the relation between the papacy and the state, and the possible reunion of Protestants and Catholics, that an acquaintance with this author is essential for the student of Christian historiography. The "second part" of Bossuet's work, *The Continuity of Religion*, has recently ap-

peared in English translated by Victor Day. Helena: Victor Day, 1930. xvi+233 pages.)

105. **Tillemont, S. de.** *Memoires pour servir à l'histoire ecclésiastique.* 16 vols. Paris: Robustel, 1693–1712. (The last 12 volumes were published after the author's death; not strictly a history but a laborious assembling of texts strung together to cover the period to 513 A.D.; valuable for documentation.)

106. **Fleury, C.** *Histoire ecclésiastique.* 20 vols. Paris: Marin, 1691–1720. (Originally to 1414; carried to 1594 in 16 more volumes by J. C. Fabre, 1726–37; re-edited with a 4-volume Index by Rondet, 1769–74. The work in whole or in part has been widely translated; the latest English rendering was by J. H. Newman in 3 volumes [Oxford, 1842–44]. Fleury was a vigorous exponent of Gallicanism against the Italian party in the Catholic church.)

107. **Rohrbacher, R. F.** *Histoire universelle de l'église catholique.* 29 vols. Nancy, 1842–49. (Also many later editions and translations into different languages. Through its use the ultra-montane interest gained pre-eminence over the Gallican influence of Fleury [Item 106].)

108. **Darras, J. E.** *Histoire générale de l'église, depuis la création jusqu'à nos jours* (twelfth century), continued by J. Bareille and J. Fèvre. 44 vols. Paris, 1862–89.

109. *Dictionnaire de l'histoire universelle de l'église, embrassant ... l'histoire des idées, des faits, des actes, des personnages, etc., que appartiennent aux annales de l'église depuis la naissance de Notre-Seigneur Jésus-Christ jusqu'au temps present.* 6 vols. *MTET* (Item 130), Vols. LI–LVI. (A vast compilation of statistical information.)

110. **Mourret, F.** *Histoire générale de l'église.* 9 vols. Paris: Bloud, 1909–25. (Comes down to 1903; interprets church history comprehensively, as including dogma, organization, liturgy, biographical narrative, and similar aspects of Christian activities and interests; not unlike the manuals of Alzog, Funk, Hergenröther, Marion, and Kirsch, mentioned above.) (In English translation: *A History of the Catholic Church*, Vol. V. St. Louis, Missouri: Herder, 1930. Other volumes to follow.)

DICTIONARIES AND ENCYCLOPEDIAS

111. *Catholic Dictionary.* By W. E. Addis and T. Arnold, revised by T. B. Scannell. 6th ed. London: Kegan Paul, 1903. viii+961 pages.

112. *Catholic Encyclopedia.* By C. G. Herbermann and Others. 17 vols. (including Index and Supplement.) New York: Encyclopedia Press, 1907–22. (*CE*)

113. *Cyclopedia of Biblical, Theological, and Ecclesiastical Literature.* By J. M'Clintock and J. Strong. 12 vols. (including Supplement). New York: Harper, 1867–91.

114. *Dictionary of Christian Antiquities.* By W. Smith and S. Cheetham. 2 vols. London: Murray, 1875–80.

115. *Dictionary of Christian Biography, Literature, Sects and Doctrines.* By W. Smith and H. Wace. 4 vols. London: Murray, 1877–87. (Covers first eight centuries of Christianity. Published in an abbreviated form for first six centuries by W. C. Piercy and H. Wace. London: Murray, 1911. xii+1028 pages.) (*DCB*)

116. *Dictionary of Ecclesiastical Terms: Being a History and Explanation of Certain Terms Used in Architecture, Ecclesiology, Liturgiology, Music, Ritual, Cathedral Constitution, etc.* By J. S. Bumpus. London: Laurie, 1910. 328 pages.

117. *Dictionary of Religion and Ethics.* By S. Mathews and G. B. Smith. New York: Macmillan, 1921. vii+513 pages.

118. *Dictionnaire apologétique de la foi catholique.* By A. d'Alès. 4 vols. 4th ed. Paris: Beauchesne, 1925–28.

119. *Dizionario di erudizione storico-ecclesiastica da S. Pietro sino ai nostri giorni.* By G. Moroni. 109 vols. (including 6 vols. of indexes). Venice: Emiliana, 1840–79.

120. *Encyclopedia of Religion and Ethics.* By J. Hastings. 13 vols. (including Index). Edinburgh: Clark, 1917–27. (*ERE*)

121. *Encyclopédie des sciences ecclésiastiques.* Published by Letouzey in Paris, a product of the best Roman Catholic scholarship and embracing five series of dictionaries as follows:

122. (1) *Dictionnaire de la Bible.* By F. Vigouroux. 5 (10) vols., with Supplement in progress. 1894——.

123. (2) *Dictionnaire de théologie catholique.* By A. Vacant, E. Mangenot, and (at present) E. Amann. 1909——. Vols. I–IX (*A–L*) with Index completed in 1929.

124. (3) *Dictionnaire d'archéologie chrétienne et de liturgie.* By F. Cabrol and H. Leclercq. 1903——. Vols. I–VIII (A–*Lexique*) completed in 1930. (*DACL*)

125. (4) *Dictionnaire d'histoire et de géographie ecclésiastiques.* By A. de Meyer and E. van Cauwenbergh. Vol. I had reached "Athaulf" in 1930.

126. (5) *Dictionnaire de droit canonique.* By A. Villien, E. Magnin, and (now) A. Amanieu. 1924——. Vol. I had reached "Anathème" in 1926.

127. *Encyclopédie des sciences religieuses.* By F. Lichtenberger. 13 vols. Paris: Fischbacher, 1877–82. (Represents Protestant scholarship.)

128. *Encyclopédie théologique, ou série de dictionnaires sur toutes les parties de la science religieuse.* Edited by J. P. Migne. 50 (52) vols. Paris: Migne, 1844–49. (*MET*). Continued in:

129. *Nouvelle encyclopédie théologique.* 52 (53) vols. 1851–55. (*MNET*). Further continued in:

130. *Troisième et dernière encyclopédie théologique.* 67 vols. 1855–73. (*MTET*). (For a student who has the patience and skill to separate the gold from the dross, this mine of older uncritical Roman Catholic erudition in 172 volumes [Items 128–30] may still be worked with much profit.)

131. *Kirchliches Handlexikon.* By C. Mensel and Others. 7 vols. Leipzig: Naumann, 1887–1902. (A work of Lutheran scholars.)

132. *Lexikon für Theologie und Kirche.* By K. Hofmann and M. Buchberger. Freiburg: Herder, 1930——. (New edition in progress; 2 volumes published; Roman Catholic.)

133. *New Schaff-Herzog Encyclopedia of Religious Knowledge.* By S. M. Jackson and Others. 12 vols. (including an appendix). New York: Funk & Wagnalls, 1908–12. (Based on the older *PRE* [Item 135].)

134. *Protestant Dictionary.* By C. H. H. Wright and C. Neil. xv+832 pages. London: Hodder & Stoughton, 1904.

135. *Realencyklopädie für protestantische Theologie und Kirche.* By J. J. Herzog and re-edited by A. Hauck. 3d ed. 24 vols. (including 2 supplementary vols). Leipzig: Hinrichs, 1896–1913. (Represents critical Protestant scholarship.) (*PRE*)

136. *Religion in Geschichte und Gegenwart.* By H. Gunkel and L. Zscharnack. 2d extensively revised edition. 5 vols. Tübingen: Mohr, 1927——. (In 1930 complete to end of Volume IV; general, but with much attention to Christianity; Protestant.) (*RGG*)

137. *Wetzer und Westes Kirchenlexikon, oder Encyklopädie der katholischen Theologie und ihrer Hülfswissenschaft.* Begun by J. Hergenröther and continued by F. Kaulen. 12 vols. and Register. Freiburg: Herder, 1882–1903. (Roman Catholic.)

BIBLIOGRAPHIES

138. *Bibliographisches Beiblatt der theologischen Literaturzeitung.* Leipzig: Hinrichs, 1922——. (An excellent guide; see Item 157.)

139. **Bratke, E.** *Wegweiser zur Quellen- und Litteratur-Kunde der Kirchengeschichte.* Gotha: Perthes, 1890. vii+282 pages. (Useful, but not complete.)

140. *Bulletin de littérature ecclésiastique.* Paris: Lathielleux, 1899——. (A publication of the Catholic Institute of Toulouse.)

141. *Dictionnaire de bibliographie catholique, présentant l'indication et les titres complets de tous les ouvrages qui ont été publiés dans les trois langues grecque, latine, et française depuis la naissance du christianisme, en tous pays, mais principalement en France.* 6 vols. Paris: Migne, 1858–66. (*MTET* [Item 130], Vols. XXXIX–XLIV.)

142. *Die evangelische Theologie, ihr jetziger Stand und ihre Aufgaben.* Teil 3: *Die Kirchengeschichte:* (1) *Allgemeines, Die alte Kirche, Das Mittelalter;* (2) *Die Reformation und Gegenreformation,* by G. Krüger; (3) *Die Neuzeit,* by L. Zscharnack. Halle (Salle): Buchhandlung des Waisenhauses, 1928–30. Classification and critical evaluation of the more recent books in all languages.)

143. **Krüger, G.** "Literature on Church History," *HTR* (No. 149), XIV (1921), 283–374; XV (1922), 323–405; XVII (1924), 1–49, 265–95; XVIII (1925), 129–85. (A classified catalogue and brief appraisal of literature that appeared in

Germany, Austria, Switzerland, Holland, and the Scandinavian countries during the years 1914–20.)

144. *Mitteilungen aus der historischen Literatur*. Berlin: Weidmann, 1873———. (General, but includes church history.) (*MHL*)

145. *RHE* (Item 163), *II. Bibliographie*. (Comprehensive list and detailed classification; see particularly the supplementary *Tables générales* published in 1928.)

146. *Theologischer Jahresbericht*. Tübingen: Mohr, 1866–1915. (Thorough survey of all theological literature for the period.)

PERIODICALS

IN ENGLISH

147. *Catholic Historical Review*. Washington: Catholic University of America, 1915———. (The official organ of the American Catholic Association.)

148. *Church Quarterly Review*. London: Society for Promoting Christian Knowledge, 1876———. (This standard Anglican period has always given attention to historical subjects.)

149. *Harvard Theological Review*. Cambridge: Harvard University Press, 1908———. (Sponsored by the Faculty of Theology in Harvard University.) (*HRT*)

150. *Journal of Religion*. Chicago: University of Chicago Press, 1921———. (Continues the *American Journal of Theology*.) (*JR*)

151. *Journal of Theological Studies*. Oxford: Clarendon Press, 1900———. (Represents highly technical scholarship with emphasis on the earlier period of church history.)

152. *Modern Churchman*. Oxford: Blackwell, 1911———. (Represents Anglican modernism; gives attention to church history.)

153. *Review of the Churches: A Constructive Quarterly*. London: E. Benn, 1924–30. (Published in the interests of church union, but reviews a wide range of books.) (*RC*)

154. *Social Science Abstracts*. Menasha, Wisconsin, 1929———. (Summarizes articles on church history.)

155. *Theology: A Monthly Journal of Historic Christianity*. London: Society for Promoting Christian Knowledge, 1920———.

In German

156. *Römische Quartalschrift für christliche Altertumskunde und für Kirchengeschichte.* Freiburg: Herder, 1903——. (Edited by members of the Catholic Theological Faculty at Tübingen.)

157. *Theologische Literaturzeitung.* Leipzig: Hinrichs, 1876——. (Founded by the liberal Protestant scholars, E. Schürer and A. von Harnack; notices consistently books on church history.)

158. *Theologisches Literaturblatt.* Leipzig: Dörffling & Franke, 1880——. (Represents Lutheran scholarship; covers literature on church history.)

159. *Theologische Revue.* Münster: Aschendorff, 1902——. (Sponsored by the Catholic Theological Faculty at Münster.)

160. *Theologische Rundschau.* Tübingen: Mohr, 1897–1916; 1929——. (Surveys books on church history; a liberal Protestant point of view.)

161. *Zeitschrift für Kirchengeschichte.* Gotha: Perthes, 1877——. (At present represents the German Protestant Society of Church History.) *ZK*)

In French

162. *Études.* Paris, 15 Rue Monsieur, 1862——. (General in scope, but primarily historical in interest; a work of Jesuit scholarship.)

163. *Revue d'histoire ecclésiastique.* Louvain: Bureaux de la Revue, 1900——. (A publication of the Catholic University of Louvain.) (*RHE*)

164. *Revue d'histoire et de littérature religieuses.* Paris: Nourry, 1896–1922. (Represented the modernist scholarly interest of A. Loisy.)

165. *Revue d'histoire et de philosophie religieuses.* Strasbourg: Bureaux de la Revue, 1921——. (An organ of the Faculty of Protestant Theology in the University of Strassbourg.)

In Dutch

166. *Nederlandsch Archief voor Kerkgeschiedenis.* The Hague: Nijhoff, 1902——. (Published under various titles since 1829; XXII [1929], 219–82, furnishes an index covering a hundred-year period.)

167. *Acta apostolicae sedis: Commentarium officiale.* Rome: Vatican, 1909——.

168. *"Gregorianum": Commentarii de re theologica et philosophica.* Rome: Gregorian University, 1920——. (Mainly interested in dogma, but in its historical aspects.)

169. *Ricerche religiose.* Roma: Via Giulio Alberoni, 7, 1925. (Conducted by the modernist, E. Buonaiuti; devoted particularly to historical studies.)

170. *Rivista di archeologia cristiana.* Rome: Pontificio instituto di archeologia cristiana, 1924——. (Published under varying titles since 1863; along with valuable archaeological information, this authoritative Catholic periodical contains classified annotated bibliographies relating to the whole field of church history.) (*RAC*)

SPECIFIC PHASES OF CHRISTIANITY

Certain prominent items in the general history of Christianity have been studied separately, but for their intensive investigation one needs to consult the more detailed literature listed below on different periods of the history. In general, Roman Catholics view Christianity as fundamentally the story of the establishment and perpetuation of the ecclesiastical institution, particularly the papacy. One branch of Protestantism similarly emphasizes the institution, with especial interest in the episcopacy; while other groups attach chief importance to the history of dogma. Certain phases of activity, like missionary propaganda, social amelioration, or other forms of the common Christian enterprise, have in more recent years also attracted the attention of the historian.

NATURE OF ECCLESIASTICAL INSTITUTIONS

171. **Baur, F. C.** *Der Gegensatz des Katholizismus und Protestantismus nach den Principien und Hauptdogmen der beiden Lehrbegriffe.* Tübingen: Fues, 1834. viii+439 pages.

172. **Harnack, A.** *What Is Christianity?* Translated from German, *Das Wesen des Christentums.* London: Williams & Norgate, 1901. vii+301 pages.

173. **Headlam, A. C.** *The Doctrine of the Church and Christian Re-union.* London: Murray, 1920. xii+326 pages.
174. **Loisy, A.** *The Gospel and the Church.* Translated from French. New York: Scribner's, 1909. xxii+277 pages.
175. **Mozley, J. R.** *The Divine Aspect of History.* 2 vols. Cambridge: University Press, 1916. (The Christian society, in the author's opinion, is sprung from the teaching of Jesus Christ, to whom it has been true, yet it has been liable to error.)
176. **Newman, J. H.** *Essays on the Development of Christian Doctrine.* London: Longmans, 1845. xvi+445 pages. (This famous treatise has been frequently reprinted.).
177. **Sabatier, A.** *Religions of Authority and the Religion of the Spirit.* Translated from French. New York: Hodder & Stoughton, 1904. xxxii+410 pages.
178. **Simpson, P. C.** *Church Principles.* London: Hodder & Stoughton, 1923. 208 pages.
179. **Simpson, W. J. Sparrow.** *The Catholic Conception of the Church.* London: Scott, 1914. x+244 pages.
180. **Sohm, R.** *Wesen und Ursprung des Katholizismus.* 2d ed. Leipzig: Teubner, 1912. xxxiv+68 pages.

ORGANIZATION
GENERAL

181. **Allen, A. V. G.** *Christian Institutions.* New York: Scribner's, 1897. xxi+577 pages. (Includes also a survey of the history of dogma and of worship.)
182. **Cohu, J. R.** *The Evolution of the Christian Ministry.* London: Murray, 1918. x+128 pages.
183. **Gore, C.** *The Church and the Ministry.* London: Longmans, 1900. xxiii+393 pages. (Many reprintings.)
184. **Mason, A. J.** *The Church of England and Episcopacy.* Cambridge: University Press, 1914. ix+560 pages.
185. **Thompson, R. E.** *The Historic Episcopate.* Philadelphia: Westminster Press, 1910. vii+317 pages.

PAPACY

186. **Bell, Mary, I. M.** *A Short History of the Papacy.* London: Methuen, 1921. xii+390 pages.

187. **Caspar, E.** *Geschichte des Papsttums von dem Anfang bis zur Höhe der Weltherrschaft.* Vol. I, *Römische Kirche und Imperium Romanum.* Tübingen: Mohr, 1930. xv+633 pages. (Three more volumes of this important study are promised.)

188. **Chevé, C. F.** *Dictionnaire des papes, ou histoire complète de tous les souverains pontifes.* Paris: Migne, 1857 (*MTET*, [Item 130], Vol. XXXII.)

189. **Duchesne, L.** *Liber pontificalis.* 2 vols. Paris: Thorin, 1886–92. (Includes text, introduction, and commentary. There is an English translation of the *Book of the Popes* to the year 590, by Louise R. Loomis. New York: Columbia University Press, 1916. xxii+169 pages.)

190. **Krüger, G.** *The Papacy: The Idea and Its Exponents.* Translated from German. New York: Putnam's, 1909. 277 pages.

191. **Mirbt, C.** *Quellen zur Geschichte des Papsttums und des römischen Katholizismus.* 4th ed. Tübingen: Mohr, 1924. xxxii+650 pages. (Bibliography, pp. xxix–xxxii.)

192. **Mourret, F.** *La papauté.* 7th ed. Paris: Bloud, 1929. 205 pages.

SYNODS AND COUNCILS (SEE ITEM 508)

193. **Hefele, C. J.** *A History of the Councils of the Church.* Translated from German. 5 vols. Edinburgh: Clark, 1871–96. (New French edition, continued under editorship of H. Leclercq, *Histoire des conciles.* Paris: Letouzey, 1907——.) (Had reached Vol. IX [18] in 1930; extensive citations of literature.)

194. **Landon, E. H.** *A Manual of Councils of the Holy Catholic Church.* Rev. ed. 2 vols. Edinburgh: Grant, 1909.

195. **Mansi, J. D.** *Sacrorum concilorum.* 31 vols. Florence and Venice, 1759–81; publication resumed and continued Paris: Welter, 1901——.

CHURCH LAW (SEE ITEMS 698–705)

196. *Archiv für katholisches Kirchenrecht.* Mainz, 1857——.

197. "Canon Law Studies." A series of monographs. Washington, D. C.: Catholic University of America, 1916——. (Fifty-five numbers had appeared up to 1929.)

198. *Deutsche Zeitschrift für Kirchenrecht.* Berlin, 1861——. (Full in its surveys of literature.)

199. *Dictionnaire alphabétique, théorique et pratique de droit civil ecclésiastique.* Andre. 2 vols. Paris: Migne, 1873. (*MTET* [Item 130], Vols. LXIV, LXV.)

200. **Hinschius, P.** *System des katholischen Kirchenrechts.* 6 vols. Berlin: Guttentag, 1869–97.

201. *Revue catholique des institutions et droit.* (Société de jurisconsultes et de publicistes.) Lyons: Grenoble, 1872——.

202. **Sehling, E.** *Kirchenrecht I.* 2d ed. Berlin: De Gruyter, 1922. 119 pages. (A compact little book in "Sammlung Göschen"; see page 4 for literature. See also Item 943.)

203. **Sohm, R.** *Kirchenrecht.* 2 vols. Leipzig: Duncker & Humbolt, 1892–1923.

WORSHIP (SEE ITEMS 181, 495–502, 660, 665)

204. **Agrain, R.** *Liturgia: Encyclopédie populaire des connaissances liturgiques.* Paris: Bloud, 1930. 1,141 pages.

205. **Batiffol, P.** *History of the Roman Breviary.* Translated from the 3d French edition. London: Longmans, 1912. xvi+341 pages.

206. **Baudot, L.** *Le bréviaire.* Paris: Bloud, 1929. 171 pages. Also *The Roman Breviary, Its Sources and History.* London: Catholic Truth Society, 1909.

207. **Bishop, E.** *Liturgia historica: Papers on the Liturgy and Religious Life of the Western Church.* Oxford: Clarendon Press, 1918. xiv+506 pages.

208. **Braun, J.** *Liturgisches Handlexikon.* 2d ed. Freiburg: Herder, 1924. 399 pages.

209. **Casel, O.** *Jahrbuch für Liturgiewissenschaft.* Münster: Aschendorff, 1921——. (Has full lists of literature.)

210. **Clarke, C. C.** *Handbook of the Divine Liturgy: A Brief Study of the Historical Development of the Mass.* London: Kegan Paul, 1910. xiv+180 pages.

211. "Ecclesia orans." Edited by J. Herwegen. Freiburg: Herder, 1918——. (A series embracing 17 volumes up to 1930.)

212. **Fortescue, A.** *The Mass: A Study of the Roman Liturgy.* London: Longmans, 1912. xii+458 pages.

213. **Heiler, F.** *The Spirit of Worship: Its Forms and Manifestations in the Christian Churches.* Translated from German. London: Hodder & Stoughton, 1926. xv+214 pages.

214. **Lefebvre, G.** *Catholic Liturgy: Its Fundamental Principles.* Translated from French. New York: Benziger, 1929. xvii+294 pages.

215. **Macalister, A. S.** *Ecclesiastical Vestments.* London: Stock, 1896. xvi+270 pages. (Bibliography, pp. 258–61.)

216. **Richard, J. W., and Painter, F. V. N.** *Christian Worship: Its Principles and Forms.* 2d ed. Philadelphia: Lutheran Publication Society, 1908. viii+368 pages.

217. **Thalhofer, V.** *Handbuch der katholischen Liturgik.* 2d ed. by L. Eisenhofer. 2 vols. Freiburg: Herder, 1912.

218. **Walsh, J.** *The Mass and Vestments of the Catholic Church.* New York: Benziger, 1916. xvi+479 pages.

MUSIC (SEE ITEMS 1896, 1900)

219. **Agrain, R.** *Le musique religieuse.* Paris: Bloud, 1929. 204 pages.

220. **Chevalier, U.** *Reportorium hymnologicum. Catalogue des chants, hymnes, proses, sequences, tropes en usage dans l'église latine depuis les origines jusqu'à nos jours.* 4 vols. Louvain: Ceuterick, 1892–1912.

221. **Dickinson, E.** *Music in the History of the Western Church.* New York: Scribner's, 1902. ix+462 pages. Also *Study of the History of Music.* 2d ed. Scribner's, 1905. xv+415 pages.

222. *Dictionary of Hymnology, Setting Forth the Origin and History of Christian Hymns of All Ages and Nations.* Rev. ed. by J. Julian. London: Murray, 1908. xviii+1,768 pages.

223. **Leclercq, H.** Article "Hymnes" in *DACL* (Item 124), Vol. VI, cols. 2826–2928. (Extensive bibliography.)

224. **Mearns, J.** *Canticles of the Christian Church.* Cambridge: University Press, 1914. viii+105 pages. Also *Early Latin Hymnaries: An Index of Hymns and Hymnaries before 1100.* Same publisher, 1913. xx+107 pages.

225. **Ortigue, J. d'.** *Dictionnaire liturgique, historique et théorique de plain-chant et de musique de l'église au moyen âge et dans les*

temps modernes. Paris: Migne, 1853. (*MNET* [Item 129], Vol. XXIX.)

226. **Pérennès, F.** *Dictionnaire de noëls et de cantiques.* Paris: Migne, 1867. (*MTET*, Vol. LXIII.)

PREACHING (SEE ITEMS 666-68)

227. **Dargan, E. C.** *A History of Preaching.* 2 vols. New York: Hodder & Stoughton, 1905-11.

228. **Garvie, A. E.** *The Christian Preacher.* Edinburgh: Clark, 1920. xxvii+490 pages. (Part I to page 271 deals with the history of preaching.)

229. **Hering, H.** *Geschichte der Predigt.* Berlin: Reuther & Reichard, 1897. iv+253 pages.

SPECIAL CULT DEVELOPMENTS

230. **Baring-Gould, S.** *The Lives of the Saints.* 17 vols. Rev. ed. Edinburgh: Grant, 1914.

231. **Braun, J.** *Der christliche Altar in seiner geschichtlichen Entwicklung.* 2 vols. with 371 plates. Munich: Koch, 1924.

232. **Bréhier, L.** *L'art chrétien. Son développement iconographique dès origines à nos jours.* 2d ed. Paris: Laurens, 1928. 480 pages, 290 figures, and 16 plates.

233. **Bünger, F.** *Geschichte der Neujahrsfeier in der Kirche.* Göttingen: Vandenhoeck & Ruprecht, 1911. 151 pages.

234. **Dumaine, H.** *Le dimanche chrétien, ses origines, ses principaux caractères.* Brussels: Société d'études religieuses, 1922. vii+130 pages.

235. **Gwynne, W.** *The Christian Year: Its Purpose and Its History.* London: Longmans, 1915. xiv+143 pages.

236. **Herzog, G.** *La Sainte Vierge dans l'histoire.* Paris: Nourry, 1908. 163 pages.

237. **Hirn, Y.** *The Sacred Shrine: A Study of Poetry and Art of the Catholic Church.* London: Macmillan, 1912. xviii+574 pages.

238. **Holweck, F. G.** *Biographical Dictionary of the Saints.* St. Louis, Missouri: Herder, 1924. xxix+1,053 pages.

239. **Kellner, H.** *Heortologie, oder die geschichtliche Entwicklung des Kirchenjahres und die Heiligenfeste von den ältesten Zeiten bis zur Gegenwart.* 3d ed. Freiburg: Herder, 1911. xv+318 pages.

240. **Kraus, F. X.** *Geschichte der christlichen Kunst.* 2 (3) vols. Freiburg: Herder, 1896–1908.

241. **Miles, C. A.** *Christmas in Ritual Christian and Pagan.* London: Unwin, 1913. 400 pages.

242. **Seymour, W. W.** *The Cross in Tradition, History and Art.* New York: Putnam's, 1898. xxx+489 pages. (Extensive bibliography on pages xxi–xxx; also many illustrations.)

243. **Usener, H.** *Religionsgeschichtliche Untersuchungen.* 2d ed. by H. Lietzmann. Bonn: Cohen, 1911. xx+390 pages. (Chaps. i–iii, "Das Weihnachtsfest.")

DOCTRINE

GENERAL HISTORIES OF DOGMA (SEE ALSO ITEMS 503–9, 1160 f., 1221)

244. **Allen, A. V. G.** *The Continuity of Christian Thought.* 4th ed. Boston: Houghton Mifflin, 1894. xviii+438 pages.

245. **Baur, F. C.** *Lehrbuch der christlichen Dogmengeschichte.* Stuttgart: Becher, 1847. xvi+288 pages. (This book initiated a new stage in the study of dogma; for a more elaborate treatment, see his *Vorlesungen über die christliche Dogmengeschichte*, 3 [4] vols., edited by F. F. Baur. Leipzig: Fues, 1865–67.)

246. **Fisher, G. P.** *History of Christian Doctrine.* New York: Scribner's, 1896. xv+583 pages.

247. **Grandmaison, L. de.** *Le dogme chrétien, sa nature, ses formules, son développement.* Paris: Beauchesne, 1928. vi+332 pages. (A Jesuit interpretation.)

248. **Harnack, A. v.** *Lehrbuch der Dogmengeschichte.* 4th ed. 3 vols. Tübingen: Mohr, 1909–20. (Dogma is defined as a work of the Greek spirit on the basis of the gospel. An English translation in 7 volumes is entitled, *History of Dogma.* London: Williams & Norgate, 1894–1903.)

249. **Loofs, F.** *Leitfaden zum Studium der Dogmengeschichte.* 4th ed. Halle: Neimeyer, 1906. xxiii+1,002 pages.

250. **Matthews, W. R., and Others.** *Dogma in History and Thought.* London: Nisbet, 1929. xi+228 pages.

251. **Seeberg, R.** *Lehrbuch der Dogmengeschichte.* 3d ed. in 4 vols. Leipzig: Deichert, 1917–23. 4th ed. of Vol. III in 1931. Also *Grundriss der Dogmengeschichte.* 5th ed. Leipzig: Deichert,

1927. viii+173 pages. (There is an English rendering: *Text-Book of the History of Doctrines*. 2 vols. Philadelphia: United Lutheran Publishing House, 1905.)

HISTORY OF SELECTED DOCTRINES

252. **Alger, W. R.** *A Critical History of the Doctrine of the Future Life*. 10th ed. Boston: Roberts, 1880. xxii+1,008 pages. (Contains a complete bibliography collected and classified by Ezra Abbot.)

253. **Brown, W. A.** *The Christian Hope: A Study of the Doctrine of the Last Things*. New York: Scribner's, 1912. xi+216 pages.

254. **Cave, S.** *The Doctrine of the Person of Christ*. New York: Scribner's, 1925. 259 pages.

255. **Gwatkin, H. M.** *The Knowledge of God*. 2 vols., Edinburgh, Clark, 1906.

256. **Mackintosh, H. R.** *The Doctrine of the Person of Jesus Christ*. Edinburgh: Clark, 1912. xiv+540 pages.

257. **Mathews, S.** *The Atonement and the Social Process*. New York: Macmillan, 1930. 212 pages.

258. **Ottley, R. L.** *The Doctrine of the Incarnation*. 2d ed. 2 vols. London: Methuen, 1896.

259. **Paine, L. L.** *A Critical History of the Evolution of Trinitarianism*. Boston: Houghton Mifflin, 1900. xi+387 pages.

260. **Pohle, J.** *Mariology. A Dogmatic Treatise on the Blessed Virgin Mary, Mother of God*. Adopted and edited by A. Preuss. 5th ed. St. Louis, Missouri: Herder, 1926. 185 pages.

261. **Rashdall, H.** *The Idea of Atonement in Christian Theology*. London: Macmillan, 1919. xix+502 pages.

262. **Rees, T.** *The Holy Spirit in Thought and Experience*. New York: Scribner's, 1915. ix+221 pages.

263. **Robinson, H. W.** *The Christian Doctrine of Man*. Edinburgh: Clark, 1911. x+365 pages.

264. **Stevens, G. B.** *The Christian Doctrine of Salvation*. New York: Scribner's, 1905. xi+546 pages.

265. **Stone, D.** *History of the Doctrine of the Holy Eucharist*. 2 vols. London: Longmans, 1909.

CREEDS

266. **Briggs, C. A.** *Theological Symbolics.* New York: Scribner's, 1914. x+429 pages.

267. **Curtis, W. A.** *A History of Creeds and Confessions of Faith in Christendom and Beyond.* Edinburgh: Clark, 1911. xix+502 pages.

268. **Lamont, D.** *The Church and the Creeds.* London: Clarke, 1923. 256 pages.

269. **Schaff, P.** *The Creeds of Christendom.* 3 vols. 6th ed. New York: Scribner's, 1890. (Contains exposition, original texts, English translation and extensive bibliographies.)

CHRISTIANITY AND LIBERTY (INTELLECTUAL AND CIVIL)
(SEE ITEMS 803-24)

270. **Bury, J. B.** *A History of Freedom of Thought.* New York: Holt, 1913. 256 pages.

271. **Carlyle, A. J.** *The Christian Church and Liberty.* London: Clarke, 1924. 159 pages.

272. **Draper, J. W.** *The Conflict between Religion and Science.* New York: Appleton, 1862. xxiii+373 pages. (Often reprinted.)

273. **Garvie, A. E.** *Handbook of Christian Apologetics.* New York: Scribner's, 1913. xii+241 pages. (A historical treatment, with bibliographies.)

274. **Luzzatti, L.** *God in Freedom: Studies in the Relation between Church and State.* Translated from Italian. New York: Macmillan, 1930. xxxix+794 pages. (The first Italian edition, published in 1909, was entitled, *La libertà di conscienza e di scienza*).

275. **Ruffini, F.** *Religious Liberty.* Translated from Italian. London: Williams & Norgate, 1912. xxiv+563 pages.

276. **Simpson, J. Y.** *Landmarks in the Struggle between Science and Religion.* New York: Doran, 1926. xiii+288 pages.

277. **Wendland, J.** *Miracles and Christianity.* Translated from German. New York: Hodder & Stoughton, 1911. xv+299 pages.

278. **White, A. D.** *A History of the Warfare of Science with Theology in Christendom.* 2 vols. New York: Appleton, 1896. (Several later editions.)

CHRISTIAN LIVING (ASCETICISM, ETHICS, MONASTICISM)
(SEE ITEMS 527–35, 655, 706 ff.)

279. **Hall, T. C.** *History of Ethics within Organized Christianity.* New York: Scribner's, 1910. xi+605 pages.

280. **Hannah, I. C.** *Christian Monasticism.* New York: Macmillan, 1925. 270 pages.

281. **Heimbucher, M.** *Orden und Kongregation der katholischen Kirche.* 2d ed. 3 vols. Paderborn: Schöningh, 1907.

282. **Lea, H. C.** *History of Sacerdotal Celibacy in the Christian Church.* 2d ed. 2 vols. New York: Macmillan, 1907.

283. **Montrond, M. M. de.** *Dictionnaire des abbayes et monastères, ou histoire des établissements religieux.* Paris: Migne, 1856. (This is *MTET* [Item 130], Vol. XVI; see also *MET* [Item 128], Vols. XX–XXIII, containing the re-edited Helyot's *Histoire des ordres monastiques et militaires.*)

284. **Watkins, O. D.** *A History of Penance.* 2 vols. London: Longmans, 1920.

285. **Ziegler, T.** *Geschichte der christlichen Ethik.* Strassburg: Trübner, 1892. xii+607 pages.

286. **Zöckler, O.** *Askese und Mönchtum.* 2d ed. 2 vols. Frankfurt: Heyder & Zimner, 1897.

CHRISTIAN SOCIAL ACTIVITY (SEE ITEMS 520–26, 772–79)

287. **Doisy, M.** *Dictionnaire d'économie charitable, ou exposé historique, théorique et pratique de l'assistance religieuse, publique et privée, ancienne et moderne.* Paris: Migne, 1855–64. (*MTET* [Item 130], Vols. V–VIII.)

288. **Faris, E., and Others.** *Intelligent Philanthropy.* pp. 25–132. Chicago: University of Chicago Press, 1930.

289. **Gore, C.** *Christ and Society.* New York: Scribner's, 1928. 210 pages.

290. **Liese, W.** *Geschichte der Charitas.* 2 vols. Freiburg: Herder, 1922.

291. **Oliver, E. H.** *The Social Achievements of the Christian Church.* Toronto: Ryerson Press, 1930.

292. **Stead, F. H.** *The Story of Social Christianity.* 2 vols. London: Clarke, 1924.

293. **Troeltsch, E.** *Die Soziallehren der christlichen Kirchen und Gruppen.* Tübingen: Mohr, 1912. xvi+994 pages.
294. **Uhlhorn, G.** *Die christliche Liebestätigkeit.* 3 vols. Stuttgart: Gundert, 1882–90. (Volume I in English: *Christian Charity in the Ancient Church.* Edinburgh: Clark, 1883.)

SPREAD OF CHRISTIANITY (MISSIONS) (SEE ITEMS 365, 543, 615 f., 623–29, 947–54, 1222, 1258, 2263–2303)

295. **Bliss, E. M.** *A Concise History of Missions.* New York: Revell, 1897. 321 pages.
296. **Creighton, Louise.** *Missions, Their Rise and Development.* New York: Holt, 1912. 256 pages.
297. *Encyclopedia of Missions.* Edited by H. O. Dwight and others. 2d ed. New York: Funk & Wagnalls, 1904. xiv+851 pages.
298. **Fabricius, J. A.** *Salutaris lux evangelii toti orbi, etc.* Hamburg: Felgineria, 1731. 766 pages and 234 pages of indexes. (Still important as a historical source.)
299. **Millar, R.** *The History of the Propagation of Christianity, etc.* 2 vols. Edinburgh: Ruddiman, 1723. (Of value for its reproduction of documents.)
300. **Robinson, C. H.** *History of Christian Missions.* New York: Scribner's, 1915. xiv+533 pages.
301. **Ussing, H.** *Illustreret Missionshistorie.* 2d ed. Copenhagen: Gad, 1909. 602 pages.

CHAPTER III

CHRISTIANITY IN THE ROMAN EMPIRE

Intensive historical study rests fundamentally on the acquisition and interpretation of the original sources for the period under consideration. The literary and archaeological remains from which to reconstruct the history of the Christian movement during the early centuries, when it gradually attained a dominant position in the Roman Empire, are relatively abundant and have already been subjected to much diligent investigation, the results of which are now available in an extensive body of literature. An appreciative understanding of Christianity's growth is further conditioned by an acquaintance with the environment, both Jewish and gentile, within which the new religion developed and crystallized into a powerful institution. The successive stages in its growth are usually, though often somewhat arbitrarily, distinguished for convenience of treatment. Thus one may specialize on the activity of Jesus or of Paul, on the history of the "Apostolic Age" or the work of the "Apologists," and the like. While some such divisional treatment is a practical necessity, one ought never to lose sight of the basal fact of continuity in the historical stream. In order to avoid this danger, the grouping of literature cited below has been kept as simple and elastic as possible, and some of the captions will require a return to the study of certain subjects in chronological areas already traversed in connection with the investigation of previous topics. For recent and elaborate bibliographical information on the history of early Christianity, see especially Kirsch (Item 54), pp. 767–850.

SOURCES OF INFORMATION
INTRODUCTIONS TO LITERATURE

302. **Bacon, B. W.** *The Making of the New Testament.* New York: Holt, 1912. 256 pages.

303. **Bardenhewer, O.** *Patrology: The Lives and Works of the Fathers of the Church.* Translated from 2d German edition. St. Louis, Missouri: Herder, 1908. xvii+680 pages. (Covers about 100 to 750 A.D.).

304. **Ferrer, W. J.** *The Earlier Christian Books.* London: Society for Promoting Christian Knowledge, 1919. xi+108 pages. (Covers, roughly, the second century, i.e., the "Apostolic Fathers" and the early "Apologists.")

305. **Goodspeed, E. J.** *The Story of the New Testament.* Chicago: University of Chicago Press, 1916. xi+150 pages. (Concise summary for beginners.)

306. **Harnack, A.** *Geschichte der altchristlichen Litteratur bis Eusebius.* 3 vols. Leipzig: Hinrichs, 1893–1904.

307. **Krüger, G.** *Die christliche lateinische Litteratur von Augustinus, bis Gregor der Grosse.* Munich: Beck, 1921. (Reprinted from M. Schanz, *Geschichte der römischen Litteratur,* Vol. IV, chap. ii, pp. 362–645. The earlier Latin Christian writers are contained in Vol. III, pp. 240–495 [Munich, 1905], and Vol. IV, chap. i, pp. 205–550 [Munich, 1914].)

308. ———. *History of Early Christian Literature in the First Three Centuries.* Translated from German. New York: Macmillan, 1897. xxiii+409 pages.

309. **Labriolle, P. de.** *History and Literature of Christianity from Tertullian to Boethius.* Translated from French. New York: Knopf, 1925. xxiii+555 pages. (To 524 A.D.)

310. **Moffatt, James.** *An Introduction to the Literature of the New Testament.* New York: Scribner's, 1925. xxxix+659 pages. (Very full references to literature.)

311. **Puech, A.** *Histoire de la littérature grecque chrétienne depuis les origines jusqu'à la fin du quatrième siècle.* 3 vols. Paris: "Les Belles Lettres," 1928–30.

312. **Stählin, O.** *Die altchristliche griechische Litteratur.* Munich: Beck, 1924. (Reprinted from the 6th edition of W. von Christ, *Geschichte der griechischen Litteratur,* Vol. II, chap. ii, pp. 1105–1492.)

EDITIONS, COLLECTIONS, TRANSLATIONS, SOURCE BOOKS

313. *Ante-Nicene Fathers. Translation of the Writings of the Fathers down to A.D. 325.* Edited by A. Roberts and J. Donaldson. 9 vols. and 1 vol. of Bibliography and Indexes. New York: Scribner's, 1885–87. (Clement of Rome, Epistle to Diognetus, Polycarp, Ignatius, Barnabas, Papias, Justin, Irenaeus, Hermas, Tatian, Theophilus, Athenagoras, Clement of Alexandria, Tertullian, Minucius Felix, Commodian, Origen, Hippolytus, Cyprian, Caius, Novatian, Gregory Thaumaturgus, Dionysius the Great, Julius Africanus, Methodius, Arnobius, Lactantius, Teaching of the Apostles [Didache], Victorinus, Dionysius of Rome, Apostolic Constitutions. Early Liturgies, Apocryphal Gospels, etc., Clementine Writings, and other minor writings.) (*ANF*)

314. **Ayer, J. C.** *A Source Book for Ancient Church History.* New York: Scribner's, 1913. xxi+707 pages. (About 100 to 800 A.D.)

315. *Bibliothek der Kirchenväter: Eine Auswahl patristischer Werke in deutscher Übersetzung.* Edited by O. Bardenhewer and others. Munich: Kosel & Pustet, 1911——. (Sixty volumes up to 1928).

316. *Cambridge Patristic Texts.* Edited by A. J. Mason. Cambridge: University Press, 1899——. (Original text with notes; 11 volumes to 1926.)

317. *Corpus scriptorum ecclesiasticorum latinorum.* Edited by the Vienna Academy of Letters. Leipzig: Akademische Verlagsgesellschaft (G. Fock), 1866——. (Sixty-five volumes completed in 1926.) (*CSEL*)

318. *Enchiridion patristicum.* Collected by M. J. Rouet de Journel. 9th ed. Freiburg: Herder, 1923. xxvii+801 pages. (Excerpts from Didache to John of Damascus.)

319. *Florilegium patristicum tam veteris quam medii avei auctores complectens.* Edited by B. Geyer and J. Zellinger. Bonn: Hanstein, 1906——. (Twenty-seven numbers had appeared up to 1931.)

320. **Goodspeed, E. J.** *Die ältesten Apologeten: Texte mit kurzen Einleitungen.* Göttingen: Vandenhoeck & Ruprecht, 1914. ix +380 pages. (Quadratus, Aristides, Justin, Tatian, Melito, Athenagoras.)

321. *Die griechischen christlichen Schriftsteller der ersten drei Jahrhunderte.* Edited by the Kirchenväter-Commission der Preussischen Akademie der Wissenschaften. Leipzig: Hinrichs, 1905——. (Thirty-five volumes had appeared up to 1930.) (*GCS*)

322. **Hennicke, E.** (editor). *Neutestamentliche Apokryphen.* 2d ed. Tübingen: Mohr, 1924. 32+668 pages.

323. **James, M. R.** *The Apocryphal New Testament, Being the Apocryphal Gospels, Acts, Epistles and Apocalypses, with Other Narratives and Fragments Newly Translated.* Oxford: Clarendon Press, 1924. xxxi+584 pages. (Bibliography, pp. xxix–xxxi).

324. **Lake, K.** *The Apostolic Fathers, with an English Translation.* 2 vols. London: Heinemann, 1912. (Greek and English on opposite pages; in "Loeb Classical Library.")

325. **Migne, J. P.** *Patrologiae cursus completus. Series Graeca.* 161 vols. Paris: Migne, 1857–66. (An Index is in preparation by T. Hopfner and 3 parts, 288 pages, had appeared up to 1928.) (*MPG*)

326. ——. *Patrologiae cursus completus. Series Latina.* 217 vols. and 4 vols. of indexes. Paris: Migne, 1878–90. (*MPL*)

327. **Schmidt, C.** *Gespräche Jesu mit seinen Jüngern nach der Auferstehung.* 1919. 731+83 pages. (*TU* [Item 353], Vol. XLIII.)

328. *Select Library of Nicene and Post-Nicene Fathers of the Christian Church. First Series.* Edited by P. Schaff. 14 vols. New York: Scribner's, 1886–89. (Augustine and Chrysostom.) (*NPFi*)

329. *Ibid. Second Series.* Edited by H. Wace and P. Schaff. 14 vols. New York: Scribner's, 1890–1900. (Eusebius, Socrates,

Sozomen, Theodoret, Jerome, Gerundius, Rufinus, Athanasius, Gregory of Nyssa, Cyril of Jerusalem, Gregory Nazianzen, Basil, Hilary of Poitiers, John of Damascus, Ambrose, Sulpitius Severus, Vincent of Lérins, Leo the Great, Ephraim Syrus, Aphrahat, and the Seven Ecumenical Councils.) (*NPF2*)

330. **Souter, A.** *Novum Testamentum graece.* Oxford: Clarendon Press, 1910.

331. **Kidd, B. J.** *Documents Illustrative of the History of the Church (to A.D. 461).* 2 vols. London: Society for Promoting Christian Knowledge, 1920–23.

332. *Translations of Christian Literature. Series I: Greek Texts. Series II: Latin Texts. Series III: Liturgical Texts.* London: Society for Promoting Christian Knowledge, 1918——. (Translations with explanatory introductions and brief notes; still in progress; very useful.)

333. **Westcott, B. F., and Hort, F. J. A.** *The New Testament in the Original Greek. Text.* New York: Macmillan, 1881. 603 pages.

334. **Wright, F. A.** *Fathers of the Church.* New York: Dutton, 1929. vii+351 pages. (Selections from Tertullian, Cyprian, Arnobius, Lactantius, Ambrose, Jerome, Augustine.)

ARCHAEOLOGICAL REMAINS (SEE ITEM 170)

335. **Diehl, E.** *Inscriptiones latinae christianae veteres.* 2 vols. and Index. Berlin: Weidmann, 1925——. (Index not yet complete.)

336. **Jerphanion, G. de.** *La voix des monuments. Notes et études d'archéologie chrétienne.* Paris: van Oest, 1930. 331 pages, with numerous reproductions.

337. **Kaufmann, C. M.** *Handbuch der altchristlichen Epigraphik.* Freiburg: Herder, 1917. xvi+514 pages.

338. ——. *Handbuch der christlichen Archäologie.* 3d ed. Paderborn: Schöningh, 1922. xviii+684 pages. (The two books of Kaufmann are very complete in materials and literature.)

339. **Lanciani, R.** *Wanderings through Ancient Roman Churches.* Boston: Houghton Mifflin, 1924. xvi+325 pages.

340. **Lowrie, W.** *Monuments of the Early Church.* New York: Macmillan, 1901. xxii+432 pages.

341. *Monumenti di antichità christiana.* Rome: Pontificio instituo di archeologia cristiana, 1929——.

342. **Wilpert, J.** *Die Malereien der Katakomben Roms.* 2 vols. Freiburg: Herder, 1903. (Magnificent reproductions with interpretations.)

SERIES, RESEARCHES, AND MISCELLANEOUS HELPS

343 *Antike und Christentum: Kultur- und religionsgeschichtliche Studien.* By F. J. Dölger. Münster: Aschendorff, 1929——. (Appears quarterly.)

344. *Beihefte zur ZNTW* (Item 358), 1923——. (Twelve numbers to end of 1930.)

345. **Capelli, A.** *Dizionario di abbreviature latine ed italiane.* 3d ed. Milan: Hoepli, 1929. lxxiii+531 pages. (Bibliography, pp. 517–31.)

346. *Guide to the Study of the Christian Religion.* Edited by G. B. Smith. Chicago: University of Chicago Press, 1916. x+759 pages. (Out of print.)

347. **Heussi, K., and Mulert, H.** *Atlas zur Kirchengeschichte.* 66 maps. Tübingen: Mohr, 1905.

348. *Papers of the American Society of Church History.* 8 vols. New York: Putnam's, 1889–96; 2d ser., 8 vols., 1913–18. (*ASCH*)

349. **Pieper, K.** *Orbis Christianus Saeculi,* Vols. I–V. Düsseldorf: L. Schwann (no date). (A wall-map with place names underlined in different colors to show expansion of Christianity in first five centuries.)

350. **Sleumer, A.** *Kirchenlateinisches Wörterbuch.* Limburg a.d. Lahn: Steffen, 1926. 842 pages. (See also Items 592–94.)

351. **Sophocles, E. A.** *Greek Lexicon of the Roman and Byzantine Periods* (*B.C. 146–A.D. 1100*). New York: Scribner's, 1887. xv+1188 pages.

352. *Studi e testi.* Published under the direction of the officials of the Vatican Library, Rome, 1900——.

353. *Texte und Arbeiten.* I. Abt., *Beiträge zur Ergründung des älteren lateinischen christlichen Schrifttums und Gottesdienst.*

Hohenzollern: Kunstschule der Erzabtei Beuron, 1917——.
(Eighteen numbers to 1930.)

354. *Texte und Untersuchungen zur Geschichte der altchristlichen Literatur.* Edited by A. Harnack and others. Leipzig: Hinrichs, 1883——. (*TU*)

355. *Textes et documents pour l'étude historique du christianisme.* Edited by H. Hemmer and P. Lejay. Paris: Picard, 1904——.

356. *Texts and Studies.* Edited by J. A. Robinson. Cambridge: University Press, 1891——.

357. **Thompson, E. M.** *An Introduction to Greek and Latin Paleography.* Oxford: Clarendon Press, 1912. xvi+600 pages.

358. *Zeitschrift für die neutestamentliche Wissenschaft und die Kunde der älteren Kirche.* Edited by W. Lietzmann. Giessen: Töpelmann, 1900——. (*ZNTW*)

HISTORIES OF EARLY CHRISTIANITY

359. **Batiffol, P.** *L'église naissante et le catholicisme.* Paris: Lecoffre, 1909. xiv+502 pages. *La paix constantinienne et le catholicisme.* Paris: Lecoffre, 1914. viii+542 pages. *Le siège apostolique (359-451).* Paris: Lecoffre, 1924. vii+624 pages. (These volumes are by a notable Roman Catholic scholar; the first volume in English: *Primitive Catholicism.* New York: Longmans, 1911. xxviii+424 pages.)

360. **Bigg, C.** *The Origins of Christianity.* Edited by T. B. Strong. Oxford: Clarendon Press, 1909. viii+518 pages. (Nero to Constantine.)

361. **Case, S. J.** *The Evolution of Early Christianity.* Chicago: University of Chicago Press, 1914. ix+385 pages. (Gives special attention to the Jewish and gentile religious setting of Christianity in the first century; full bibliographical footnotes.)

362. ——. *Social Origins of Christianity.* Chicago: University of Chicago Press, 1923. vii+263 pages. (A rapid survey to Constantine; bibliography on pp. 255-58.)

363. **Duchesne, L.** *Early History of the Christian Church, from Its Foundation to the End of the Fifth Century.* Translated from French. 3 vols. London: Murray, 1909-24.

364. **Gwatkin, H. M.** *Early Church History to A.D. 313.* 2 vols. London: Macmillan, 1909.

365. **Harnack, A.** *Mission and Expansion of Christianity in the First Three Centuries.* 2d ed. 3 vols. London: Williams & Norgate, 1908. (A 4th edition of the original German, not greatly altered, Leipzig: Hinrichs, 1923–24.)

366. **Kidd, B. J.** *A History of the Church to A.D. 461.* 3 vols. Oxford: Clarendon Press, 1922. (Very full reference to sources.)

367. **McGiffert, A. C.** *History of Christianity in the Apostolic Age.* 2d ed. New York: Scribner's, 1899. xii+681 pages. (To about 125 A.D.)

368. **Rainy, R.** *The Ancient Catholic Church (A.D. 98–451).* Edinburgh: Clark, 1902. xii+539 pages.

369. **Scott, E. F.** *The Gospel and Its Tributaries.* New York: Scribner's, 1930. xi+295 pages. (Covers the New Testament period.)

370. **Weiss, J.** *Das Urchristentum.* 2 vols. Göttingen: Vandenhoeck & Ruprecht, 1914–17. (The 2d volume edited posthumously by R. Knopf; extends to 130 A.D.)

CHRISTIANITY AMONG JEWS

The Jewish Environment (Palestinian and Hellenistic)

371. **Bertholet, A.** *Die jüdische Religion von der Zeit Ezras bis zum Zweitalter Christi.* Tübingen: Mohr, 1911. xv+546 pages.

372. **Bousset, W.** *Die Religion des Judentums.* 3d ed. by H. Gressmann. Tübingen: Mohr, 1926. xi+576 pages.

373. **Bréhier, É.** *Les idées philosophiques et religieuses de Philon d'Alexandrie.* 2d ed. Paris: Vrin, 1925. xiv+336 pages.

374. **Charles, R. H.** *Apocrypha and Pseudepigrapha of the Old Testament in English.* 2 vols. Oxford: Clarendon Press, 1913.

375. **Derwacter, F. M.** *Preparing the Way for Paul: The Proselyte Movement in Later Judaism.* New York: Macmillan, 1930. 165 pages. (Bibliography, pp. 155–58.)

376. *Flavii Josephi opera.* Greek text edited by B. Niese. 6 vols. with Index. Berlin: Weidmann, 1888–95. (The standard critical edition.)

377. **Herford, R. T.** *The Pharisees.* London: Macmillan, 1924. 248 pages. (Supplants the author's *Pharisaism: Its Aims*

and Methods. London: Williams & Norgate, 1912. vii+340 pages.)

378. **Jackson, F. J. Foakes.** *Josephus and the Jews.* New York: R. R. Smith, 1930. x+299 pages.

379. *Josephus, with an English Translation.* By H. St. J. Thackeray. 8 vols. London: Heinemann, 1926——. (Four volumes to 1930; Greek and English on opposite pages; in "Loeb Classical Library.")

380. **Juster, J.** *Les Juifs dans l'empire romain: leur condition juridique, économique et sociale.* 2 vols. Paris: Geuthner, 1914. Wealth of detail, but lacks index.)

381. **Mathews, S.** *History of New Testament Times in Palestine.* 2d ed. New York: Macmillan, 1910. 234 pages.

382. **Moore, G. F.** *Judaism in the First Centuries of the Christian Era.* 2 vols. Cambridge: Harvard University Press, 1927. (Uses especially Talmudic sources.)

383. *Philo, with an English Translation.* By F. H. Colson and G. H. Whitaker. 10 vols. London: Heinemann, 1929——. (Two volumes to 1930; Greek and English on opposite pages; in "Loeb Classical Library.")

384. *Philonis Alexandrini opera quae supersunt.* Edited by L. Cohn and P. Wendland. 6 vols. and Index (not yet complete). Berlin: De Gruyter, 1896——. (The standard critical edition of the Greek text.)

385. **Schürer, E.** *Geschichte des judischen Volkes im Zeitalter Jesu Christi.* 4th ed. 3 vols. and Index. Leipzig: Hinrichs, 1901–11. English translation: *History of the Jewish People in the Time of Jesus Christ.* 5 vols. New York: Scribner's, 1891. (Still an indispensable work.)

386. **Smith, G. A., and Bartholomew, J. G.** *Atlas of the Historical Geography of the Holy Land.* London: Hodder & Stoughton, 1915. xxxvi pages and 60 maps.

JOHN THE BAPTIST (AND THE MANDEANS)

387. **Behm, J.** *Die mandäische Religion und das Christentum.* Leipzig: Deichert, 1927. 34 pages. (An estimate of recent literature.)

388. **Blakiston, A.** *John the Baptist and His Relation to Jesus.* London: Bennett, 1912. 273 pages.

389. **Buzy, D.** *Saint Jean-Baptiste: Études historiques et critiques.* Paris: Lecoffre, 1922. xii+411 pages.

390. **Goguel, M.** *An seuil de l'évangile Jean-Baptiste.* Paris: Payot, 1928. 304 pages.

391. **Kraeling, C. H.** "Mandaic Bibliography" and "Origin and Antiquity of the Mandeans," *Journal of the American Oriental Society* (Boston: The Society), XLVI (1926), 49–55, and XLIX (1929), 195–218.

392. **Lidzbarski, M.** *Ginza: Der Schatz oder das grosse Buch der Mandäer übersetzt und erklärt.* Leipzig: Hinrichs, 1925. xviii +619 pages.

393. **Mead, G. R. S.** *The Gnostic John the Baptizer: Selections from the Mandean John-Book.* London: Watkins, 1924. ix+ 137 pages.

394. **Stahl, R.** *Les mandéens et les origines chrétiennes.* Paris: Rieder, 1930. 216 pages.

JESUS AND HIS FOLLOWERS

395. **Abrahams, I.** *Studies in Pharisaism and the Gospels.* 2d Ser. Cambridge: University Press, 1917, 1924. (By a Jewish scholar.)

396. **Bultmann, R.** *Jesus.* Berlin: Deutsche Bibliothek, 1926. 204 pages. (On the basis of the findings of Formgeschichte; also Barthian in sympathy.)

397. **Case, S. J.** *Jesus: A New Biography.* Chicago: University of Chicago Press, 1927. vii+453 pages. (Stresses the social environment in which Jesus and his followers lived.)

398. ———. "Life of Jesus during the Last Quarter-Century," *JR* (Item 150), V (1925), 561–75. (A survey of problems and literature.)

399. **Easton, B. S.** *Christ in the Gospels.* London: Scribner's, 1930. x+210 pages. (Evaluates critically recent gospel researches.)

400. **Headlam, A. C.** *The Life and Teaching of Jesus the Christ.* London: Murray, 1923. xiii+338 pages. (Represents the more conservative Anglican scholarship.)

401. **Klausner, J.** *Jesus of Nazareth*. Translated from modern Hebrew. New York: Macmillan, 1925. 434 pages. (By a competent Jewish scholar, a professor in the Hebrew University at Jerusalem.)

402. **Nielsen, D.** *Der geschichtliche Jesus*. Translation from Danish. Munich: Meyer & Jessen, 1928. xxvii+238 pages.

403. **Riddle, D. W.** *Jesus and the Pharisees: A Study in Christian Tradition*. Chicago: University of Chicago Press, 1928. ix+193 pages.

404. **Schweitzer, A.** *The Quest of the Historical Jesus*. Translated from German. London: Black, 1910. x+410 pages. (A conspicuous representative of the "eschatological" school. The 2d German edition is considerably enlarged: *Geschichte der Leben-Jesu-Forschung*. Tübingen: Mohr, 1913. xii+659 pages.)

PAUL AND THE TRANSITION TO GENTILES

405. **Bacon, B. W.** *Jesus and Paul*. New York: Macmillan, 1921. ix+251 pages.

406. **Deissmann, G. A.** *Paul: A Study in Social and Religious History*. Translated from German. 2d ed. London: Hodder & Stoughton, 1926. xv+323 pages.

407. **Enslin, M. S.** *The Ethics of Paul*. New York: Harper, 1930. xix+335 pages.

408. **Jackson, F. J. Foakes.** *Rise of Gentile Christianity*. New York: Doran, 1927. xiii+231 pages.

409. **Jackson, F. J. Foakes, and Lake, K.** *Beginnings of Christianity*. Part I, Vol. I, *The Jewish, Gentile and Christian Backgrounds*. London: Macmillan, 1920. xi+480 pages.

410. **Knox, W. L.** *St. Paul and the Church of Jerusalem*. Cambridge: University Press, 1925. xxvii+396 pages.

411. **Morgan, W.** *The Religion and Theology of Paul*. Edinburgh: Clark, 1917. xi+272 pages.

412. **Schweitzer, A.** *Paul and His Interpreters. A Critical History*. Translated from German. London: Black, 1912. xiii+253 pages.

413. **Toussaint, C.** *L'hellénisme et l'Apôtre Paul*. Paris: Nourry, 1921. 366 pages.

414. **Wagenmann, J.** *Die Stellung des Apostels Paulus neben den Zwölf in den ersten zwei Jahrhunderten.* Giessen: Töpelmann, 1926. xv+224 pages.

415. **Wilson, T. W.** *St. Paul and Paganism.* Edinburgh: Clark, 1927. vii+285 pages.

CHRISTIANITY AMONG GENTILES
GENERAL SOCIAL CONDITIONS

416. **Barrow, R. H.** *Slavery in the Roman Empire.* London: Methuen, 1828. xvi+259 pages. (Sources and bibliography on pp. 237–46.)

417. **Capot, V.** *The Roman World.* Translated from French. New York: Knopf, 1928. xix+444 pages. (Extensive bibliographies, pp. 427–35.)

418. **Davis, W. S.** *The Influence of Wealth in Imperial Rome.* New York: Macmillan, 1910. xi+340 pages.

419. **Dill, S.** *Roman Society from Nero to Marcus Aurelius.* London: Macmillan, 1904. xxii+639 pages.

420. **Friedländer, L.** *Roman Life and Manners under the Early Empire.* Translated from 7th German edition. 4 vols. London: Routledge, 1908–13.

421. **Keipert, H.** *Atlas antiquus: Twelve Maps on the Ancient World.* Taken from the German edition. New York: Rand, McNally (no date).

422. **Pöhlmann, R. v.** *Geschichte der sozialen Frage und des Sozialismus in der antiken Welt.* 2 vols. Munich: Beck, 1912.

423. **Rostovtzeff, M.** *The Social and Economic History of the Roman Empire.* Oxford: Clarendon Press, 1926. xxv+695 pages, with 60 illustrations.

424. **Waltzing, J. P.** *Étude historique sur les corporations professionelles chez les Romains depuis les origines jusqu'à la chute de l'empire d'occident.* 4 vols. Louvain: Peeters, 1895–1900.

CHRISTIANITY AND THE GRAECO-ROMAN RELIGIONS
(SEE ITEM 361)

425. **Angus, S.** *The Mystery-Religions and Christianity: A Study in the Religious Background of Early Christianity.* New York: Scribner's, 1925. xvi+357 pages. (Bibliography, pp. 315–50.)

426. **Angus, S.** *The Religious Quests of the Graeco-Roman World: A Study in the Historical Background of Early Christianity.* New York: Scribner's, 1929. xx+444 pages.

427. **Case, S. J.** *Experience with the Supernatural in Early Christian Times.* New York: Century, 1929. vii+341 pages.

428. **Cumont, F.** *After Life in Roman Paganism.* New Haven: Yale University Press, 1922. xv+225 pages.

429. ————. *Oriental Religions in Roman Paganism.* Translated from French. Chicago: Open Court, 1911. xxv+298 pages. (There is much additional information in the 3d edition of the German translation: *Die orientalischen Religionen im römischen Heidentum.* Leipzig: Teubner, 1931. xvi+334 pages, with 8 tables of illustrations.)

430. **Farnell, L. R.** *Greek Hero Cults and Ideas of Immortality.* Oxford: Clarendon Press, 1921. xvi+434 pages.

431. **Fowler, W. W.** *The Religious Experience of the Roman People.* London: Macmillan, 1911. xviii+504 pages.

432. **Halliday, W. R.** *The Pagan Background of Early Christianity.* Liverpool: University Press, 1925. xvi+334 pages.

433. **Leipoldt, J.** *Die Religionen in der Umwelt des Urchristentums. BAR* (Item 2359), Lieferung 9-11, 1926. xxii pages and 193 illustrations.

434. **Loisy, A.** *Les mystères païens et le mystère chrétien.* 2d ed. Paris: Nourry, 1930. 352 pages.

435. **Lucius, E.** *Die Anfänge des Heiligenkults in der christlichen Kirche.* Edited by G. Anrich. Tübingen: Mohr, 1904. xi+526 pages.

436. **Murray, G.** *Five Stages of Greek Religion.* New York: Columbia University Press, 1925. 276 pages.

437. **Nilsson, M. P.** *A History of Greek Religion.* Translated from Swedish. Oxford: University Press, 1925. 310 pages.

438. **Nock, A. D.** "Early Gentile Christianity and Its Hellenistic Background" in *Essays on the Trinity and the Incarnation,* edited by A. E. J. Rawlinson (London: Longmans, 1928), pp. 51-156.

439. **Reitzenstein, R.** *Die hellenistischen Mysterienreligionen nach ihren Grundgedanken und Wirkungen.* 3d ed. Leipzig: Teubner, 1927. viii+438 pages.

440. **Salvatorelli, L.** "From Locke to Reitzenstein: the Historical Investigation of the Origins of Christianity," *HTR* (Item 149), XXII (1929), 263–369.

441. **Willoughby, H. R.** *Pagan Regeneration: A Study of Mystery Initiations in the Graeco-Roman World.* Chicago: University of Chicago Press, 1929. xi+307 pages. (Bibliography at end of each chapter.)

CHRISTIANITY AND THE GRAECO-ROMAN LEARNING
(CULTURE AND PHILOSOPHY)

442. **Arnold, E. V.** *Roman Stoicism.* Cambridge: University Press, 1911. iii+468 pages. (Comprehensive bibliography, pp. 437–50.)

443. **Bigg, C.** *The Christian Platonists of Alexandria.* 2d ed. Oxford: Clarendon Press, 1913. xxvii+304 pages.

444. *Boethius, with an English Translation.* By H. F. Stewart and E. K. Rand. London: Heinemann, 1918. xiv+420 pages. (Latin and English on opposite pages; contains "The Theological Tractates" and "The Consolation of Philosophy"; in "Loeb Classical Library.")

445. **Bultmann, R.** *Der Stil der Paulinischen Predigt und die kynisch-stoische Diatribe.* Göttingen: Vandenhoeck & Ruprecht, 1910. 110 pages.

446. **Fitzgerald, A.** *The Letters of Synesius of Cyrene, Translated into English with Introduction and Notes.* Oxford: University Press, 1926. 272 pages.

447. **Geffcken, J.** *Der Ausgang des griechisch-römischen Heidentums.* Heidelberg: Winter, 1920. 347 pages.

448. **Haarhoff, T.** *Schools of Gaul: A Study of Pagan and Christian Education in the Last Century of the Western Empire.* London: Oxford University Press, 1920. xii+272 pages.

449. **Hatch, E.** *Influences of Greek Ideas and Usages upon the Christian Church.* London: Williams & Norgate, 1890. xxiii+359 pages.

450. **Hicks, R. D.** *Stoic and Epicurean.* New York: Scribner's, 1910. xix+412 pages. (Bibliography, pp. 401–4.)

451. **Rand, E. K.** *Founders of the Middle Ages.* Cambridge: Harvard University Press, 1928. ix+365 pages. (Discusses Chris-

tianity and pagan culture, Ambrose, Jerome, Boethius, the new poetry and education, Augustine and Dante.)

452. **Walden, J. W. H.** *The Universities of Ancient Greece.* New York: Scribner's, 1910. xiv+367 pages. (To the end of paganism.)

453. **Wendland, P.** *Die hellenistisch-römische Kultur in ihrer Beziehung zu Judentum und Christentum.* 2d ed. Tübingen: Mohr, 1912. x+256 pages.

454. **Whittaker, T.** *The Neoplatonists.* 2d ed. Cambridge: University Press, 1918. xv+318 pages.

455. **Wilkins, A. S.** *Roman Education.* Cambridge: University Press, 1905. viii+100 pages.

CHRISTIANITY AND ROMAN IMPERIALISM
GENERAL

456. **Boissier, G.** *La fin du paganisme.* 2 vols. 8th ed. Paris: Hachette, 1923. (Still standard; from Constantine to the "fall" of the Western Empire.)

457. **Broglie, A. de.** *L'église et l'empire romain au IVe siècle.* 6 vols. Paris: Perrin, 1900–1904. (From Constantine to Theodosius.)

458. **Bury, J. B.** *History of the Later Roman Empire from the Death of Theodosius I to the Death of Justinian.* (395–565). 2 vols. London: Macmillan, 1923. Also *Invasion of Europe by the Barbarians.* Macmillan, 1928. xii+296 pages.

459. *CMH* (Item 562), Vol. I. *The Christian Roman Empire and the Foundation of the Teutonic Kingdoms.* (Detailed bibliographical information on pp. 615–95.)

460. **Dalton, O. M.** *The Letters of Sidonius, Translated with Introduction and Notes.* 2 vols. Oxford: Clarendon Press, 1915.

461. **Dill, S.** *Roman Society in the Last Century of the Western Empire.* London: Macmillan, 1899. xxviii+459 pages.

462. **Glover, T. R.** *Life and Letters in the Fourth Century.* Cambridge: University Press, 1901. xvi+398 pages.

463. **Hodgkin, T.** *The Dynasty of Theodosius, or Eighty Years' Struggle with the Barbarians.* Oxford: Clarendon Press, 1889. xiii+239 pages.

464. **Seeck, O.** *Geschichte des Untergang der antiken Welt.* 6 (12) vols. Berlin: Siemenroth & Troschel, 1895–1921. (From Con-

stantine to end of Western Empire: several of the earlier volumes have been revised and supplemented since their first publication.)

465. **Zeiller, J.** *L'empire romain et l'église.* Paris: Boccard, 1928. iv+360 pages. (Bibliographies, mostly in French and German at end of each chapter.)

Persecution of Christians

466. **Canfield, L. H.** *The Early Persecutions of the Christians.* New York: Longmans, 1913. 215 pages. (Surveys the problems, sources, and modern literature to time of Hadrian.)

467. **Case, S. J.** *The Revelation of John: A Historical Interpretation.* Chicago: University of Chicago Press, 1919. xii+419 pages.

468. *DACL* (Item 124), articles "Accusations contre les chrétiens," Vol. I., cols. 265–307; and "Droit persécuteur," Vol. IV, cols. 1565–1648.

469. **Hardy, E.** *Christianity and the Roman Government.* London: Longmans, 1894. Reprinted in "Studies in Roman History," First Series, London: Allen, 1910, pp. 1–161. (To Marcus Aurelius.)

470. **Healy, P. J.** *The Valerian Persecution: A Study of the Relations between Church and State in the Third Century A.D.,* Boston: Houghton Mifflin, 1905. xv+285 pages.

471. **Linsenmayer, A.** *Die Bekämpfung des Christentums durch den römischen Staat bis zum Tode des Kaisers Julian (363).* Munich: Lentner, 1905. 301 pages. (Critical and well documented.)

472. **Manaresi, A.** *L'impero romano e il cristianesimo.* Turin: Bocca, 1914. xv+597 pages. (A good summary of the findings of critical study, with full bibliography on pp. 565–77.)

473. **Owen, E. C. E.** *Some Authentic Acts of the Early Martyrs.* Oxford: Clarendon Press, 1927. 183 pages. (In English translations.)

474. **Workman, H. B.** *Persecution in the Early Church.* London: Kelly, 1906. xx+382 pages. (Somewhat popularly presented, but rich in references to sources and modern literature.)

Constantine and Christianity

475. **Baker, G. P.** *Constantine the Great and the Christian Revolution.* New York: Dodd Mead, 1930. 351 pages.

476. **Case, S. J.** "Acceptance of Christianity by the Roman Emperors," *ASCH* (Item 348), 2d Ser., VIII (1928), 43–64.

477. **Coleman, C. B.** *Constantine the Great and Christianity.* New York: Longmans, 1914. 258 pages.

478. **Huttmann, Maude A.** *The Establishment of Christianity and the Proscription of Paganism.* New York: Longmans, 1914. 257 pages.

479. **Maurice, J.** *Constantin le Grand: L'origine de la civilisation chrétienne.* Paris: "Editions Spes," 1924. xi+307 pages.

480. **Schwartz, E.** *Kaiser Constantin und die christliche Kirche.* Leipzig: Teubner, 1913. vii+171 pages. (Five noteworthy lectures.)

Julian

481. **Bidez, J.** *La vie de l'Empereur Julien.* Paris: "Les Belles Lettres," 1930. x+408 pages. (A sympathetic interpretation; full bibliography.)

482. *CMH* (Item 562), Vol. I, chap. iii. (Bibliography on pp. 633–35.)

483. *The Works of the Emperor Julian, with an English Translation.* By W. C. Wright. 3 vols. London: Heinemann, 1913–23. (Greek and English on opposite pages; in "Loeb Classical Library.")

EARLY CHRISTIAN INSTITUTIONS
(See Also Items 181–269)
General

484. **Beet, W. E.** *The Early Roman Episcopate to A.D. 384.* London: Kelly, 1913. xii+332 pages. And *The Rise of the Papacy. 385–461.* Kelly, 1910. 334 pages.

485. **Chapman, J.** *Studies on the Early Papacy.* New York: Benziger, 1928. 238 pages.

486. **Dudden, F. H.** *Gregory the Great: His Place in History and Thought.* 2 vols. London: Longmans, 1905.

487. **Fulton, J.** *Index canonum: The Greek Text, an English Translation and a Complete Digest of the Entire Code of Canon Law*

of the Undivided Primitive Church. 3d ed. New York: Whittaker, 1892. xxx+393 pages.

488. **Goodspeed, E. J.** *Formation of the New Testament.* Chicago: University of Chicago Press, 1926. ix+210 pages. (The story of the formation of a New Testament canon; selected bibliography, p. 186.)

489. **Harnack, A.** *Constitution and Law of the Church in the First Two Centuries.* London: Williams & Norgate, 1910. xiv+349 pages.

490. **Hatch, E.** *The Organization of the Early Christian Churches.* London: Longmans, 1881. xxviii+222 pages. (Inaugurated a new type of approach among Protestant students.)

491. **Lietzmann, H.** *Petrus und Paulus in Rom.* 2d ed. Berlin: De Gruyter, 1927. viii+315 pages.

492. **Regnier, A.** *St. Léon le Grand.* Paris: Lecoffre, 1910. 210 pages.

493. **Shotwell, J. T., and Loomis, Louise R.** *The See of Peter,* New York: Columbia University Press, 1927. xxvi+737 pages.

494. **Streeter, B. H.** *The Primitive Church: Studied with Special Reference to the Origins of the Christian Ministry.* New York: Macmillan, 1929. xiii+323 pages.

WORSHIP AND SACRAMENTS (SEE ALSO ITEMS 204–18, 660–65)

495. **Cabrol, F.** *La priére des premiers chrétiens.* 3d ed. Paris: Grasset, 1929. 279 pages. (Bibliography, pp. 268–88.)

496. **Duchesne, L.** *Christian Worship: Its Origin and Evolution.* Translated from French. 2d ed. London: Society for Promoting Christian Knowledge, 1912. xx+595 pages. (To Charlemagne.)

497. **Gavin, F.** *The Jewish Antecedents of the Christian Sacraments.* London: Society for Promoting Christian Knowledge. 1928. viii+120 pages.

498. **Harnack, A.** *Bible Reading in the Early Church.* Translated from German. London: Williams & Norgate, 1912. x+159 pages.

499. **Oesterley, W. O. E.** *The Jewish Background of the Christian Liturgy.* Oxford: Clarendon Press, 1925. 343 pages.

500. **Poschmann, B.** *Die abendländische Kirchenbusse im Ausgang des christlichen Altertums.* Munich: Kösel & Pustet, 1928. viii+316 pages.

501. **Reitzenstein, R.** *Die Vorgeschichte der christlichen Taufe.* Leipzig: Teubner, 1929. viii+399 pages. (See also Items 387–94.)

502. **Wetter, G. P.** *Altchristliche Liturgien: I. Das christliche Mysterium. II. Das christliche Opfer.* Göttingen: Vandenhoeck & Ruprecht, 1921–22.

DOGMA, CREEDS, AND COUNCILS (SEE ALSO
ITEMS 193–95; 244–69)

503. **Bethune-Baker, J. F.** *An Introduction to the Early History of Christian Doctrine.* 4th ed. London: Methuen, 1929. XXVI +452 pages.

504. **Bousset, W.** *Kyrios Christos: Geschichte der Christusglaubens von den Anfängen des Christentums bis Irenaeus.* 2d ed. Göttingen: Vandenhoeck & Ruprecht, 1921. xxii+394 pages.

505. **Lebreton, J.** *Histoire du dogme de la trinité des origines au concile de Nicée.* Paris: Beauschesne, 1927——. (Two volumes have appeared, the first in a 7th edition; now to *Irenaeus.*)

506. **McGiffert, A. C.** *The God of the Early Christians.* New York: Scribner's, 1924. 200 pages.

507. **Moody, C. N.** *The Mind of the Early Converts.* London: Hodder & Stoughton, 1920. xiii+310 pages.

508. *NPF2* (Item 329), Vol. XIV: *The Seven Ecumenical Councils, Their Canons and Dogmatic Decrees.* (In English translation.)

509. **Tixeront, J.** *History of Dogmas.* Translated from French. 3 vols. 2d ed. St. Louis, Missouri: Herder, 1923.

SEPARATIST LEADERS AND GROUPS (HERESIES)

510. **Bousset, W.** *Hauptprobleme der Gnosis.* Göttingen: Vandenhoeck & Ruprecht, 1907. vi+398 pages.

511. **Buonaiuti, E.** *Gnostic Fragments.* London: Williams & Norgate, 1924. 114 pages. (In English translations.)

512. **Burkitt, F. C.** *The Religion of the Manichees.* Cambridge: University Press, 1925. viii+129 pages.

513. **Faye, E. de.** *Gnostiques et Gnosticisme.* 2d ed. Paris: Geuthner, 1925. 547 pages.

514. **Harnack, A.** *Marcion: Das Evangelium vom fremden Gott.* 2d ed. Leipzig: Hinrichs, 1924. xv+235 pages, and "Beilagen" 455 pages. (*TU* [Item 353], Vol. XLV.)

515. **Hilgenfeld, A.** *Ketzergeschichte des Urchristentums.* Leipzig: Fues, 1884, x+644 pages.

516. **Labriolle, P. de.** *Le crise montaniste.* Paris: Leroux, 1913. xx+607 pages. (Full bibliography, pp. vii-xx.) Also *Les sources de l'histoire du montanisme. Textes grecs, latins, syriaques publiés avec une introduction critique, une traduction française des notes et des "Indices."* Leroux, 1913. cxxxviii+282 pages.

517. **McLean, N.** "Marcionism," *ERE* (Item 120), VIII (1916), 407-9.

518. **Scott, E. F.** "Gnosticism," *ERE* (Item 120), VI (1914), 231-42.

519. **Vassall-Phillips, O. R.** *The Work of St. Optatus against the Donastists.* London: Longmans, 1917. xxxv+438 pages.

THE CHRISTIAN LIFE
Ideals and Social Practices (See Items 279-94)

520. **Allard, P.** *Les esclaves chrétiens depuis les premiers temps de l'église jusqu'à la fin de la domination romaine en occident.* 6th ed. Paris: Lecoffre, 1914. xiii+484 pages.

521. **Bigelmair, A.** *Die Beteiligung der Christen am öffentlichen Leben in vorconstantinischer Zeit.* Munich: Lentner, 1902. 340 pages.

522. **Cadoux, C. J.** *The Early Church and the World.* Edinburgh: Clark, 1925. liii+675 pages. (To Constantine; bibliography, pp. xxxiii-li.)

523. **Dobschütz, E. v.** *Christian Life in the Primitive Church.* Translated from German. London: Williams & Norgate, 1904. xxxix+438 pages.

524. **Preisker, H.** *Christentum und Ehe in den ersten Jahrhunderten.* Berlin, Trowitzsch, 1927. viii+260 pages. (To Constantine.)

525. **Raymond, I. W.** *Teaching of the Early Church on the Use of Wine and Strong Drink.* New York: Columbia University Press, 1927. 170 pages.

526. **Scullard, H. H.** *Early Christian Ethics in the West.* London: Williams & Norgate, 1907. xiv+308 pages.

EARLY MONASTICISM

527. **Budge, E. A. W.** *The Paradise, or the Garden of the Holy Fathers, Being Histories of the Anchorites, Recluses, Monks, Cenobites and Ascetic Fathers of the Deserts of Egypt between 250 A.D. and ca. 400.* 2 vols. London: Chatto & Windus, 1907 (English translation of Syriac texts.)

528. **Butler, E. C.** "Monasticism," *CMH* (Item 562), I, 521–42, and bibliography on pp. 683–87.

529. **Chapman, J.** *St. Benedict and the Sixth Century.* London: Sheed & Ward, 1929. vii+239 pages. (See Item 722.)

530. **Clark, W. K. L.** *St. Basil the Great: A Study in Monasticism.* Cambridge: University Press, 1913. ix+176 pages.

531. ———. *The Lausiac History of Palladius.* London: Society for Promoting Christian Knowledge, 1918. xii+188 pages.

532. **Gasquet, F. A.** *The Rule of St. Benedict Translated with an Introduction.* London: Chatto & Windus, 1925. xxviii+130 pages.

533. **Hasluck, F. W.** *Athos and Its Monasteries.* New York: Dutton, 1924. xii+213 pages.

534. **Mackean, W. H.** *Christian Monasticism in Egypt to the Close of the Fourth Century.* London: Society for Promoting Christian Knowledge, 1920. 160 pages.

535. **Mason, A. J.** *Fifty Spiritual Homilies of St. Marcarius the Egyptian.* London: Society for Promoting Christian Knowledge, 1921. li+316 pages. (Introduction and English translation.)

LEADERS AND CHURCHES IN DIFFERENT REGIONS

536. **Arcy, M. C. d', and Others.** *A Monument to Saint Augustine.* London: Sheed & Ward, 1930. 367 pages.

537. **Bayard, L.** *Tertullien et Saint Cyprien.* Paris: Lecoffre, 1930. 285 pages.

538. **Bardy, G.** *Saint Athanase (296–373).* Paris: Lecoffre, 1914. xvi–207 pages.

539. **Baur, C.** *Der heilige Johannes Chrysostomus und seine Zeit.* 2 vols. Munich: Hueber, 1929–30.

540. **Boyer, C.** "Bulletin augustinien," *Gregorianum* (Item 168), X (1929), 102–11.

541. **Buonaiuti, E.** *Il cristianesimo nell' Africa romana.* Bari: Latzera, 1928. xxiv+454 pages.

542. **Burkitt, F. C.** *Early Eastern Christianity: St. Margaret's Lectures, 1904, on the Syriac-speaking Church.* London: Murray, 1904. viii+228 pages.

543. **Couling, C. E.** (Mrs.). *The Luminous Religion. A Study of Nestorian Christianity in China with a Translation of the Inscriptions upon the Nestorian Tablet.* London: Carey Press, 1925. 63 pages. (Reprinted from the *Chinese Recorder* [Item 2225], LV [1924], 215–24, 308–17; the translation of the inscriptions is that of Professor Saeki of Tokyo.)

544. **Donaldson, S. A.** *Church Life and Thought in North Africa A.D. 200.* Cambridge: University Press, 1909. xii+200 pages.

545. **Driver, G. R.** and **Hodgson, L.** *Nestorius: The Bazaar of Heracleides.* Oxford: Clarendon Press, 1925. xxxv+425 pages.

546. **Faye, E. de.** *Origen and His Work.* Translated from French. New York: Columbia University Press, 1929. 192 pages. (Popular presentation.)

547. ———. *Origène: Sa vie, son œuvre, sa pensée.* 3 vols. Paris: Leroux, 1923–28. (Important detailed study.)

548. **Holme, L. R.** *The Extinction of the Christian Churches in North Africa.* London: Clay, 1898. vii+263 pages.

549. **Holmes, T. S.** *The Origin and Development of the Christian Church in Gaul during the First Six Centuries.* New York: Macmillan, 1911. xiv+584 pages.

550. **Hughes, L.** *The Christian Church in the Epistles of St. Jerome.* London: Society for Promoting Christian Knowledge, 1923. viii+117 pages.

551. **Labriolle, P. de.** *The Life and Times of St. Ambrose.* Translated from French. St. Louis, Missouri: Herder, 1928. xxv+293 pages.

552. **Leigh-Bennett, E.** *Handbook of the Early Christian Fathers.* London: Williams & Norgate, 1920. xii+340 pages. (Clement of Rome; Ignatius, Polycarp, Irenaeus, Justin, Tertullian, Clement of Alexandria, Origen, Cyprian, Athanasius, Hilary of Poitiers, Cyril of Jerusalem, Basil, Gregory of Nazianzus, Gregory of Nyssa, Chrysostom, Jerome, Ambrose, Augustine.)

553. **Loofs, F.** *Nestorius and His Place in the History of Christian Doctrine.* Cambridge: University Press, 1914. vii+132 pages.

554. ———. *Paulus von Samosata.* Leipzig: Hinrichs, 1924. xx+346 pages. (*TU* [Item 353], LXIV, 5.)

555. **Robinson, J. A.** *St. Irenaeus: The Demonstration of the Apostolic Preaching.* London: Society for Promoting Christian Knowledge, 1920. ix+154 pages. (Introduction and English rendering of this newly discovered Armenian document.)

556. **Simpson, W. J. Sparrow.** *St. Augustine and African Church Divisions.* London: Longmans, 1910. v+154 pages.

557. ———. *St. Augustine's Conversion: An Outline of His Development to the Time of His Ordination.* New York: Macmillan, 1930. ix+276 pages. (Bibliography, pp. 273 f.).

558. **Tollinton, R. B.** *Clement of Alexandria: A Study in Christian Liberalism.* 2 vols. London: Williams & Norgate, 1914.

559. **Zeiller, J.** (Item 465), chaps. iv–xii. (Bibliography at close of each chapter; treats "Christianity outside the Empire," "Egypt," "Asia Minor," "The Hellenic Peninsula and Constantinople," "Provinces on Danube," "Gaul and Britain," "Spain and Africa," "Rome, Italy, and the Papacy.")

CHAPTER IV

CHRISTIANITY IN WESTERN CONTI-
NENTAL EUROPE, TO 1517

The plan adopted for the medieval period in western
Continental Europe is based upon the simple classification of works dealing with the expansion of Christianity,
those which mainly treat church organization and institutions, and those which describe the special agencies
and manifestations of the religious and cultural life. A
section on general works is placed at the beginning; and
the prominent aspects of the period from 1303 to 1517
are separately treated at the close of the chapter. An
attempt is made to offset the obvious over-simplification
of this division by means of cross-references by numbers.
Books which manifestly apply to more than one subsection but are not sufficiently general to be placed in the
"General" section, have usually been mentioned in the
first subsection for which they are useful, and thereafter
referred to by number. Exceptions to this occur where a
work is regarded as chiefly of value for a later section; in
such cases a forward reference has usually been inserted.
In many instances the decision to assign a book to a
specific subsection has had to be made somewhat arbitrarily. Books of a miscellaneous character have been
placed where they seemed likely to yield most service;
valuable chapters of such books have in some cases been
specifically indicated.

GENERAL

This section consists of a representative selection of works of a general character. Under "General" are listed works of general history to cover approximately the whole period; under "Special," works of general history which cover only a limited section of the period, or treatises on special aspects of the field. In the latter are included general works on economic history. A number of works on economic, political, or cultural history of more limited range are noted in later sections.

WORKS ON THE POLITICAL, SOCIAL, AND CULTURAL HISTORY
GENERAL (SEE ITEM 90)

560. **Adams, G. B.** *Civilization during the Middle Ages Especially in Relation to Modern Civilization.* New York: Scribner's, 1894; rev. ed., 1914. vi+455 pages.

561. **Bryce, James.** *The Holy Roman Empire.* Oxford, 1864. Final revision, New York: Macmillan, 1919. lix+571 pages. Also in "Home University Library," New York: Holt; London: Williams & Norgate, 1921. (A classic of historical interpretation.)

562. *The Cambridge Medieval History.* Planned by J. B. Bury. Edited by H. M. Gwatkin, J. P. Whitney, J. R. Tanner, C. W. Previté-Orton, and Z. N. Brooke. Cambridge: University Press; New York: Macmillan, 1911–29. Vols. I–VI. (An indispensable work valuable for many topics of church history and provided with ample bibliographies and numerous maps. Volume VI deals mainly with the thirteenth century.) (*CMH*)

563. **Fisher, H. A. L.** *The Medieval Empire.* 2 vols. New York: Macmillan, 1898.

564. **Lavisse, E., and Rambaud, A.** *Histoire générale du IV siècle à nos jours.* 12 vols. Paris: Colin, 1893–1901. (Volumes I–IV to 1559. A dependable work. Bibliographies now antiquated but useful for the earlier literature.)

565. **Munro, D. C.** *The Middle Ages, 395–1272.* New York: Century, 1921; reprinted 1924. 446 pages. (Working bibliography classified by chapters.)

566. **Thompson, J. W.** *The Middle Ages, 300–1500.* 2 vols. New York: Knopf, 1931. (A substantial general history.)

567. **Thorndike, L.** *The History of Medieval Europe*. New York: Houghton Mifflin, 1917. xx+682 pages. London: Harrap, 1920. viii+666 pages. (The English edition is entitled *Medieval Europe, Its Development and Civilization*.) (A widely used textbook, with bibliographies.)

568. **Tout, T. F.** *The Empire and the Papacy, 918–1273*. 2d ed. London: Rivington, 1899; 9th impression, 1921. vii+526 pages.

SPECIAL

569. **Abrahams, I.** *Jewish Life in the Middle Ages*. New York: Macmillan, 1896; reprinted 1917. xxvi+452 pages.

570. **Boissonnade, P.** *Life and Work in Medieval Europe*. Translated from French by E. Power. London: Kegan Paul, 1927. 415 pages. (An informing account of the rise of the arts and industry. Stresses the destruction of civilization by the barbarians.)

571. **Crump, P. G., and Jacob, E. F.** *The Legacy of the Middle Ages*. Oxford: Clarendon Press, 1926. viii+549 pages. (Valuable chapters by experts on art, education, status of women, political thought, etc.)

572. **Cutts, E. L.** *Scenes and Characters of the Middle Ages*. London: Virtue, 1872. xiii+546 pages. 4th ed., London: O'Connor, 1922. (Interesting and informing. Has many illustrations.)

573. **Grätz, H.** *Geschichte der Juden von den ältesten Zeiten bis auf die Gegenwart*. 13 vols. Leipzig, 1894–1908. Translated by Löwy, B., *History of the Jews*. 6 vols. Philadelphia: Jewish Publication Society of America, 1891–98. London: D. Nutt, 1891–92. 5 vols. 3d ed., New York: Hebrew Publishing Co., 1926. 6 vols.

574. **Imbart de la Tour, P.** *Questions d'histoire, sociale et religieuse, époque féodale*. Paris: Hachette, 1907. xvi+293 pages. (Social and economic issues, evolution of social ideas, organization of French church, etc.)

575. **Kötzschke, R.** *Allegemeine Wirtschaftsgeschichte des Mittelalters*. Jena: Fischer, 1924. xiv+626 pages. (Fifth to fifteenth century.)

576. **Little, A. G., and Powicke, F. M.** (editors). *Essays on Medieval History Presented to Thomas Frederick Tout.* Manchester: University Press, 1925. ix+432 pages.

577. **Luchaire, A.** *Social France at the Time of Philip Augustus.* Translated by E. B. Krehbiel from the 2d French edition (*La société française au temps de Philippe-Auguste* [Paris: Hachette, 1909]). New York: Holt, 1912. viii+441 pages.

578. **Pirenne, H.** *Medieval Cities: Their Origin and the Revival of Trade.* Translated from French by F. D. Halsey. Princeton: Princeton University Press, 1925. 249 pages. (Lectures delivered in America. French edition, Brussels: Lamertin, 1927.)

579. **Thompson, J. W.** *An Economic and Social History of the Middle Ages.* New York: Century, 1928. ix+900 pages. (Includes sections on the economic history of the church and monasticism.)

TEXTBOOKS AND GENERAL WORKS ON CHURCH HISTORY FOR THE PERIOD (SEE ITEMS 43–66, 93, 98–101, 106–10)

580. **Deansley, M.** *A History of the Medieval Church, 590–1500.* London: Methuen, 1925. viii+280 pages. (A well-written general sketch.)

581. **Foakes-Jackson, F. J.** *An Introduction to the History of Christianity, A.D. 590–1314.* New York: Macmillan, 1921. ix+390 pages. (Treats, with some fulness, well-chosen topics of ecclesiastical history. Sections on social life.)

582. **Lagarde, A.** *The Latin Church in the Middle Ages.* Translated from the French by A. Alexander. New York: Scribner's, 1915. vi+600 pages. (A compressed, factual history. Has a good summary of papal finances. Shows research throughout.)

583. **Pullan, L.** *From Justinian to Luther,* A.D. *518–1517,* Oxford: Clarendon Press, 1930. 256 pages. (Does not attempt to cover all phases. Some chapters offer fresh or unfamiliar material.)

584. **Schnürer, G.** *Kirche und Kultur im Mittelalter.* 3 vols. Paderborn: F. Schöningh, 1924–26. (Systematic treatment of the social, economic, political, and cultural aspects of Christianity from the fourth to the fifteenth century.)

585. **Trench, R.** *Lectures on Medieval Church History.* 2d ed. London: Paul, 1886. x+453 pages. New York: Scribner's, 1888 (?). x+444 pages. (Nineteen lectures on topics so arranged as to constitute virtually a complete history of the medieval church. Scholarly and judicial, but becoming antiquated.)

Reference Helps
Historical (See Items 111–46)

586. **Chevalier, U.** *Répertoire des sources historiques du moyen âge: Bio-bibliographie.* 2 vols. Paris, 1883–88. New ed., Paris: Picard, 1903–7. (Bibliographies arranged alphabetically by biographies.)

587. ———. *Répertoire des sources historiques du moyen âge: Topo-bibliographie.* Paris: Picard, 1894–1903. (Similar treatment of places and topics.)

588. **Dahlmann, F. C., and Waitz, G.** *Quellenkunde der deutschen Geschichte.* 8th ed. (Edited by P. Heere.) Leipzig: Koehler, 1912. xx+1,290 pages.

589. **Paetow, L. J.** *Guide to the Study of Medieval History for Students, Teachers and Libraries.* Berkeley: University of California Press, 1917. xvi+552 pages. Revised ed. New York: Crofts, 1931. xvii+643 pages. (Reliable and well indexed.)

590. **Potthast, A.** *Bibliotheca historica medii aevi. Wegweiser durch die Geschichtswerke des europäischen Mittelalters bis 1500.* Berlin: Weber, 1862. 2d ed., 2 vols., 1986. (A reliable guide to the sources and literature of medieval history to the time of its appearance. Now partly superseded by Paetow's *Guide* [Item 589] but contains much material not in the latter work.)

591. **Thompson, J. W.** *Reference Studies in Medieval History.* Chicago: University of Chicago Press, 1907. 2d ed., 1914; rev. and enlarged ed., 1923–24. 3 vols. paged continuously. (Extensive selection of references to works in English, including periodical articles conveniently classified.)

For Medieval Latin (See Items 345, 350, 357)

592. **Beeson, C. H.** *A Primer of Medieval Latin.* Chicago: Scott, Foresman, 1925. 389 pages. (This book consists mainly of selections from religious and secular authors. It contains a

short grammatical introduction, footnotes on the texts, and a vocabulary of the distinctly medieval words.)

593. **Ducange, C. du F.** *Glossarium ad scriptores mediae et infimae latinitatis* (1678; 3 vols.). L. Favre's edition, 10 vols., Niort: Favre, 1883–87.

594. **Nunn, H. P. V.** *Ecclesiastical Latin.* Cambridge: University Press, 1922; 2d ed., 1927. xv+162 pages. (This is a combined grammar and reader, and is suitable for private reference or class use.)

GENERAL SOURCE WORKS (SEE ITEMS 317, 319, 326)

595. **Achéry, L. d'.** *Specilegium sive collectio veterum aliquot scriptorum.* 13 vols. Paris, 1655–77. New ed., 4 vols., Paris: Montalant, 1713.

596. *Acta Sanctorum quotquot toto orbe coluntur.* . . . . Antwerp and Brussels, 1643——. (This work of the Bollandists—Jesuit successors of John Bollandus who instituted it—gives the lives of the saints, in the Latin originals, in order of their places in the calendar. Sixty-five heavy volumes have been published, bringing the work to November 10. Besides supplying biographical data, more or less reliable, the lives reveal useful facts connected with the habits, beliefs and social environment of the religious men who wrote them.)

597. *Analecta Bollandiana.* Brussels: Société des Bollandistes, 1882——. (Primarily for hagiography. Contains additions to the *Acta Sanctorum* [Item 596]. Also reviews the literature of church history in general.)

598. **Coulton, G. G.** *Life in the Middle Ages.* London: Constable, 1910. 2d ed., Cambridge: University Press, 1928. 4 vols. Reprinted in 1 volume, same publisher, and New York: Macmillan, 1930. xxv+446 pages. (A wide range of source selections in translation. Includes folk lore, science, art, monasteries, etc.)

599. **Henderson, E. F.** *Select Historical Documents of the Middle Ages.* London: Macmillan, 1892. 2d ed., London: G. Bell & Sons, 1903. xiv+477 pages.

600. **Jaffé, P.** *Regesta pontificum Romanorum ab condita ecclesia ad annum 1198.* 2d ed., 2 vols. Leipzig, 1885–88. Continua-

tion by A. Potthast, 1198–1304. Berlin: De Decker, 1874–75.
2 vols. New ed., Berlin: Weidmann, 1906——; and by P. F.
Kehr, *Italia pontificia*, Berlin: Weidmann, 1906–25. 7 vols.
And by A. Brockmann, *Germania pontificia*. Berlin: Weidmann, 1910——.

601. *Magnum bullarium romanum*: *Bullarum diplomatum et privi-
legiorum sanctorum romanorum pontificum*. 24 vols. and 1 appendix vol. Turin: S. Franco and H. Dalmazzo, 1857–72·
(Bulls and other authoritative papal documents, A.D. 431–
1740. A continuation was undertaken, to consist of 5 volumes,
only one of which appeared [1760–78]. Naples: Caposaso,
1885.)

602. **Marténe, E.** *Veterum scriptorum et monumentorum histori-
corum, dogmaticorum, moralium, amplissima collectio*. Paris:
Montalant, 1724–33. 9 vols. (A miscellaneous collection.)

603. *Monumenta Germaniae Historica*. Edited by G. H. Pertz and
others. Hanover and Berlin, 1826. (This comprehensive collection contains a vast amount of church history source material. It is subdivided into about sixteen sections of from 1
to 30 volumes each. The four sections, comprising about 50
volumes, which are devoted to the *auctores* and *scriptores* of
various periods, contain the works of many ecclesiastical
writers. Where these duplicate the collection of Migne, the
Monumenta editions are usually preferable.) (*MGH*)

604. **Robinson, J. H.** *Readings in European History*. 2 vols. New
York: Ginn, 1904–6. (A selection of interesting source readings in English, for the student of general history. Volume
I covers the period from the fourth to the fifteenth century.)

605. *Scriptores rerum Germanicorum in usum scholarum, ex monu-
mentis Germaniae historicis recusi*. Hanover, 1840——. (A
selection of documents from *MGH* [Item 603] chiefly in im-
proved editions, octavo size.)

606. **Thatcher, O. J., and McNeal, E. H.** *A Source Book of Medieval History*. New York: Scribner's, 1905. xix+619 pages.
(Features constitutional documents. Much of the material is
of direct interest for the church-history student.)

PERIODICALS (SEE ITEMS 23–26, 147–70, 597, 833, 835)

607. *Bibliothèque de l'école des Chartes: revue d'érudition consacrée specialement à l'étude du moyen âge.* Paris: Decourchant, 1839——. Now published by Picard. (Indexed by ten-year periods.)

608. *Le moyen âge. Revue d'histoire et de philosophie.* Paris: Bouillon, 1888. Bi-monthly since 1897. Now published by Champion. (Lists new books and contents of periodicals.)

609. *Speculum, a Journal of Medieval Studies.* Cambridge: Medieval Academy of America, 1926——. (A quarterly, valuable for medieval literature, science, and society.)

THE EXPANSION OF CHRISTIANITY
(SEE ITEMS 295–301, 2224 ff.)
CHRISTIANITY AMONG THE FRANKS AND VISIGOTHS

610. **Dalton, O. M.** *Gregory of Tours: the History of the Franks.* 2 vols. Oxford: Clarendon Press, 1927. (Volume II contains a translation with critical notes. A work of importance.)

611. **Dill, S.** *Roman Society in Gaul in the Merovingian Age.* London: Macmillan, 1926. xiii+566 pages.

612. **Gaskoin, C. J. B.** *Alcuin, His Life and His Work.* London: Clay, 1904. xxii+275 pages.

613. **Hauck, A.** *Kirchengeschichte Deutschlands.* Leipzig: Hinrichs. Vols. I–III, 1887–96. Vols. III² and IV, 1904–6. Vol. V, 1903. (Bibliography with each volume.)

614. **Hodgkin, T.** *Italy and Her Invaders.* 8 vols. Oxford: Clarendon Press, 1880–99. Volumes V and VI have been revised (1916) by R. H. Hodgkin. (This work acquaints the reader with the Barbarian peoples and the process of their Christianization and appropriation of Latin culture to the time of Charlemagne.)

615. **Maclear, G. F.** *A History of Christian Missions during the Middle Ages.* London: Macmillan, 1863. xxi+466 pages.

616. **Robinson, C. H.** *The Conversion of Europe.* New York: Longmans, 1917. xxiii+640 pages. (Condensed—*How the Gospel Spread through Europe.* London: Society for Promoting Christian Knowledge, 1919. v+184 pages.)

617. **Robinson, G. W.** (translator). *The Life of St. Boniface by Willibald.* Cambridge: Harvard University Press, 1916. 114 pages.

618. —— (translator). *Eugippius, The Life of Saint Severinus.* Cambridge: Harvard University Press, 1914. 141 pages.

619. **Schubert, H. v.** *Geschichte der christlichen Kirche im Frühmittelalter.* Tübingen: Mohr, 1921. xxiv+808 pages. (Detailed and critical history to *ca.* 900.)

620. **Wells, C. L.** *The Age of Charlemagne.* New York: Christian Literature Co., 1898. x+472 pages. (Epochs of church history.)

THE CONVERSION OF THE SCANDINAVIAN PEOPLES
(SEE ITEM 679)

621. **Arup, E.** *Danmark's historie.* Vol. I. Copenhagen: Hagerup, 1925. 350 pages. (To 1282.)

622. **Hallendorff, C. J. H., and Schück, A.** *History of Sweden.* London: Cassell, 1929. 485 pages. (Translated from the Swedish manuscript by Mrs. Lajla Yapp.)

623. **Jörgensen, A. D.** *Den nordiske Kirkes Grundlaeggelse og förste Udvikling.* 2 vols. Copenhagen: Selspabet, 1874–78.

624. **Robinson, C. H.** *St. Anskar the Apostle of the North. 801–865.* London: Society for the Propagation of the Gospel, 1921. 139 pages. (Translation of the *Life* by Rimbert [d. 888].)

LATER MISSIONS AND EXPANSION OF THE WESTERN CHURCH

625. **Lemmens, L.** *Die Heidenmission des Spätmittelalters.* Münster: Aschendorff, 1919. x+112 pages.

626. **Maschke, E.** *Die deutschen Orden und die Preussen. Bekehrung und Unterwerfung in der preussish-baltischen Mission des 13. Jahrhunderts.* ("Historische Studien," No. 176.) Berlin: Ebering, 1928. xii+100 pages.

627. **Peers, E. A.** *Ramon Lull: A Biography.* London: Society for Promoting Christian Knowledge, 1929. xviii+454 pages. (Scholarly. Has extensive bibliography.)

628. **Robinson, C. H.** (translator). *The Life of Otto the Apostle of Pomerania, 1060–1139.* London: Society for Promoting Christian Knowledge, 1921. 193 pages. (Translation of the *Life* by Ebo and Herbordus.)

629. **Rockhill, W. W.** *The Journey of William of Rubruck to the Eastern Parts of the World, 1253–55, with Two Accounts of the Earlier Journey of John of Pian de Corpine.* London: Hakluyt Society, 1900. vi+304 pages.

HISTORY OF CHURCH ORGANIZATION

The works selected under this head do not include works on the institutions of monasticism and of social amelioration. These are supplied in the appropriate parts of the section "Religious Life and Worship." A number of titles of works not strictly devoted to "organization" have been included in the first subdivision of this section, in order, without further complicating the outline, to enable the reader to keep himself aware of the general development of Christianity.

The Advance and Development of the Papacy to 1303
(See Items 181, 186–92)

To the Beginning of the Crusades, 1095

630. **Barry, W.** *The Papal Monarchy from St. Gregory the Great to Boniface VIII (590–1303).* "Story of the Nations Series." London: Fisher; New York: Putnam's, 1902.

631. **Brockmann, A.** (editor). *Papsttum und Kaisertum: Forschungen zur politischen Geschichte und Geisteskultur des Mittelalters.* Munich: Verlag der Müncher Drucke, 1926. viii+707 pages. (A miscellany of scholarly essays.)

632. **Davenport, E. H.** *The False Decretals.* Oxford: Blackwell, 1916. xx+111 pages.

633. **Duchesne, L.** *The Beginnings of the Temporal Sovereignty of the Popes, A.D. 754–1073.* Translated from French by A. H. Matthew. London: Kegan Paul, 1908. xi+312 pages.

634. **Gay, J.** *Les papes du XIᵉ siècle et la chrétienté.* Paris: Lecoffre (Gabalda), 1926. xvii+428 pages. (Bibliography favors French titles.)

635. **Greenwood, T.** *Cathedra Petri: a Political History of the Great Latin Patriarchate.* 6 vols. London: Steward, 1856–72. (Incorporates much source material; extends to *ca.* 1413. Unsympathetic but not controversial.)

636. **Gregorovius, F.** *Geschichte der Stadt Rom im Mittelalter.* 8 vols. Berlin: Cotta, 1859–72. Volume I in 5th ed., Vols. II–VIII, 4th ed., 1889–1903. (Translated from the 4th edition by A. Hamilton, *History of the City of Rome in the Middle Ages.* 8 [13] vols. London: Bell, 1894–1902.) (A monumental work, constituting virtually a history of Western Europe and reviewing notable religious movements in the light of the political and social environment.)

637. **Halphen, L.** *Étude sur l'administration de Rome au moyen âge, 751–1252.* (Bibliothèque de l'école des hautes études. Sciences historiques et philologiques, 166.) Paris: Champion, 1907. xvi+190 pages.

638. **Hinschius, P.** *Decretales pseudo-Isidorianae, et capitula Angilramni.* Leipzig: Pauchnitz, 1863. ccxxxviii+771 pages.

639. **Mann, H. K.** *The Lives of the Popes in the Middle Ages.* 12 vols. London: Kegan Paul, 1902. 2d ed., 1925. (Gregory the Great to Innocent III.)

640. **McCabe, J.** *Crises in the History of the Papacy.* New York: Putnam's, 1916. xiv+459 pages.

641. **Poole, R. L.** *Lectures on the History of the Papal Chancery down to the Time of Innocent III.* Cambridge: University Press, 1915. xvi+211 pages.

642. **Vincent, Marvin R.** *The Age of Hildebrand.* New York: Christian Literature Co., 1896. xxii+457 pages.

643. **Voosen, E.** *Papauté et pouvoir civil à l'époque de Grégoire VII.* Gembloux: Duculot, 1927. xii+342 pages.

644. **Whitney, J. P.** "Pope Gregory VII and the Hildebrandine Ideal," *Church Quarterly Review,* LXX (1910), pp. 414–46.

645. **Wurm, H. I.** *Die Papstwahl, ihre Geschichte und Gebräuche.* Köln: Bachem, 1902. 136 pages. (Principles and practice in papal elections, entire period.)

FROM 1095 TO THE FALL OF BONIFACE VIII, 1303
(SEE ITEMS 691, 695)

646. **Almedingen, E. M.** *The English Pope (Adrian IV).* London: Heath, 1925. xvii+204 pages. (Enlarges on Breakspeare's work in Scandinavia.)

647. **Archer, T. A., and Kingsford, C. L.** *The Crusades: The Story of the Latin Kingdom of Jerusalem.* New York: Putnam's, 1900. xxx+467 pages.

648. **Barker, E.** "The Crusades," *Encyclopædia Britannica.* 13th ed.. Separately published London: Milford, 1923. 112 pages. Reprinted 1925.

649. **Finke, H.** *Aus den Tagen Bonifaz VIII. Funde und Forschungen.* Münster: Aschendorff, 1902. 296+ccxxiii pages.

650. **Luchaire, A.** *Innocent III.* Paris: Hachette, 1905-8. Six volumes, separately entitled. Vols. I, III, and IV revised 1911. (An authoritative work.)

651. **Paetow, L. J.** *The Crusades and Other Historical Essays Presented to D. C. Monro.* New York: Crofts, 1928. x+419 pages.

The Clergy and Their Functions

General

652. **Eubel, C.** *Hierarchia catholica medii aevi . . . . 1198-1605.* 3 vols. Regensburg: Monastery, 1898-1910. Volume III appeared in 2d edition, 1923. (Tabulated lists of bishops with dates and historical footnotes. Arranged in alphabetical order of dioceses.)

653. **Gams, P. B.** *Series episcoporum ecclesiae catholicae.* Ratisbon: Manz, 1873. 2d ed., 1931. xxiv+963 pages.

654. **Imbart de la Tour, P.** *Les élections épiscopales dans l'église de France du IXᵉ au XIIᵉ siècle 814-1150.* Paris: Hachette, 1891. xxxi+554 pages.

655. **Lea, H. C.** *History of Sacerdotal Celibacy in the Christian Church.* (See Item 282.)

656. **Lee, G. C.** "Hincmar: an Introduction to the Study of the Revolution in the Organization of the Church in the Ninth Century," *Papers of the American Society of Church History,* Series I, VIII, 231-60. Baltimore: Knickerbocker, 1897.

657. **Lesne, E.** *La hiérarchie épiscopale; provinces, metropolitains primats en Gaule et Germanie ... 742-822.* Lille: Facultés catholiques; Paris: Picard, 1905. xv+350 pages.

658. **Vacandard, E.** "Les origines du célibat ecclésiastique," *Études de critique et d'histoire religieuse,* 1st Ser. (Paris: Le-

coffre, 1905; viii+390 pages), pp. 71–120. (To the twelfth century.)

659. **Wordsworth, J.** *The Ministry of Grace.* New York: Longmans, 1901. xxiv+488 pages.

SACRAMENTS AND PREACHING
SACRAMENTS (SEE ITEMS 231, 284)

660. **Batiffol, P.** *Leçons sur la messe.* 4th ed. Paris: Gabalda, 1919. xi+330 pages.

661. **Chardon, C. M.** *Histoire des sacrements.* 6 vols. Paris: Desprey, 1745. 2d ed. Paris, 1840.

662. **Lea, H. C.** *History of Auricular Confession and Indulgences in the Latin Church.* 3 vols. Philadelphia: Lea Bros., 1796.

663. **Paulus, N.** *Geschichte des Ablasses im Mittelalter.* 3 vols. Paderborn: Schoningh, 1922–23.

664. **Saltet, L.** *Les réordinations; études sur le sacrement de l'ordre.* Paris: Gabalda, 1907. 419 pages.

665. **Schmitz, H. J.** *Die Bussbücher.* In 2 vols.: *Die Bussbücher und die Bussdisciplin der Kirche,* and *Die Bussbücher und die kanonische Bussverfassung.* Mainz: Kirchheim, 1883 and 1898. (Schmitz has good editions of the Penitentials, but his introductions are biased in favor of a theory of their Roman origin.)

PREACHING (SEE ITEMS 227–29)

666. **Albert, F. R.** *Die Geschichte der Predigt in Deutschland bis Luther.* 3 (1) vols. Gütersloh: Bertelsmann, 1892–96.

667. **Walter, J.** *Die ersten Wanderprediger Frankreichs.* Leipzig: Böhme, 1906. 182 pages. (Itinerant preaching monks, 1095–1145.)

668. **Zawart, A.** "The History of Franciscan Preaching . . . 1209–1927," *Franciscan Studies,* No. VII, pp. 241–596. New York: Wagner, 1928.

NATIONAL AND TERRITORIAL CHURCH INSTITUTIONS
IN GERMANY AND FRANCE

669. **Chénon, É.** *Histoire des rapports de l'église et de l'état.* Paris: Bloud, 1913. 252 pages. (France—entire history.)

670. **Goyau, G.** *Histoire religieuse.* Paris: Société de l'histoire nationale, 1922. vi+639 pages. (In the "National History Series," edited by G. Hanotaux.)

671. **Koeniger, A. M.** *Burchard I von Worms und die deutsche Kirche seiner Zeit (1000–1025).* Munich: Lentner, 1905. xii +244 pages. (A study of the conditions of the German church and society in the time of Burchard.)

672. **Longueval, J., and Others.** *Histoire de l'église gallicane.* 24 (15) vols. 4th ed. Paris: Bureau de la bibliothèque catholique, 1825–27. (An elaborate chronicle by four Jesuits.)

673. **Sainte-Marthe, S., and Continuators.** *Gallia christiana in provincias ecclesiasticas distributa . . . . ab origine ecclesiarum ad nostra tempora.* Paris: Congregatio de Propagande Fide, 1656, 4 vols. *Gallia Christiana nova,* Paris: Didot, 1715– 1865, 16 vols. *Gallia Christiana novissima,* Monbeliard and Valence, 1895–1916, 6 vols. (Essential for provincial, diocesan, and local history of France.)

674. **Werminghoff, A.** *Verfassungsgeschichte der deutschen Kirche im Mittelalter.* 2d ed. Leipzig: Teubner, 1913. A revision of the author's *Geschichte der Kirchenverfassung Deutschlands . . . . 1905.*)

675. ———.. *Nationalkirchliche Bestrebungen im deutschen Mittelalter.* Stuttgart: Enke, 1910. xviii+180 pages. (Deals with German national tendencies and concordats with the popes. The study is carried beyond the Reformation.)

IN OTHER COUNTRIES

676. **Blok, S. J.** *History of the People of the Netherlands.* Translated from the Dutch by O. A. Bierstadt and R. Putnam. 5 vols. New York: Putnam's, 1898–1912. (Volumes I and II cover this period.)

677. **Bull, E.** *Folk og Kirke i Middelalderen; Studier til Norges historie.* Christiania and Copenhagen: Gyldendal, Nordisk Forlag, 1912. 271 pages. (Priests and people, miracles, etc., in Norway, from the middle of the eleventh to the beginning of the sixteenth century.)

678. **Florez, H.** (editor), **and Others.** *España Sagrada.* 51 vols. Madrid: R. Academie de la historia, 1754–89.

679. **Friis, A., and Others.** *Det danske Folks Historie.* 8 vols. Copenhagen: Erichsen, 1927–29. (Volumes I–III for the Middle Ages, to 1531.)

680. **Gams, S. B.** *Die Kirchengeschichte von Spanien.* 3 vols. Regensburg: Manz, 1862–79. (Volumes II and the first part of Volume III treat our period. A Roman Catholic view.)

681. **McCracken, W. D.** *The Rise of the Swiss Republic.* 2d ed. New York: Holt, 1901. x+423 pages.

682. **Meyrick, F.** *The Church in Spain.* London: Gardner, 1892. xiv+450 pages. (An introductory sketch, poorly annotated.)

683. **Moll, W.** *Kerkgengeschiednis van nederland voor de hervorming.* 4 vols. Utrecht: Kemink, 1864–69.

684. **Montelius, O., and Others.** *Sveriges Historia till vara Dagar.* 14 vols. Stockholm: Nostedt, 1919–26. (Volumes I–V for the Middle Ages.)

685. **Monticelli, G.** *Italia religiosa. La religione del populo italiano nel suo sviluppo storico.* Turin: Bocca, 1927. xvi+474.

686. **Muratori, L. A.** *Rerum Italicarum scriptores. (500–1500).* 25 vols. Milan, 1723–51. New ed., Citta di Castello and Bologna: Lapi, 1900.

687. **Sedgwick, H. D.** *Italy in the Thirteenth Century.* 2 vols. New York: Houghton Mifflin, 1912.

688. **Ughelli, F.** *Italia sacra sive de episcopis Italiae et Insularum adjacentium etc.* 10 vols. Venice: Coleti, 1717–22.

689. **Watts, H. E.** *The Christian Recovery of Spain.* New York: Putnam's, 1894. xxvii+315 pages.

690. **Westman, K. B.** *Den Svenska Kyrkans utveckling från St. Bernhards tidevarv till Innocentius III's.* Stockholm: Norstedt, 1915. xii+301 pages.

691. **Willson, T. B.** *History of the Church and State in Norway from the Tenth to the Sixteenth Century.* Westminster: Constable, 1903. xii+382 pages.

692. **Wordsworth, John.** *The National Church of Sweden.* London: Mowbray; Milwaukee: Young Churchman Co., 1911. xix+459 pages.

Local Church Organization

693. **Collins, R. W.** "The Parish Priest and His Flock as Depicted in the Councils of the Twelfth and Thirteenth Centuries." *JR* (Item 150), X (1930), 313–32.

694. **Dobiache-Rojdestvensky, O.** *La vie paroissale en France au XIIIe siècle.* Paris: Picard, 1911. 190 pages.

695. **Imbart de la Tour, P.** *Les origines religieuses de la France. Les paroisses rurales du IVe au XIe siècle.* Paris: Picard, 1900. 354 pages. (Deals with the organization of local churches and their relations to feudalism.)

696. **Prévost, G. A.** *L'église et les campagnes au môyen âge.* Paris: Champion, 1892. 292 pages.

697. **Schäfer, H.** *Pfarrkirche und Stift im deutschen Mittelalter. Eine Kirchenrechtsgeschichtliche Untersuchung.* Stuttgart: Enke, 1903. xiv+210 pages.

Church Law (See Items 196–203)

698. **Hazeltine, H. D.** "Roman and Canon Law in the Middle Ages," *CMH* (Item 562), Vol. V, chap. xxi.

699. **Lea, H. C.** *Studies in Church History: The Rise of the Temporal Power.* Philadelphia: Lea, 1883. xv+603 pages. (Benefit of clergy, excommunication, etc.)

700. **MacKinney, L. C.** "The Laity in the French Councils of the Eleventh Century," *JR* (Item 150), IX (1929), 568–88.

701. **Maitland, F. W.** *Collected Papers.* Edited by H. A. L. Fisher. Cambridge: University Press, 1911.

702. **Richter, A. L.** *Lehrbuch des katholischen und evangelischen Kirchenrechtes.* 8th ed. Leipzig: Tauchnitz, 1886.

703. **Sägmüller, J. B.** *Lehrbuch des katholischen Kirchenrechts.* 2 vols. Freiburg: Herder, 1900–1904. 3d ed. 1914.

704. **Schulte, A.** *Der Adel und die deutsche Kirche im Mittelalter.* (Kirchenrechtliche Abhandlungen 63, 64.) Stuttgart: Enke, 1910. xii+460 pages.

705. **Vinogradoff, P.** *Roman Law in Medieval Europe.* 1909. New ed. (F. de Zulneta). Oxford: Clarendon Press, 1929. 155 pages.

RELIGIOUS LIFE AND WORSHIP
Western Monastic Orders and Monastic Life
General

706. **Berlière, U.** *L'ordre monastique dès origines au XII siècle.* 3d ed. Lille: Desclée, xii+310 pages. (Bibliographies by chapters. A well-informed sympathetic sketch.)

707. **Coulton, G. G.** *Medieval Studies.* 1st Ser. 2d ed. London: Simpkin, 1915. vi+132 pages. 3d ed., Cambridge: Cambridge University Press, 1930. 273 pages.

708. **Montalambert, C. F. R., Comte de.** *The Monks of the West from St. Benedict to St. Bernard.* 6 vols. London: Nimmo. 1896. (The work of an enthusiastic admirer. Original French edition: *Les Moines d'Occident.* Paris, 1869–70.)

709. **Wishart, A. W.** *A Short History of Monks and Monasteries,* 2d ed. Trenton, New Jersey: Brandt, 1902. 462 pages.

710. **Workman, H. B.** *The Evolution of the Monastic Ideal . . . . to the Coming of the Friars.* London: Kelly, 1913. xxi+368 pages.* (An objective study and interpretation.)

Monastic Orders and Rules

711. **Chaumont, L.** *Histoire de Cluny depuis les origines jusqu'à la ruine de l'abbaye.* 2d ed. Paris: Gigord, 1911. ii+260 pages.

712. **Holsten, L.** *Codex regularum monasticarum.* 6 vols. Rome, 1661. 2d ed., Vienna, 1759.

713. **Leclercq, H.** *L'ordre Bénédictin.* Paris: Rieder, 1930. 80 pages.

714. **Lefèbvre, F. A.** *Saint Bruno et l'ordre des Chartreux.* 2 vols. Paris: Librairie Saint Paul, 1884.

715. **Prutz, H.** *Die geistlichen Ritterorden.* Berlin: Mittler, 1908. xviii+549 pages.

716. **Sackur, E.** *Die Cluniacenser . . . . bis zur Mitte des XIten Jahrhunderts.* 2 (1) vols. Halle: Niemeyer, 1892–94.

717. **Smith, L. M.** *Cluny in the Eleventh and Twelfth Centuries.* London: Allan, 1930. xxviii+348 pages.

718. **Winter, F.** *Die Prämonstratenser des 12. Jahrhunderts und ihre Bedeutung für das nordöstliche Deutschland.* Berlin: Schweigger, 1865. vi+386 pages.

719. **Woodhouse, F. C.** *The Military Religious Orders of the Middle Ages.* London: Society for Promoting Christian Knowledge, 1879. xvii+360 pages. (Well informed but undocumented.)

CLOISTER LIFE (SEE ITEMS 279–86)

720. **Arbois de Jubainville, H. d', and Pigotte, L.** *Études sur l'état intérieure des abbayes cisterciennes et principalemant de Clairvaux au XIIᵉ et au XIIIᵉ siècle.* Paris: Durand, 1858. xviii+489 pages.

721. **Bühler, J.** (editor). *Klosterleben im deutschen Mittelalter nach zeitgenössischen Aufzeichnungen.* Leipzig: Insel, 1921. Enlarged edition 1923, xxiii+546 pages. (Source selections in German translation. Includes friars.)

722. **Butler, E. C.** *Benedictine Monachism. Studies in Benedictine Life and Rule.* London: Longmans, 1919. viii+387 pages. (See Item 529.)

723. **Coulton, G. G.** *Five Centuries of Religion.* 2 vols. Cambridge: University Press, 1923——. To be completed in 4 volumes. (Treats unsympathetically, with great learning, most phases of the history of monasticism and the mendicants from the beginning of the twelfth century.)

724. **Eckenstein, I.** *Women under Monasticism: Chapters on Saint-lore and Convent Life, 500–1500.* Cambridge: University Press, 1896. xv+496 pages.

725. **Monticelli, G.** *Due secoli di vita religiosa in Italia (800–1000).* Turin: Bocca, 1928. 383 pages.

726. **Scott, E., and Bland, C. C. A** (translators). *The Dialogue of Caesarius of Heisterbach.* 2 vols. London: Routledge, 1929. (A treasury of well-told stories by a Cistercian of the early thirteenth century.)

THE FRIARS, CA. 1209–1517

ST. FRANCIS OF ASSISI AND THE FRANCISCANS

For Franciscan periodicals see the *CMH* (Item 562), VI, 692. The Series "Franciscan Studies," New York: J. F. Wagner, and the publications of the British Society of Franciscan Studies (Manchester: University Press) should also be consulted.

727. **Boehmer H.** *Analekten zur Geschichte des Franciscus von Assisi.* S. Francisci opuscula, etc. Editio major. Tübingen: Mohr, 1904. lxxii+166 pages. The minor edition, published at the same time, has been revised by F. Wiegand, Tübingen: Mohr, 1930. xii+75 pages.

728. **Coulton, G. G.** *From St. Francis to Dante, a Translation of All That Is of Primary Interest in the Chronicle of the Franciscan Salimbene, etc.* London: Nutt, 1906. vi+264 pages.

729. **Felder, H.** *Die Ideale des heiligen Franciscus von Assisi.* Paderborn: Schöningh, 1923. 2d ed., 1924. xv+445 pages. Translated by B. Bittle: *The Ideals of St. Francis of Assisi.* New York: Benziger, 1925. xvi+518 pages.

730. **Freer, A. S. B.** *The Early Franciscans and Jesuits: A Study in Contrasts.* London: Society for Promoting Christian Knowledge, 1922. 141 pages. (Features missions of both orders.)

731. **Goetz, W.** *Die Quellen zur Geschichte des heiligen Franz von Assisi.* Gotha: Perthes, 1904. x+259 pages.

732. **Jörgensen, J.** *St. Francis of Assisi.* Translated from the Danish by T. O. Sloane. New York: Longmans, 1912; reprinted 1926. xv+428 pages.

733. **Le Monnier, L.** *Histoire de Saint François d'Assisi.* 7th ed. 2 vols. Paris: Librairie Saint François, 1922.

734. **Little, A. G.** *Guide to Franciscan Studies.* London: Society for Promoting Christian Knowledge, 1920. New York: Macmillan, 1921. v+63 pages.

735. *The Little Flowers and the Life of St. Francis, with the Mirror of Perfection.* "Everyman" edition. London: Dent, 1910; reprinted 1927.

736. **Muzzey, D. S.** *The Spiritual Franciscans.* New York: Columbia University Press, 1907. 76 pages.

737. **Reinmann, G. J.** *The Third Order Secular of St. Francis.* Washington, D.C.: Catholic University of America, 1928. 200 pages.

738. **Robinson, P.** *The Life of Saint Clare Ascribed to Fr. Thomas of Celano . . . . with an Appendix Containing the Rule of Saint Clare.* Philadelphia: Dolphin Press; London: Unwin, 1910. xliv+170 pages.

739. **Sabatier, P.** *Life of Francis of Assisi.* Translated from the French (1893) by L. S. Houghton. New York: Scribner's, 1894; reprinted 1917. (Still the most essential life of St. Francis.)

740. **Salter, E. G.** *The Coming of the Friars to England and Germany.* London: Dent, xxxvi+198 pages. (Chronicles of Eccleston and Jordan of Giano in translation.)

741. **Salvatorelli, L.** *The Life of St. Francis of Assisi.* Translated by E. Sutton. New York: Knopf, 1928. 313 pages. (From the Italian: *Vita di Francesco d'Assisi.* Bari: Laterza, 1926. 250 pages.) (A vivid biography.)

St. Dominic and the Dominicans

742. **Aron, M.** *Un animateur de la jeunesse au XIIIe siècle.* Paris: Desclée, 1930. 396 pages. (On Jordan of Saxony.)

743. **Drane, A. T.** *The History of St. Dominic.* New York: Longmans, 1891. xvii+485 pages.

744. **Galbraith, G. R.** *The Constitution of the Dominican Order.* Manchester: The University Press. New York: Longmans, 1925. xvi+286 pages.

745. **Herkless, J.** *Francis and Dominic and the Mendicant Orders.* New York: Scribner's, 1901. 237 pages.

746. **Mortier, P.** *Histoire des maîtres généraux de l'ordre des Frères-Prêcheurs.* 7 vols. Paris: Picard, 1903–13.

747. **Scheeben, H. C.** *Der heilige Dominikus.* Freiburg: Herder, 1927. xvi+459 pages.

The Brotherhoods in the Netherlands and Germany

748. **Barnikol, E.** *Studien zur Geschichte der Brüder vom gemeinsamen Leben.* Tübingen: Mohr, 1917. xii+215 pages.

749. **Greven, J.** *Die Anfänge der Beguinen; ein Beitrag zur Geschichte der Volksfrömmigkeit und des Ordenswesen.* Münster: Aschendorff, 1912. xv+227 pages.

750. **Hyma, A.** *The Christian Renaissance. A History of the Devotio Moderna.* Grand Rapids: The Reformed Press, 1924. New York: Century, 1925. xviii+501 pages.

751. **Jones, R. M.** *Studies in Mystical Religion.* New York: Macmillan, 1909. xxxviii+518 pages.

752. **Kettlewell, S.** *Thomas à Kempis and the Brothers of Common Life.* 2d ed. London: Kegan Paul, 1885. viii+392 pages.

753. **Leete, F. D.** *Christian Brotherhood.* New York: Eaton & Mains, 1912. 415 pages. (Attempts a complete history of religious brotherhoods to the present day. From secondary sources.)

754. **Ullmann, K.** *Reformers before the Reformation, Principally in Germany and the Netherlands.* 2 vols. 3d ed. Edinburgh: Clark, 1863.

755. **Vernet, F.** "Beghards, Beguines hétérodoxes," article in *Dictionnaire de Théologie Catholique* (Item 123), II, 528–35. "Frères du libre esprit." *Ibid.*, VI, 800–809.

756. **Winkworth, S.** *The History and Life of Dr. John Tauler with Twenty-five of his Sermons.* London: Smith Elder & Co., 1857. xi+415 pages. New York: Willy & Halstead, 1858. xxxix+481 pages.

MYSTICISM, DEVOTION, AND PIETY (SEE ITEMS 230, 596)

757. **Butler, A.** *The Lives of the Saints.* New edition by H. Thurston. London: Burns, 1926. xix+412 pages.

758. **Butler, C.** *Western Mysticism.* London: Constable, 1923. xii+344 pages. (Augustine, Gregory I, Bernard.)

759. **Dobbins, D.** *Franciscan Mysticism.* "Franciscan Studies," No. VII. New York: Wagner, 1927. 207 pages. (On Bonaventura.)

760. **Dunbar, A. B. C.** *A Dictionary of Saintly Women.* 2 vols. London: Bell, 1904–5.

761. **Fleming, W. K.** *Mysticism in Christianity.* New York: Revell, 1913. x+282 pages.

762. **Hardman, O.** *The Ideals of Asceticism.* New York: Macmillan, 1924. xvi+232 pages. (A scholarly appreciation and exposition of ascetic devotion.)

763. **Hyma, A.** *Thomas à Kempis, Imitation of Christ. Edited by A. Hyma from Hitherto Undiscovered Sources.* New York: Century, 1927. xxxviii+182 pages.

764. **Inge, W. R.** *Christian Mysticism Considered in Eight Lectures Delivered before the University of Oxford.* New York: Scribner's, 1899. xv+379 pages. (A work of first importance.)

765. **Leuba, J. H.** *The Psychology of Religious Mysticism.* London: Kegan Paul, 1925. xii+336 pages.

766. **Pourrat, P.** *Christian Spirituality.* Vol. II, *In the Middle Ages.* Translated from the French by S. P. Jacques. New York: Kennedy, 1922. (The whole work is in 3 volumes, the third being in two parts, of which Part I only has appeared, 1927.)

767. **Preger, W.** *Geschichte der deutschen Mystik im Mittelalter.* 3 vols. Leipzig: Dorffling, 1874–93. (Important.)

768. **Underhill, E.** *Mysticism: A Study in the Nature and Development of Man's Spiritual Consciousness.* 12th ed. London: Methuen, 1930. 504 pages.

769. ———. *The Mystics of the Church.* New York: Doran, 1926. 259 pages.

770. **Vernet, F.** *La spiritualité médiévale.* Paris: Bloud, 1929. 211 pages. (Treats popularly the various forms of medieval devotion.)

771. **Winkworth, S.** *Theologia Germanica.* Translated by S. Winkworth from F. Pfeiffer's edition. Andover: Draper, 1855. lxxii+202 pages. (Pfeiffer's 3d German edition, Gütersloh: Bertelsmann, 1875.)

THE CHURCH AND SOCIAL AMELIORATION
(SEE ITEMS 387–94)

772. **Brace, C. L.** *Gesta Christi, or a History of Humane Progress.* London: Hodder, 1882. 2d ed., 1884. 4th American ed., New York: Armstrong, 1885. xxiii+520 pages.

773. **Chadwick, W. E.** *The Church, the State and the Poor. A Series of Historical Sketches.* London: Scott, 1914. viii+223 pages.

774. **Dubois, P.** *Les asseuréments au XIII siècle.* Paris: Rousseau. 1900, 237 pages. (Discusses the *Peace of God.*)

775. **Duval, F. V.** *De la paix de Dieu à la paix le fer.* Paris: Paillard, 1923. 103 pages.

776. **Hausrath, A.** *Weltverbesserer im Mittelalter.* 3 vols. Leipzig: Breitkopf, 1893–95.

777. *Historical Illustrations of the Social Effects of Christianity.* New York: Longmans, 1924. xii+171 pages. (A report of the Conference on Christian Politics, Economics, and Citizenship, Birmingham, 1924.)

778. **Mackinney, L. C.** "The People and Public Opinion in the Eleventh Century Peace Movement," *Speculum* (Item 609), V (1930), 181–200.

779. **Prutz, H.** *Die Friedensidee. Ihr Ursprung, anfänglicher Sinn und allmählicher Wandel.* Munich and Leipzig: Duncker, 1917. 213 pages.

Worship, Church Architecture, and Art

Liturgy and Ritual (See Items 204–26, 232, 234, 237, 240, 660)

780. **Dowden, J.** *The Church Year and Calendar.* Cambridge: University Press, 1910. xxvi+160 pages. (A sketch of the development of the church year.)

781. **Frere, W. H.** *The Principles of Religious Ceremonial.* London: Longmans, 1906. x+324 pages. (In part historical.)

782. **Gougaud, L.** *Devotions et pratiques ascétiques du moyen âge.* Lille and Bruges: Desclée; Paris: P. Lethielleux, 1925. vii+237 pages. (Discussion by a learned Benedictine of medieval piety in its ritual expression.)

783. (Publications of) *The Henry Bradshaw Society, Founded . . . . 1890 for the Editing of Rare Liturgical Texts.* London: printed for the Society 1891. (Sixty-six volumes to 1928. Critical editions with some translations.)

784. **Strappel, R.** *Liturgie und geistliche Dichtung, 1050–1300.* Frankfort: Diesterweg, 1927. xvii+216 pages. (Useful for the development of hymnody.)

785. **Thomas, W.** *Der Sonntag im frühen Mittelalter.* Göttingen: Vandenhoeck & Ruprecht, 1929. 120 pages.

786. **Thurston, R. P.** *The Stations of the Cross: An Account of Their History and Devotional Purpose.* London: Burns, 1906. xii+183 pages. (Has been translated into French by A. Boudinhon. Paris: Letouzey, 1907. xi+286 pages.)

787. **Will, R.** *Le culte: Étude d'histoire et de philosophie religieuse.* Volume I, Strassbourg: Librairie Istra, 1925. Volume II. Paris: Alcan, 1929. (A Protestant scholar's interpretation of the history and functions of various elements in worship. Illuminating and uncontroversial.)

CHURCH ARCHITECTURE AND ART

788. **Durand, G.** (d. 1296). *The Symbolism of the Churches and Church Ornaments*. Critical translation by J. M. Neale of Durand's *Rationale divinorum officiorum*. Book I. New York: Scribner's, 1893. cxxxv+209 pages.

789. **Jackson, T. G.** *Gothic Architecture in France, England and Italy*. 2 vols. Cambridge: Cambridge University Press, 1915. (A work of distinction.)

790. **Jameson, Mrs. A. B.** *Legends of the Monastic Orders as Represented in the Fine Arts*. New York: Mifflin, 1898. xv+489 pages.

791. **Lethaby, W. R.** *Medieval Art from the Peace of the Church to the Eve of Renaissance*. New ed. London: Duckworth, 1912. xviii+315 pages.

792. **Michel, A.** *Histoire de l'art depuis les premiers temps chrétiens jusqu'à nos jours*. 8 vols. Paris: Colin, 1905–29.

793. **Reinach, S.** *Apollo: an Illustrated Manual of the History of Art throughout the Ages*. Translated by F. Simmonds from French. (Published in England, 1904, as *The Study of Art*.) Rev. ed., New York: Scribner's, 1924. xvi+350 pages.

POPULAR CULTS AND FOLK BELIEFS
(SEE ITEMS 230, 233, 238, 239, 241, 243)

794. **Baring-Gould, S.** *Curious Myths of the Middle Ages*. (1866.) Boston: Little, 1904. 453 pages.

795. **Beissel, S.** *Die Verehrung der Heiligen und ihre Reliquien in Deutschland*. Freiburg: Herder, 1890. 143 pages. (To *ca.* 1200.)

796. **Français, J.** (pseudonym). *L'église et la sorcellerie*. Paris: Nourry, 1910. 272 pages. (Based in part on evidence in Lea's *History of the Inquisition*.)

797. **Gougaud, L.** "La danse dans les églises," *RHE* (Item 163), XV (1914), 5–22, 229–45.

798. **Heath, S. H.** *Pilgrim Life in the Middle Ages*. London: Unwin, 1911. 351 pages.

799. **Hyde, D.** *Legends of Saints and Sinners*. London: Unwin, 1915. xiv+295 pages.

800. **Lea, H. C.** *Superstition and Force.* Philadelphia: Lea, 1866. 4th ed., 1892. xvi+627 pages.

801. **Thorndike, L.** *A History of Magic and Experimental Science during the First Thirteen Centuries of Our Era.* 2 vols. New York: Macmillan, 1923.

802. **Trier, J.** "Patrozinienforschung und Kulturgeographie," *HZ* (Item 25), CXXXIV (1926), 319-49.

EDUCATION, LEARNING, AND THEOLOGY
Schools and Universities (See Item 929)

803. **Abelson, P.** *The Seven Liberal Arts. A Study in Medieval Culture.* . . . . New York: Columbia University Press, 1906. viii+151 pages.

804. **Deansley, M.** "Medieval schools," *CMH* (Item 563), Vol. V, chap. xxii.

805. **Denifle, H.** *Geschichte der Universitäten im Mittelalter.* Berlin: Weidmann, 1885. xlv+814 pages.

806. **McCabe, J.** *Peter Abélard.* New York: Putnam, 1901. ix+402 pages.

807. **Maitre, L.** *Les écoles épiscopales et monastiques en occident avant les universités.* 2d ed. Paris: Abbaye Saint Martin, 1924. x+226 pages.

808. **Mullinger, J. B.** *The University of Cambridge.* 3 vols. Cambridge: University Press, 1873-1911. (Volume I comes to 1535. Contains material on the early universities in general.)

809. ————. *The Schools of Charles the Great and the Restoration of Education in the Ninth Century.* London: Longmans, 1877, xix+193 pages. Reprinted, New York: Stechert, 1904.

810. **Norton, A. V.** *Readings in the History of Education. Medieval Universities.* Cambridge: Harvard University, 1909. x+155 pages. (Source materials.)

811. **Poole, R. L.** "The Masters of the Schools at Paris and Chartres in John of Salisbury's Time," *EHR* (Item 24), XXXV (1920), 321-42.

812. **Rait, R. S.** *Life in a Medieval University.* Cambridge: University Press, 1912. viii+164 pages.

813. **Rashdall, H.** *The Universities of Europe in the Middle Ages* 2 (3) vols. Oxford: Clarendon Press, 1895.

814. **Symonds, J. A.** *Wine, Women and Song.* London: Chatto, 1925. xiii+208 pages. (Medieval student songs.)

815. **West, A. F.** *Alcuin and the Rise of the Christian Schools.* New York: Scribner's, 1892. vii+205 pages. Reprinted 1912.

The Advance of Learning and of Science

816. **Brehaut, E.** *An Encyclopedist of the Dark Ages: Isidore of Seville.* ("Columbia University Studies," Vol. XLVIII, No. 1.) New York: Longmans, 1912. 274 pages.

817. **Graves, F. P.** *A History of Education during the Middle Ages and the Transition to Modern Times.* New York: Macmillan, 1910; reprinted 1916. xv+328 pages.

818. **Haskins, C. H.** *The Renaissance of the Twelfth Century.* Cambridge: Harvard University Press, 1927. x+437 pages.

819. **Little, A. G.** *Roger Bacon: Essays Contributed by Various Writers.* Oxford: Clarendon Press, 1914. viii+425 pages. (Fourteen essays on Bacon and thirteenth-century science and learning.)

820. **Marique, P. J.** *History of Christian Education.* 2 vols. New York: Fordham University Press, 1924–26.

821. **O'Leary, de L. E.** *Arabic Thought and Its Place in History.* London: Kegan Paul; New York: Dutton, 1922. vii+320 pages.

822. **Sandys, J. E.** *A History of Classical Scholarship from the Sixth Century B.C. to the End of the Middle Ages.* 3 vols. Cambridge: University Press, 1905–8. Volume I in 2d edition, 1906; in 3d edition, 1921 (to 1400).

823. **Sartiaux, F.** *Foi et science au moyen âge.* Paris: Rieder, 1926. 255 pages.

824. **Taylor, H. O.** *The Medieval Mind.* 2 vols. New York: Macmillan, 1911. 2d ed., 1914. (Treats leaders and tendencies in medieval thought and culture. With copious extracts.)

825. **Zimmer, H.** *The Irish Element in Medieval Culture.* (Translated by J. L. Edmonds from an essay in *Preussische Jährbücher,* 1887.) New York: Putnam's, 1891. vii+139 pages.

SCHOLASTIC THEOLOGY AND PHILOSOPHY
(SEE ITEMS 244–65)

826. *Beiträge zur Geschichte der Philosophie und Theologie des Mittelalters.* Münster: Aschendorf, 1891——. (Thirty-seven volumes to 1930.)

827. **Bett, H.** *John Scotus Erigena.* Cambridge: University Press, 1925. 204 pages.

828. **Grabmann, M.** *Geschichte der scholastischen Methode.* 2 vols. Vol. I. Freiburg and St. Louis, Missouri: Herder, 1909.

829. ——. *Thomas Aquinas, His Personality and Thought.* Translated by V. Michel. New York: Longmans, 1928. ix+ 191 pages.

830. **Husik, I.** *A History of Medieval Jewish Philosophy.* New York: Macmillan, 1916. vii+462 pages.

831. **MacDonald, A. J.** *Berengar and the Reform of Sacramental Doctrine.* London: Longmans, 1930. xii+444 pages. (A thorough treatment. Follows the controversy to 1215.)

832. **Mandonnet, P.** *Siger de Brabant et l'averrosïme latin.* 2 vols. Louvain: Institut superieur de philosophie de l'Université, 1911.

833. *The New Scholasticism: A Quarterly Review of Philosophy.* Washington, D.C.: Catholic University Press, 1927——.

834. **Reade, M. W. V.** "Philosophy in the Middle Ages," *CMH* (Item 562), Vol. V, chap. xxiii.

835. *Recherches de théologie ancienne et médiévale.* Louvain: Abbaye de Mont César, 1929——. (Quarterly.)

836. **Seeberg, R.** *Lehrbuch der Dogmengeschichte* (Item 251). Vol. III, *Die Dogmengeschichte des Mittelalters.* 4th ed. Leipzig: Deichert, 1931. xvii+797 pages.

837. **Wicksteed, P. H.** *Dante and Aquinas.* London: Dent, 1913. xii+271 pages.

838. **Workman, H. B.** *Christian Thought to the Reformation.* New York: Scribner's, 1911. 256 pages.

839. **Wulf, M. de.** *History of Medieval Philosophy.* Translated by Ernest C. Messenger. 2 vols. New York: Longmans, 1925– 26. (From the fifth French edition, 1924–25. Deals with Scholastics and their opponents.)

840. **Wulf, M. de.** *Philosophy and Civilization in the Middle Ages.* Princeton: Princeton University Press; London: Milford; Oxford: University Press, 1922. x+313 pages.

POLITICAL THOUGHT (SEE ITEMS 270–78)

841. *CMH* (Item 562), Vol. VI, chap. xviii.

842. **Carlyle, R. W. and A. J.** *A History of Medieval Political Theory in the West.* 5 vols. London: Blackwood, 1903–28.

843. **Dunning, W. A.** *A History of Political Theories, Ancient and Medieval.* New York: Macmillan, 1902. xxv+360 pages.

844. **Emerton, E.** *Humanism and Tyranny: Studies in the Italian Trecento.* Cambridge: Harvard University Press, 1925. vii+377 pages.

845. **Gierke, O.** *Political Theories of the Middle Ages.* Translated by F. W. Maitland. Cambridge: University Press, 1900. lxxx+197 pages. From Volume III of the author's *Das deutsche Genossenschaftsrecht.* 3 vols. Berlin: Weidman, 1868–81. (Important.)

846. **Hearnshaw, F. T. C., and Others.** *The Social and Political Ideas of Some Great Medieval Thinkers.* London: Harrap, 1923. 224 pages. (A set of lectures of variant quality.)

847. **Jarrett, B.** *Social Theories of the Middle Ages. 1200–1500.* London: Benn, 1926. ix+280 pages.

848. **Mackinnon, J.** *A History of Modern Liberty.* 2 vols. New York: Longmans, 1906.

RELIGION IN POPULAR LITERATURE AND DRAMA

849. **Cargill, O.** *Drama and Liturgy.* New York: Columbia University Press, 1930. ix+151 pages. (Combats the "liturgical theory" of the origin of the mystery plays. Useful bibliography.)

850. **Chambers, E. K.** *The Medieval Stage.* 2 vols. Oxford: Clarendon Press, 1903. 2d ed., 1913.

851. **Dinsmore, C. A.** *Aids to the Study of Dante.* New York: Houghton Mifflin, 1903. xiv+435 pages.

852. **Evans, S.** (translator). *The High History of the Holy Grail.* (From the Old French of Percival le Gallois.) 2 vols. 2d ed.

London: Dent, 1899; reprinted 1907. (One-volume edition London: Dent, 1910. xxii+379 pages.)

853. **Fitzmaurice, K. J.** *A History of Spanish Literature.* New York: Appleton, 1898; reprinted 1915 and 1921. ix+423 pages.

854. **Moore, E.** *Tutte le opere di Dante Alighieri.* Oxford: University Press, 1894. 2d ed., 1897. viii+490 pages.

855. **Putnam, G. H.** *Books and Their Makers in the Middle Ages.* 2 vols. New York: Putnam's, 1896–97. Volume I in 2d edition 1898.

856. **Scherer, W.** *History of German Literature.* Translated by F. C. Conybeare from the 11th German edition. 2 vols. New York: Scribner's, 1901.

THE DECLINE OF THE MEDIEVAL CHURCH, AND ITS STRUGGLE TO MAINTAIN ITSELF

(SEE ITEMS 98, 101, 110, 186, 191, 192–95, 560–68, 591, 597–606, 630, 635)

HERESY AND THE SECTS

857. **Böhmer, H.** "Waldenser," *PRE* (Item 135), XX, 799 ff.

858. **Bussel, F. W.** *Religious Thought and Heresy in the Middle Ages.* London: Scott, 1918. xiii+873 pages.

859. **Comba, Enrico.** *History of the Waldenses of Italy.* Translated from Italian by T. E. Comba. London: Truslove, 1889. viii+357 pages.

860. **Comba, Ernesto.** *Storia dei Valdesi.* Torre Pellice: Liberia "La Luce," 1923. 291 pages. (A general history of the Waldensians.)

861. **Davison, E. S.** *Forerunners of Saint Francis and Other Studies.* New York: Houghton Mifflin, 1927. xvi+425 pages.

862. **Döllinger, J.** *Beiträge zur Sektengeschichte des Mittelalters.* 2 vols. Munich: Beck, 1890.

863. **Gebhart, E.** *L'Italie mystique.* Paris: Hachette, 1890. Translated by E. M. Hulme, *Mystics and Heretics of Italy at the End of the Middle Ages.* London: Allen & Unwin, 1922. 283 pages.

864. **Jones, R. M.** *The Church's Debt to Heretics.* New York: Doran, London: Clark, 1925. ix+225 pages.

865. **Newman, L. I.** *Jewish Influence on Christian Reform Movements.* New York: Columbia University Press, 1925. xxvii+707 pages. (An argument for Jewish influence, involving a detailed study of many heresies.)

866. **Vedder, H. C.** "The Origin and Early History of the Waldenses," *American Journal of Theology* (see Item 150), IV, (1900), 465–99.

867. **Warner, J. H.** *The Albigensian Heresy.* 2 vols. London: Society for Promoting Christian Knowledge, 1922–28. (Volume I deals with the origins and doctrines; Volume II, with the Crusade and extermination.)

REPRESSION AND THE INQUISITION

868. **Frédéricq, P.** "Les récents, historiens catholiques de l'Inquisition en France," *RH* (Item 26), CIX (1912), 307–34.

869. **Krehbiel, E. B.** *The Interdict, Its History and Operation, with Special Attention to the Time of Innocent III (1198–1216.)* Washington: American Historical Association, 1909. viii+184 pages. (Full bibliography.)

870. **Lea, H. C.** *A History of the Inquisition in the Middle Ages.* 3 vols. New York: Harper, 1888. 2d ed., 1906, Vol. I by Macmillan; Vols. II and III by Harper. (The most complete treatise. Exposes the abuses of the Inquisition.)

871. **Maycock, A. L.** *The Inquisition from Its Establishment to the Great Schism, with an Introduction by Father Ronald Knox.* London: Constable, 1926. xxiii+276 pages. New York: Harper, 1927.

872. **Mollat, G.** (editor). *Manuel de l'inquisiteur.* 2 vols. Paris: Champion, 1927. (A French critical edition and translation of the essential parts of the *Practica inquisitionis hereticae pravitatis* of Bernard Gui [d. 1317]. A source for heresies and the Inquisition.)

873. **Turberville, A. S.** *Medieval Heresy and the Inquisition.* London: Lockwood, 1920. vi+264 pages. (A good short account.)

874. **Vacandard, É.** *The Inquisition.* Translated from French by B. L. Conway. London and New York: Longmans, 1908. xiv+284 pages. New edition 1918. xiv+195 pages. (A representative Roman Catholic view.)

DISTRESS, DECLINE, AND ATTEMPTED REFORM OF
PAPACY, CA. 1304–1517
THE CAPTIVITY, THE SCHISM, AND THE REFORMING COUNCILS

875. **Baluzius, Stephanus.** *Vitae paparum avionensium* . . . .
1305–1394. The "new edition according to the manuscripts,"
by G. Mollat (Paris: Letouzey, 1914–28; 4 vols.) should be
used. The original work appeared in 1693. (A first-rate authority, but favorable to France.)

876. **Creighton, M.** *A History of the Papacy during the Period of
the Reformation.* 5 vols. New York: Longmans, 1887–94. 2d
ed., 1897, with title *A History of the Papacy from the Great
Schism to the Sack of Rome.* 6 vols. Reprinted 1919.

877. **Emerton, E.** *The Beginnings of Modern Europe (1250–1450).*
New York: Ginn, 1917. xiv+550 pages.

878. **Finke, H.** *Acta concilii Constantiensis.* 4 vols. Münster:
Regensberg, 1896–1928.

879. ———. *Forschungen und Quellen zur Geschichte des Kon-
stanzer Konzils.* Paderborn: Schöningh, 1889. v+347 pages.

880. **Flick, A. C.** *The Decline of the Medieval Church.* 2 vols. New
York: Knopf, 1930. (Covers the period 1300–1500. Well
organized but defective in research.)

881. **Haller, J., and Others.** *Concilium Basilience: Studien und
Quellen zur Geschichte des Konzils von Basel:* 7 vols. Basel:
Reich, 1896–1926.

882. ———. *Papsttum und Kirchenreform.* Vol. I. Berlin: Weidmann, 1903. xx+556 pages. (Examines papal finances and
other causes of dissatisfaction with the Avignon papacy. Sug-
gests English influence in the rise of Gallicanism. Only Volume I appeared.)

883. **Jordan, G. J.** *The Inner History of the Great Western Schism;
a Problem in Church Unity.* London: Williams, 1930. 216
pages. (Has valuable source studies.)

884. **Lazarus, P.** *Das Basler Konzil.* Berlin: Ebering, 1912. 359
pages.

885. **Locke, C.** *The Great Western Schism.* New York: Christian
Literature Co., 1896. x+314 pages.

886. **Mollat, G.** *Les papes d'Avignon (1305–1378) 1912.* 3d ed.
Paris: Lecoffre, 1920. xv+439 pages. (Intimate account of
the persons and policies of the seven Avignon popes.)

887. **Previté-Orton, C. W.** *The Defensor Pacis of Marsilius of Padua.* Cambridge: University Press, 1928. vi+517 pages. (Introduction and critical text.)

888. **Rocquain, F.** *La cour de Rome et l'esprit de reforme avant Luther.* 3 vols. Paris: Thorin, 1893–97.

889. **Salembier, L.** *Le grand Schisme d'occident.* Paris: Lecoffre, 1900. xii+430 pages. 3d ed., 1902. (General treatment of the papal schism and the councils held to end it; strongly favorable to the Roman popes.)

890. **Valois, Noël.** *La crise religieuse du XVᵉ siècle. Le pape et le concile. (1418–1450).* 2 (1) vols. Paris: Picard, 1909. (Serves as a continuation of the following.)

891. ———. *La France et le grand schisme d'occident.* 4 vols. Paris: Picard, 1896–1901. (A work of special importance.)

892. **Wirz, C.** (editor). *Bullen und Breven.* ("Quellen zur Schweizergeschichte," Vol. XXI.) Basel: Basler Buchhandlung, 1902. cxiii+654 pages.

893. **Workman, H. B.** *The Foundation of Modern Religion: A Study in the Task and Contribution of the Medieval Church.* New York: Revell, 1916. 249 pages.

THE PAPACY AND THE RENAISSANCE (SEE ITEMS
909 [VOL. I], 923–26)

894. **Allen, P. S.** *The Age of Erasmus.* Oxford: Clarendon Press, 1914. 303 pages.

895. **Burckhardt, J. C.** *The Civilization of the Renaissance in Italy.* Translation by S. G. C. Middlemore of *Die Cultur der Renaissance in Italien.* (1877–78). 2 (1) vols. London: Sonnenschein, 1892 and 1909. New York: Macmillan, 1909. xvi+559 pages.

896. **Burdach, K.** *Reformation, Renaissance, Humanismus.* 2d ed. Berlin: Paetel, 1918. xiii+207 pages. (Defines historically the terms of the title.)

897. **Guirard, Jean.** *L'église et les origines de la renaissance.* Paris: Lecoffre, 1902. 339 pages.

898. **Huizinga, J.** *The Waning of the Middle Ages. A Study of the Forms of Life, Thought and Art in France and the Nether-*

lands in the Fourteenth and Fifteenth Centuries. London: Arnold, 1924. viii+328 pages.

899. **Hulme, E. M.** *The Renaissance, the Protestant Revolution and the Catholic Reformation.* New York: Century, 1914. Rev. ed., 1915. 629 pages.

900. **Janssen, J.** *Geschichte des deutschen Volkes seit dem Ausgang des Mittelalters.* Freiburg: Herder, 1893–99. Translated by M. A. Mitchell and A. M. Christie, *History of the German People at the Close of the Middle Ages.* London: Kegan Paul, 1896–1925, 17 vols. (For a critique of this Roman Catholic work see E. Emerton, *Papers of the American Historical Association*, Vol. I [New York, 1886], pp. 442–46.)

901. **Lindeboom, J.** *Het Bijbelsch Humanisme in Nederland.* Leiden: Adriani, 1913. viii+280 pages.

902. **Owen, J.** *The Sceptics of the Italian Renaissance.* London: Sonnenschein, 1893. 3d ed., 1909. 476 pages.

903. **Pater, W.** *The Renaissance: Studies in Art and Poetry.* New York: Macmillan, 1903; reprinted 1906. xvi+252 pages.

904. **Van Dyke, P.** *The Age of the Renaissance.* New York: Christian Literature Co., 1897. xxii+397 pages.

905. **Whitcomb, M.** *A Literary Source Book of the German Renaissance.* Philadelphia: University of Pennsylvania Press, 1899. 112 pages.

906. ———. *A Literary Source Book of the Italian Renaissance.* Philadelphia: University of Pennsylvania Press, 1898; reprinted 1900. 118 pages.

MORAL ABUSES (SEE ITEMS 598, 655, 662, 663, 681, 683, 691, 693, 699, 707, 717, 723, 726, 728, 754, 798, 800, 854, 870, 875–95, 898–900, 907, 910, 916, 955–60, 979)

ADVOCATES OF REFORM (SEE ITEMS 1114, 1354)

907. **Aygalliers, W. d'.** *Ruysbroeck l'admirable.* Paris: Perrin, 1923. 452 pages. Translated by F. Rothwell, *Ruysbroeck the Admirable.* London: Dent, 1925. xliii+326 pages. (Some critical apparatus omitted in the translation. Examines the whole social and intellectual environment of Ruysbroeck and emphasizes the survival and reemergence of Platonism.)

908. **Bonet, M. G.** *Les précurseurs de la réforme et de la liberté de conscience dans les pays latins du XIIe au XVe siècle.* Paris: Fischbacher, 1904. viii+268 pages.

909. **Dacheux, L.** *Jean Geiler de Kaysersberg, prédicateur de la cathedrale de Strasbourg, 1478–1510.* Paris: Delgrave, Strasbourg: Derivaux, 1876. 583+xcv pages.

910. **Miller, E. W., and Scudder, J. W.** *Wessel Gansfort; Life and Writings.* 2 vols. New York: Putnam's, 1917.

911. **Nelson, E. W.** "Recent Literature concerning Erasmus," *Modern History*, I (1929), 88–102. (Lists studies 1923–29.)

912. **Noël, E. P.** *Œuvres complets de Jean Tauler.* Paris: Tralin, 1911. 437 pages. (A French translation from the Latin version made by Surius.)

913. **Renaudet, A.** *Préréforme et humanisme à Paris. 1494–1517.* Paris: Champion, 1916. xlviii+739 pages. (Exceptionally informing.)

914. **Roeder, R.** *Savonarola.* New York: Brentano, 1930. 307 pages.

915. **Schnitzer, J.** *Savonarola: Ein Kulturbild aus der Zeit der Renaissance.* 2 vols. München: Reinhardt, 1924. (The best work on Savonarola and his times.)

916. **Smith, P.** *Erasmus; a Study of his Life, Ideals and Place in History.* New York: Harper, 1923. xiv+479 pages.

917. **Thureau-Dangin, P. M. P.** *Un prédicateur populaire: Saint Bernardine de Sienne, 1380–1444.* Paris: Bloud, 1896. New ed., 1926. xv+332 pages.

918. **Vansteenberghe, E.** *Le Cardinal Nicholas de Cues.* Paris: Champion, 1920. xix+506 pages.

CHAPTER V

CHRISTIANITY IN WESTERN EUROPE SINCE THE REFORMÅTION

Research in the history of modern Christianity is very complicated. Abundant source material is available, but it is difficult to derive from it a unified view of the historical development. Only certain phases of the modern church—e.g., the Reformation, the French Revolution, or the development of nineteenth-century theology, particularly in Germany—have been so thoroughly investigated that it is possible to give adequate analyses of the course of events. It would be beyond the scope of this selective bibliography to list the numerous works on special problems and data of the modern church. A student could hardly derive therefrom guidance to further study. He will find reference to them in the works mentioned in this guide; most of them contain a detailed bibliography.

It should be mentioned that *general* works on the political or ecclesiastical history of the *countries* are listed only where the first reference to these countries is made.

GENERAL

WORKS ON MODERN POLITICAL AND CULTURAL HISTORY
POLITICAL

919. *The Cambridge Modern History.* 12 vols. London: Macmillan, 1902–10.
920. **Meinecke, F.** *Die Idee der Staatsraison in der neueren Geschichte.* Munich: Oldenbourg, 1929. vii+575 pages.

921. **Robinson, J. H., and Beard, C. A.** *Outline of European History.* Part 2, "From the Seventeenth Century to the Present Time." 2d ed. Boston: Ginn, 1927. 886 pages.
922. **Schäfer, D.** *Weltgeschichte der Neuzeit.* (In 2 parts.) 11th ed. Berlin: Mittler, 1922.

CULTURAL

923. **Dilthey, W.** *Gesammelte Schriften.* Vol. II, *Weltanschauung und Analyse des Menschen seit Renaissance und Reformation.* Leipzig: Teubner, 1914. 528 pages.
924. **Friedell, E.** *Kulturgeschichte der Neuzeit.* Three volumes are planned, 2 volumes published, covering the period from the Renaissance to the French Revolution. Munich: Beck, 1928. (English translation: *A Cultural History of the Modern Age,* Vol. I. New York: Knopf, 1930.)
925. **Paulsen, F.** *Geschichte des gelehrten Unterrichts auf deutschen Schulen und Universitäten bis zur Gegenwart.* 2 vols. Leipzig: Veit, 1885. 3d ed., Berlin, 1926.
926. **Randall, J. H.** *The Making of the Modern Mind.* A survey of the intellectual background of the present age. Cambridge, Massachusetts: Riverside Press, 1926. 653 pages.
927. **Smith, P.** *A History of Modern Culture.* Vol. I, *The Great Renewal, 1543–1687.* New York: Holt, 1930, 653 pages. (Bibliography.)
928. **Ueberweg, F.** *Grundriss der Geschichte der Philosophie.* Bearbeitet by M. Heinze and others. Parts 3–5, 12th ed. Berlin: Mittler, 1926.
929. **Windelband, W.** *History of Philosophy.* Translated from German by J. H. Tufts. London: Macmillan, 1901; and many other editions. 726 pages.

WORKS ON THE HISTORY OF MODERN CHRISTIANITY
GENERAL (SEE ITEMS 43–66, 86–89, 94–101, 106–10)

930. **Cheetham, S.** *A History of the Christian Church since the Reformation.* London: Macmillan, 1907. 474 pages.
931. **Ehrhard, A.** *Katholisches Christentum und Kirche Westeuropas in der Neuzeit.* (See Item 66, pp. 298–430.)
932. **Pullan, L.** *Religion since the Reformation.* Oxford: Clarendon Press, 1923. 291 pages.

933. **Troeltsch, E.** *Protestantisches Christentum und Kirche in der Neuzeit.* (See Item 66, pp. 431–792.)

934. ———. *Protestantism and Progress.* Translated from German. New York: Putnam, 1912. x+207 pages.

935. **Wand, J. W. C.** *A History of the Modern Church from 1500 to the Present Day.* London: Methuen, 1930. x+340 pages.

DOCTRINAL (SEE ITEMS 244–51, 291–93)

936. **Seeberg, R.** *Lehrbuch der Dogmengeschichte.* Vol. IV, Parts 1 and 2. Leipzig: Deichert, 1920. (A new edition is in preparation. See Item 251.)

937. **Werner, K.** *Geschichte der katholischen Theologie seit dem Trienter Konzil bis zur Gegenwart.* 2d ed. Munich: Oldenbourg, 1889. 656 pages.

SOCIAL AND INSTITUTIONAL (SEE ITEMS 220–23, 227–29, 820, 848)

938. **Dunning, W. A.** *A History of Political Theories from Luther to Montesquieu.* New York: Macmillan, 1905. 459 pages.

939. **Hering, C. W.** *Geschichte der kirchlichen Unionsversuche seit der Reformation bis auf unsere Zeit.* 2 vols. Leipzig: Fleischer, 1836–38.

940. **Hirsch, E.** *Die Reich-Gottes-Begriffe des neueren europäischen Denkens.* Göttingen: Vandenhoeck & Ruprecht, 1921. 35 pages.

941. **Kühn, Joh.** *Toleranz und Offenbarung.* Eine Untersuchung der Motive und Motivformen der Toleranz im offenbarungsgläubigen Protestantismus; zugleich ein Versuch zur neueren Religions- und Geistesgeschichte. Leipzig: Meiner, 1923. xvi+473 pages.

942. **Moser, H. J.** *Die evangelische Kirchenmusik in volkstümlichem Überblick.* Stuttgart: Engelhorn, 1926. 188 pages.

943. **Sehling, E.** *Geschichte der protestantischen Kirchenverfassung.* 2d ed. Leipzig: Teubner, 1914. 50 pages. (See also Item 202.)

944. **Werdermann, H.** *Der evangelische Pfarrer in Geschichte und Gegenwart.* Leipzig: Quelle & Meyer, 1925. 150 pages.

945. **Westphal, J.** *Das evangelische Kirchenlied nach seiner geschichtlichen Entwicklung.* 6th ed. Berlin: Union, 1925. 272 pages.

946. **Uhlhorn, F. G. W.** *Die christliche Liebestätigkeit seit der Reformation.* Vol. III. viii+520 pages. (See Item 294.)

MISSIONS (SEE ITEMS 295–301, 1222, 1259, 2263–2303)

947. **Arens, B.** *Handbuch der katholischen Missionen.* 2d ed. Freiburg: Herder, 1930. xx+510 pages.

948. **Brown, W.** *The History of the Christian Missions over the Sixteenth, Seventeenth, Eighteenth and Nineteenth Centuries.* 3 vols. 3d ed. London: Baker, 1864.

949. **Frick, H.** *Die evangelische Mission. Ursprung, Geschichte, Ziel.* Bonn: K. Schroeder, 1922. 445 pages.

950. **Graham, J. A.** *Missionary Expansion since the Reformation.* New York: Revell, 1899. xv+244 pages.

951. **Jann, A.** *Die katholischen Missionen in Indien, China und Japan.* Ihre Organization und das portugiesische Patronat vom 15. bis ins 18. Jahrhundert. Paderborn: Schöningh, 1915. 540 pages.

952. **Moore, E. C.** *The Spread of Christianity in the Modern World.* Chicago: University of Chicago Press, 1919. xi+352 pages.

953. **Thompson, A. C.** *Protestant Missions. Their Rise and Early Progress.* New York: Scribner's, 1894. vii+314 pages.

954. **Warneck, G.** *Outline History of Protestant Missions from the Reformation to the Present Time.* Translated from German. New York: Revell, 1901. xiv+364 pages.

THE REFORMATION
GENERAL
TEXTBOOKS (SEE ITEM 899)

955. **Below, G. v.** *Die Ursachen der Reformation.* 3d ed. Munich: Oldenbourg, 1917. 187 pages.

956. **Hauser, H., and Renaudet, A.** *Les débuts de l'âge moderne.* Paris: Alcan, 1929. 639 pages.

957. **Kidd, B. J.** *Documents Illustrative of the Continental Reformation.* Oxford: Clarendon Press, 1911. 742 pages.

958. **Lindsay, T. M.** *A History of the Reformation.* 2 vols. New York: Scribner's, 1906–7.

959. **Smith, P.** *The Age of the Reformation.* New York: Holt, 1920. xii+861 pages.

960. **Walker, W.** *The Reformation.* New York: Scribner's, 1900. 478 pages.

SPECIAL PHASES OF THE REFORMATION (SEE ITEMS 171, 266–69)

961. **Allen, J. W.** *History of Political Thought in the Sixteenth Century.* New York: Dial Press, 1928. xxii+625 pages.

962. **Beard, C.** *The Reformation in its Relation to Modern Thought and Knowledge.* London: Williams & Norgate, 1885. 451 pages.

963. **Dorner, I. A.** *History of Protestant Theology, Particularly in Germany.* Translated from German. 2 vols. Edinburgh: Clark, 1871.

964. **Holstein, G.** *Die Grundlagen des evangelischen Kirchenrechts.* Tübingen: Mohr, 1928. xi+408 pages.

965. **McNeill, J. T.** *Unitive Protestantism.* New York: Abingdon, 1939. 345 pages.

966. **Murray, R. H.** *The Political Consequences of the Reformation.* London: Benn Bros., 1926, 352 pages.

967. **Paulus, N.** *Protestantimus und Toleranz im 16. Jahrhundert.* Freiburg: Herder, 1911. vi+374 pages. (Catholic.)

968. **Ritschl, O.** *Dogmengeschichte des Protestantismus.* 4 vols. Göttingen: Vandenhoeck & Ruprecht, 1908–27.

969. **Schweizer, A.** *Die protestantischen Centraldogmen in ihrer geschichtlichen Entwicklung innerhalb der reformierten Kirche.* 2 vols. Zurich, 1854–56.

970. **Völker, K.** *Toleranz und Intoleranz im Zeitalter der Reformation.* Leipzig: Hinrichs, 1912. viii+279 pages.

GERMANY

GENERAL HISTORY (SEE ITEMS 588, 856, 900)

971. *Archiv für Reformationsgeschichte.* Edited by W. Friedensburg. Leipzig: Heinsius, 1906——.

972. **Bezold, F. v.** *Geschichte der deutschen Reformation.* Berlin: Grote, 1890. 883 pages.

973. **Brandi, K.** *Deutsche Reformation und Gegenreformation.* 2 vols. Leipzig: Quelle & Meyer, 1927, 1930.

974. **Haller, J.** *Die Epochen der deutschen Geschichte.* 4th ed. Stuttgart: Cotta, 1925. xii+375 pages.

975. **Lamprecht, K.** *Deutsche Geschichte.* 5 vols. 6th ed. Berlin: Gaertner, 1891–96.

976. **Ranke, L.** *Deutsche Geschichte im Zeitalter der Reformation.* 6 vols. Berlin: Duncker & Humblot, 1839–44.

977. ———. *History of the Reformation in Germany.* Translated from German. New York: Dutton, (1905) 1920. xxiv+792 pages.

978. *Schriften des Vereins für Reformationsgeschichte.* Vols. I–XCIII published since 1883 in Halle; Vols. XCIV——, in Leipzig byHeinsius. Numerous valuable monographs, which are periodically published, treat of all phases of the history of the Reformation, particularly in Germany. The collection represents a mine of information.

979. **Wolf, G.** *Quellenkunde der deutschen Reformationsgeschichte.* 3 vols. Gotha: Perthes, 1915, 1922.

LUTHER
WORKS

980. **Luther, M.** *Werke.* Kritische Gesamtausgabe. Weimar: Böhlau, 1883——. (Almost completed.) This is the famous Weimar edition (W.A.). It is indispensable to the Luther student.

981. ———. *Sämtliche Werke.* Edited by E. L. Enders and K. Irmischer. 67(25) vols. Frankfurt, a. M. and Erlangen: Heyder & Zimmer, 1832–85.

982. ———. *Exegetica opera latina.* Edited by C. S. T. Elsperger, H. Schmidt, J. C. Jrmischer, J. Linke. 28(16) vols. Erlangen: Heyder, 1829–86. The last two titles are those of the Erlangen edition (E.A.). It is still generally recognized as authoritative.

983. ———. *Werke in Auswahl.* Unter Mitwirkung von Albert Leitzmann. Edited by Otto Clemen. 4 vols. Berlin: Gruyter, 1912–13. Four more volumes are to be published. Vol. VIII (table-talk) appeared in 1930.

984. ———. *Works*. With introductions and notes. Edited by H. E. Jacobs. 3 vols. Philadelphia: Holman, 1915–30. (To be continued.)

985. ———. *Colloquia*. Edited by H. E. Bindseil. 3 vols. Detmold: Meyer, 1863–66.

986. ———. *Briefwechsel*. Edited by L. Enders and others. 18 vols. Leipzig: Heinsius, 1884–1923.

987. ———. *Correspondence and Other Contemporary Letters*. Translated and edited by P. Smith. 2 vols. Philadelphia: Lutheran Publication Society, 1913.

988. **Scheel, O.** *Dokumente zu Luthers Entwicklung*. 2d ed. Tübingen: Mohr, 1929. xii+364 pages.

MONOGRAPHS

989. **Boehmer, H.** *Der junge Luther*. Gotha: Flamberg, 1925. 394 pages.

990. ———. *Luther in the Light of Recent Research*. 5th ed. Translated from the German. London: Bell, 1930. xi+380 pages.

991. **Fife, R. H.** *Young Luther; the Intellectual and Religious Development of Martin Luther to 1518*. New York: Macmillan, 1928. 232 pages.

992. **Grisar, H.** *Luther*. 3 vols. 3d ed. Freiburg: Herder, 1924–25. (Catholic.)

993. ———. *Luther*. Adapted from the second German edition. London and St. Louis: Herder, 1930. xi+609 pages. (Abbreviated edition.)

994. **Holl, K.** *Luther*. ("Gesammelte Aufsätze," Vol. I.) 4th and 5th eds. Tübingen: Mohr, 1927. xi+590 pages.

995. **Jacobs, H. E.** *Martin Luther*. New York: Putnam, 1898. 454 pages.

996. **Köstlin, J.** *Martin Luther, sein Leben un seine Schriften*. Edited by G. Kawerau. 2 vols. Berlin: 1903. (English translation: *Life of Luther*. New York: Scribner's, 1903. xvi+587 pages.)

997. **Mackinnon, J.** *Luther and the Reformation*. 4 vols. London: Longmans, Green, 1925–30.

998. **Murray, R. H.** *Erasmus and Luther: Their Attitude to Toleration.* London: Society for Promoting Christian Knowledge, 1920. 503 pages.

999. **Scheel, T.** *Martin Luther: Vom Katholizismus zur Reformation.* Vol. I, 3d ed.; Vol. II, 2d ed. Tübingen: Mohr: 1917, 1930.

1000. **Smith, P.** *The Life and Letters of M. Luther.* Boston and New York: Houghton Mifflin, 1911. xvi+490 pages.

1001. **Strohl, H.** *L'évolution religieuse de Luther jusqu'à 1515.* Strasbourg: Librairie Istra, 1922, 174 pages.

1002. ———. *L'épanouissement de la pensée religieuse de Luther de 1515 à 1520.* Strasbourg: Librairie Istra, 1924. 424 pages.

MELANCHTHON
WORKS

1003. **Melanchton, Ph.** *Opera.* Edited by Bretschneider and Bindseil. ("Corpus Reformatorum," Vols. I–XXVII.) Halle: Schwetschke, 1834–60.

1004. *Supplementa Melanchthoniana* (Works of Melanchthon not printed in "Corpus Reformatorum.") Edited by O. Clemen and others. 5 vols. Leipzig: Heinsius, 1910–26.

MONOGRAPHS

1005. **Ellinger, G.** *Philipp Melanchthon.* Berlin: Gaertner, 1902. 624 pages.

1006. **Hartfelder, V.** *Philipp Melanchthon als Praeceptor Germaniae.* Berlin: Hofmann, 1889. xxviii+687 pages.

1007. **Richard, J. W.** *Philip Melanchthon.* New York: Putnam, 1898. 399 pages.

OTHER PERSONALITIES

1008. **Anrich, G.** *Martin Bucer.* Strassbourg: Trübner, 1914. 147 pages.

1009. **Held, P.** *Ulrich von Hutten. Seine religiös-geistige Auseinandersetzung mit Katholizismus, Humanismus, Reformation.* Leipzig: Heinsius, 1928. vii+169 pages.

1010. **Hirsch, E.** *Die Theologie des Andreas Osiander und ihre geschichtlichen Voraussetzungen.* Göttingen: Vandenhoeck & Ruprecht, 1919. 296 pages.

1011. **Kalkoff, P.** *Ulrich von Hutten und die Reformation.* Eine kritische Geschichte seiner wichtigsten Lebenszeit und die Entscheidungsjahre der Reformation (1517–23). Leipzig: Haupt, 1920. 601 pages.

1012. **Müller, K.** *Luther und Karlstadt.* Tübingen: Mohr, 1906. xi+243 pages.

1013. **Walter, L. G.** *Thomas Münzer et les luttes sociales à l'époque de la Réforme.* Paris: Plon, 1927. 365 pages.

SPECIAL PHASES OF THE GERMAN REFORMATION

1014. **Cornelius, A.** *Geschichte des Münsterischen Aufruhrs.* 2 vols. Leipzig: Weigel, 1855–60.

1015. **Matthes, K.** *Das Corpus Christianum bei Luther im Lichte seiner Erforschung.* Berlin: Curtius, 1929. 134 pages. (A discussion of the literature on the social views of Luther.)

1016. **Meyer, J.** *Historischer Kommentar zu Luthers Kleinem Katechismus.* Gütersloh: Bertelsmann, 1929. xii+364 pages.

1017. **Reu, J. M.** *Quellen zur Geschichte des kirchlichen Unterrichts in der evangelischen Kirche Deutschlands zwischen 1530 und 1600.* 7 vols. Gütersloh: Bertelsmann, 1904.

1018. ———. *D. Martin Luther's Kleiner Katechismus.* Die Geschichte seiner Entstehung, seiner Verwirklichung und seines Gebrauchs. Munich: Kaiser, 1929. x+377 pages.

1019. **Rieker, K.** *Die rechtliche Stellung der evangelischen Kirche Deutschlands in ihrer geschichtlichen Entwicklung bis zur Gegenwart.* Leipzig: Hirschfeld, 1893. xv+488 pages.

1020. **Schubert, H.** *Anfänge der evangelischen Bekenntnisbildung.* Leipzig: Heinsius, 1928. 39 pages.

1021. ———. *Revolution und Reformation im 16. Jahrhundert.* Tübingen: Mohr, 1927. 53 pages.

1022. ———. *Der Kommunismus der Wiedertäufer in Münster und seine Quellen.* Heidelberg: Winter, 1919. 58 pages.

1023. **Sehling, E.** (editor). *Die evangelischen Kirchenordnungen der 16. Jahrhunderts.* 5 vols. Leipzig: Reisland, 1902–13.

1024. **Stern, A.** *Quellen und Darstellungen der Geschichte des grossen deutschen Bauernkrieges.* ("Sitzungsberichte der Berliner Akademie der Wissenschaften," 1929, pp. 184–90.) Berlin: Gruyter, 1929.

1025. **Winckelmann, O.** *Das Fürsorgewesen der Stadt Strassburg vor und nach der Reformation bis zum Ausgang des 16. Jahrhunderts.* Leipzig: Heinsius, 1922. 301 pages.

SWITZERLAND
GENERAL HISTORY

1026. **Blösch, E.** *Geschichte der schweizerisch reformierten Kirchen.* 2 vols. Bern: Schmid & Francke, 1898-99.

1027. **Dändliker, K.** *Geschichte der Schweiz mit besonderer Rücksicht auf die Entwicklung des Verfassungs- und Kulturlebens.* 3 vols. Zurich: Schulthess, 1900-1904.

1028. **Hadorn, W.** *Die Reformation in der deutschen Schweiz.* Frauenfeld: Huber, 1928. 207 pages.

1029. **Rieker, K.** *Grundsätze reformierter Kirchenverfassung.* Leipzig: Hirschfeld, 1883. vii+208 pages.

1030. **Ruchat, A.** *Histoire de la réformation de la Suisse.* 7 vols. Paris: 1835-38.

ZWINGLI
WORKS

1031. **Zwingli, H.** *Opera* ("Corpus Reformatorum," Vols. LXXXVIII–XCVI). Edited by M. Schuler and J. Schulthess. 8 vols. Zurich: Schulthess, 1828-42. (Supplement volume edited by J. Schulthess and Marthaler, 1861.)

1032. ———. *Sämtliche Werke.* Edited by E. Egli, G. Finsler, W. Köhler, and O. Farner. Vols. I–XI. Leipzig: Heinsius, 1926——.

1033. ———. *The Latin Works and Correspondence together with Selections from His German Works.* Edited by S. M. Jackson. New York: Putnam, 1912——. (Three volumes to 1929; 2 or 3 more promised.)

MONOGRAPHS

1034. **Jackson, S.** *Huldreich Zwingli.* New York: Putnam, 1907. 519 pages.

1035. **Köhler, W.** *Die Geisteswelt Ulrich Zwinglis.* Christentum und Antike. Gotha: Perthes, 1920. 156 pages.

1036. ———. *Zwingli und Luther*. Der Streit über das Abendmahl bis zum Marburger Religionsgespräch 1529. Leipzig: Heinsius, 1929. 851 pages.

1037. **Stähelin, R.** *Huldreich Zwingli*, 2 vols. Basel: Schwabe, 1895–97.

CALVIN AND GENEVA

WORKS

1038. **Calvin, J.** *Opera quae supersunt omnia*. ("Corpus Reformatorum," Vols. XXIX–LXXXVII.) Edited by G. Baum, E. Cunitz, and E. Reuss. 59 vols. Brunswick: Schwetschke, 1863–1900.

1039. ———. *Works*. 51 vols. Printed for the Calvin Translation Society. Edinburgh, 1844–56.

1040. ———. *Opera selecta*. Edited by Peter Barth. Four volumes are planned. Volumes I and III are published. Munich: Kaiser, 1926———.

1041. ———. *Institutes of the Christian Religion*. Translated by Henry Beveridge. 2 vols. Edinburgh: Clark, 1895.

1042. ———. *Letters*. Edited by J. Bonnet. 4 vols. Philadelphia: Presbyterian Board of Publication, 1858.

1043. **Herminjard, A. L.** *Correspondance des réformateurs dans les pays de langue français*. Geneva: Georg, 1866–97.

MONOGRAPHS

1044. **Bauke, H.** *Probleme der Theologie Calvins*. Leipzig: Hinrichs, 1922. 108 pages.

1045. **Beyerhaus, G.** *Studien zur Staatsanschauung Calvins*. Berlin: Trowitzsch, 1910. 162 pages.

1046. **Dide, A.** *Michel Servet et Calvin*. Paris: Flammarion, 1907. viii+322 pages.

1047. **Doumergue, E.** *Jean Calvin. Ses hommes et les choses de son temps*. 7 vols. Lausanne: Bridel, 1899–1928.

1048. **Henry, P.** *Life and Times of John Calvin*. Translated from German. 2 vols. London: Whittaker, 1849.

1049. **Hunter, A.** *The Teaching of Calvin*. Glasgow: Maclehose, Jackson, 1920. 304 pages.

1050. **Kampschulte, F. W.** *Johann Calvin, seine Kirche und sein Staat*. 2 vols. Leipzig: Duncker & Humblot, 1869–99. (Catholic.)

1051. **Lang, A.** *Zwingli und Calvin.* Bielefeld und Leipzig: Velhagen & Klasing, 1915. 128 pages.

1052. **Pannier, J.** *Recherches sur l'évolution religieuse de Calvin jusqu'à sa conversion.* 3 vols. Strasbourg: Imprimerie alsacienne, 1924.

1053. **Walker, W.** *John Calvin.* New York: Putnam, 1906. 456 pages.

BEZA

1054. **Baird, H. M.** *Theodore Beza.* New York: Putnam, 1899. 376 pages.

1055. **Choisy, E.** *L'état Calviniste à Genève au temps de Théodore de Bèze.* Geneva: Eggiman, 1902. 620 pages.

ANABAPTISTS AND SOCINIANS

THE ANABAPTISTS

1056. **Bax, E. B.** *Rise and Fall of the Anabaptists.* London: Sonnenschein, 1903. 407 pages.

1057. **Bergmann, C.** *Die Täuferbewegung im Kanton Zürich bis 1660.* Leipzig: Heinsius, 1916. x+176 pages.

1058. **Blaupot ten Cate, S.** *Geschiedenis der Doopsgezinden in Holland, Zeeland, Utrecht en Gelderland.* 2 vols. Amsterdam: van Kampen, 1847.

1059. **Brons, A.** *Ursprung, Entwicklung und Schicksale der Taufgesinnten oder Mennoniten in kurzen Zügen dargestellt.* Edited by S. M. ten Cate. 3d ed. Amsterdam: Müller, 1913. xxii+391 pages.

1060. **Burrage, H. S.** *History of the Anabaptists in Switzerland.* Philadelphia: Baptist Publication Society, 1881. xvi+231 pages.

1061. **Corpus Schwenckfeldianorum.** Published under the auspices of the Schwenckfelder Church of Pennsylvania, and the Hartford Theological Seminary, Hartford, Connecticut. 8 vols. Leipzig: Breitkopf & Hartel, 1907–27.

1062. **Correll, E. H.** *Das Schweizerische Täufermennonitentum.* Ein sozialer Bericht. Tübingen: Mohr, 1925. 145 pages.

1063. **Coutts, A.** *Hans Denck.* Edinburgh: Macniven & Wallau, 1927. 262 pages.

1064. **Dosker, H. E.** *The Dutch Anabaptists*. Philadelphia: Judson Press, 1921. 310 pages.

1065. **Horsch, J.** *Menno Simons*. Scottdale, Pennsylvania: Mennonite Publication House, 1916. 324 pages.

1066. **Loserth, J.** *Balthasar Hubmaier und die Anfänge der Wiedertaufe in Mähren*. Brünn: Winiker, 1893. viii+217 pages.

1067. *Mennonitisches Lexikon*. Edited by Chr. Hege and Chr. Neff. In process of publication; Volume I is completed. Frankfurt am Main: Chr. Hege, 1913.

1068. **Mueller, E.** *Geschichte der Bernischen Täufer*. Nach den Urkunden dargestellt. Frauenfeld, Switzerland: Huber, 1895. 411 pages.

1069. *Quellen zur Geschichte der Wiedertäufer*. Vol. I, *Herzogtum Württemberg*. Edited by G. Bossert. Leipzig: Heinsius, 1930. xvi+1199 pages.

1070. **Sachsse, C.** *Doctor Balthasar Hubmaier als Theologe*. Berlin: Trowitzsch, 1914. 274 pages.

1071. **Smith, C. H.** *The Mennonites*. Berne, Indiana: Mennonite Book Concern, 1920. 340 pages.

1072. **Vedder, H. C.** *Balthasar Hubmaier*. New York: Putnam, 1905. 333 pages.

1073. ———. *A Short History of the Baptists*. Philadelphia: Baptist Publication Society, 1907. 431 pages.

SOCINIANISM

1074. **Fock, O.** *Der Socinianismus*. Kiel: Schröder, 1847. 722 pages.

1075. **Wallace, R.** *Antitrinitarian Biography*. 3 vols. London: Whitfield, 1850.

SCANDINAVIA
DENMARK (SEE ITEM 679)

1076. **Helveg, L. M.** *Den danske Kirkes Historie elfter Reformationen*. 2 vols. 2d ed. Copenhagen: Iversen, 1880.

1077. **Joergensen, G.** *Reformationen i Danmark: Dan danske Kirkes historie 1517–1537*. Copenhagen: Gad, 1919. 276 pages.

1078. **Koch, H. L. S. P., and Rordam, H. F.** *Danmarks Kirkehistorie 1517–1848*. 2 vols. Copenhagen: Gad, 1889.

SWEDEN (SEE ITEMS 622, 684, 692)

1079. **Bergendorff, C.** *Olavus Petri and the Ecclesiastical Transformation in Sweden.* New York: Macmillan, 1928. 264 pages. (Bibliography.)

1080. **Holmquist, H.** *Den svenska reformationens begynnelse 1523–1537.* Stockholm, Sveriges Kristl. studentrörelses förl., 1923. 157 pages. (Also in German translation: *Die schwedische Reformation.* Leipzig: Heinsius, 1925.)

1081. **Schück, H.** *Olavus Petri.* 4th ed. Stockholm: Geber, 1923. 72 pages.

NORWAY

1082. **Bang, A. C.** *Den norske Kirkes Historie i reformations Aarhundredet.* Christiania: Bigler, 1895. 434 pages.

1083. ———. *Udsigt over den norske Kirkes histoire elfter Reformationen.* Christiania: Cammermeyer, 1883. 314 pages.

ICELAND

1084. **Helgason, J.** *Islands Kirke fra Reformationen til vore Fage: Rn historisk Fremstilling.* Copenhagen: Gad, 1922. 251 pages.

FRANCE

GENERAL HISTORY (SEE ITEMS 127, 670)

1085. **Brémond, H.** *Histoire littéraire du sentiment religieux en France depuis le fin des guerres de religion jusqu'à nos jours.* 6 vols. Paris: Bloud, 1916–22.

1086. ———. *A Literary History of Religious Thought.* Translated from French. Vol. I, *Devout Humanism.* Vol. II, *The Coming of Mysticism. 1590–1620.* New York: Macmillan, 1928–30.

1087. **Edwards, W.** *Notes on European History.* Vol. II, *The Reformation and the Ascendency of France, 1494–1715.* London: Rivingtons, 1926. 652 pages.

1088. **Galton, A. H.** *Church and State in France, 1300–1907.* London: Arnold, 1907. 290 pages.

1089. **Jervis, W. H.** *The Gallican Church. A History of the Church of France from the Concordat of Bologna, 1516, to the Revolution.* 2 vols. London: Murray, 1872.

1090. **Lavisse, E.** *Histoire de France depuis les origines jusqu'à la révolution.* 9 vols. Paris: Hachette, 1903–11.

THE HUGUENOTS

1091. **Baird, H. M.** *History of the Rise of the Huguenots of France.* 2 vols. New York: Scribner's, 1907.

1092. **Benoît, E.** *Histoire de l'édit de Nantes.* 5 vols. Delft: A. Beman, 1693–95.

1093. **Imbart de la Tour, P.** *Les origines de la Réforme.* 3 vols. Paris: Hachette, 1905–14. (Catholic, unprejudiced.)

1094. **Rocquain, T.** *La France et Rome pendant les guerres de religion.* Paris: Champion, 1924. 551 pages.

1095. **Romier, L.** *Catholiques et Huguénots à la cour de Charles IX.* Paris: Perrin, 1924. 359 pages.

1096. **Thompson, J. W.** *The Wars of Religion in France. 1559–1576.* Chicago: University of Chicago Press, 1909. 635 pages.

1097. **Vienot, J.** *Histoire de la Réforme française des origines à l'édit de Nantes.* Paris: Fischbacher, 1926. 476 pages. (Popular, but scientific.)

1098. **Whitehead, A. W.** *Gaspard de Coligny, Admiral of France.* London: Methuen, 1904.

THE NETHERLANDS
GENERAL HISTORY

1099. **Blok, P. J.** *History of the People of the Netherlands.* (See Item 676, Vols. III–V.)

1100. **Motley, J. L.** *History of the United Netherlands. 1584–1609.* 4 vols. London: Harper's, 1860–67.

THE REFORMATION

1101. *Bibliotheka Reformatoria Neerlandica.* Edited by S. Cramer and F. Pijper. 10 vols. The Hague: Nijhoff, 1903——.

1102. **Brandt, G.** *History of the Reformation and Other Ecclesistical Transactions, in and about the Low Countries from the Beginning of the Eighth Century Down to the Famous Synod of Dort, inclusive.* Translated from the Dutch. 4 vols. London: Childe, 1720–23.

1103. **Knappert, L.** *Het ontstaan en de vestiging van het protestantisme in de Nederlanden.* Utrecht: Osthoek, 1924. 450 pages.

1104. ———. *Geschiedenis der Nederlanske Hervormde Kerk gedurende de 16ᵉ en 17ᵉ Eeuw.* 2 vols. Amsterdam: Meulenhoff, 1911.

1105. **Pont, W.** *Geschiedenis van het Lutheranisme in de Nederlanden tot 1618.* Harlem: Bohn, 1911. xvi+632 pages.

1106. **Reitsma, J.** *Geschiedenis van de Hervorming en de Hervormde Kerk der Nederland.* 3d ed. Groningen: Wolters, 1893. 452 pages.

SPAIN (SEE ITEMS 680, 1115)

1107. **McCrie, T.** *History of the Progress and the Suppression of the Reformation in Spain.* Edinburgh: Blackwood, 1829. 2d ed., 1855. 162 pages.

1108. **Schäfer, E.** *Beiträge zur Geschichte des spanischen Protestantismus und der Inquisition im 16. Jahrhundert.* 3 vols. Gütersloh: Bertelsmann, 1902.

ITALY

1109. **Buschbell, G.** *Reformation und Inquisition in Italien um die Mitte des 16. Jahrhunderts.* Paderborn: Schöningh, 1910, 344 pages.

1110. **Chiminelli, P.** *Bibliografia della storia della riforma religiosa in Italia.* Rome: Bilychnis, 1921. 301 pages.

1111. **Comba, E.** *I nostri Protestanti avanti la riforma e durante la riforma.* 2 vols. Firenze: Tipografia Claudiana, 1895–97.

1112. **McCrie, T.** *History of the Progress and Suppression of the Reformation in Italy.* Philadelphia: Presbyterian Board of Publication, 1842. 2d ed., Edinburgh, 1856.

THE CATHOLIC REFORMATION
GENERAL (SEE ITEM 190)

1113. *Corpus Catholicorum.* Werke katholischer Schriftsteller im Zeitalter der Glaubensspaltung. Edited by J. Greving and A. Ehrhard. Münster: Aschendorff, 1919———.

1114. **Jourdan, G. V.** *The Movement towards Catholic Reform in the Early Sixteenth century.* London: Murray, 1914. 336 pages.

1115. **Lea, H. C.** *A History of the Inquisition in Spain.* 4 vols. New York: Macmillan, 1906.

1116. **Pastor, L. v.** *History of the Popes from the Close of the Middle Ages.* Translated from German. Fourteen volumes are published. St. Louis: Herder, 1891——.

1117. **Ranke, L.** *History of the Popes, Their Church and Their State, in the Sixteenth and Seventeenth Centuries.* Translated from German. Philadelphia: Lea & Blanchard, 1844. xi+ 644 pages.

THE COUNCIL OF TRENT (SEE ITEMS 193–95)

1118. *Concilium Tridentinum: Diariorum actorum, epistularum, tractatuum nova collectio.* Edited by S. Merkle and others. In progress. Freiburg: Herder, 1911——.

1119. **Froude, J. A.** *The Council of Trent.* New York: Scribner's, 1896. 294 pages.

1120. **Schmidt, K. D.** *Studien zur Geschichte des Konzils von Trient.* Tübingen: Mohr, 1925. 220 pages.

THE JESUITS (SEE ITEMS 281, 730)
IGNATIUS OF LOYOLA

1121. **Boehmer, H.** *Studien zur Geschichte der Gesellschaft Jesu.* Vol. I, *Loyola.* Bonn: Falkenroth, 1914. vi+447 pages.

1122. **Dyke, P. van.** *Ignatius Loyola, Founder of the Jesuits.* New York and London: Scribner's, 1927. 381 pages.

1123. **Gothein, E.** *Ignatius von Loyola und die Gegenreformation.* Halle: Niemeyer, 1895. xii+795 pages.

HISTORY OF THE ORDER (SEE ITEM 1485)

1124. **Boehmer, H.** *The Jesuits.* Translated from German. Philadelphia: Castle Press, 1928. 192 pages.

1125. **Campbell, T.** *The Jesuits 1534–1921.* New York: Encyclopedia Press, 1922. xvi+937 pages.

1126. **Duhr, B.** *Geschichte der Jesuiten in den Ländern deutscher Zunge.* 4 vols. Regensburg: Manz, 1907——.

1127. **Hoensbroech, P.** *Der Jesuitenorden. Eine Encyclopädie aus den Quellen zusammengestellt.* 2 vols. Bern und Leipzig: Haupt, 1926–27.

1128. **Touqueray, H. S. J.** *Histoire de la Compagnie de Jésus en France des origines à la suppression (1528–1762).* 5 vols. Paris: Firmion-Didot, 1925.

1129. **Tracchi-Venturi, P.** *Storia della Compagnia di Gesù in Italia.* 2 vols. Rome: Soc. edit. Dante Alighieri, 1910–22.

PERSONALITIES

1130. **Braunsberger, O.** *Petrus Canisius.* Freiburg: Herder, 1917. xi+333 pages.

1131. **Coleridge, H. J.** *The Life and Letters of St. Francis Xavier.* 2 vols. 2d ed. London: Burns, 1890.

1132. **Cros, L. J. M.** *Saint François de Xavier. La vie et ses lettres.* 2 vols. Toulouse: Privat, 1900.

THE CHURCH IN THE SEVENTEENTH CENTURY
GENERAL

1133. **Müller, K.** *Kirchengeschichte.* Vol. II, Part 2. (See Item 60.) (From the age of the Counter-Reformation to the end of the eighteenth century. The best work on this period.)

1134. **Ward, A. W.** *The Counter-Reformation.* London: Longmans, Green, 1883. (1906) x+203 pages.

GERMANY

1135. **Bornkamm, H.** *Luther und Böhme.* Berlin: Gruyter, 1925. vii+300 pages.

1136. **Kahnis, K. F. A.** *Der innere Gang des deutschen Protestantismus.* Leipzig: Dörffling & Franke, 1854. 2d ed. 1874. xi+262 pp.

1137. **Leube, H.** *Kalvinismus und Luthertum im Zeitalter der Orthodoxie.* Leipzig: Deichert, 1928. xiii+402 pages.

1138. **Mejer, O.** *Zur Geschichte der römisch-deutschen Frage.* 3 vols. Freiburg: Herder, 1885.

1139. **Ritter, M.** *Deutsche Geschichte im Zeitalter der Gegenreformation und des dreissigjährigen Krieges.* 3 vols. Stuttgart: Cotta, 1889–1908

HOLLAND

1140. **Duker, D. A. C.** *Gisbertus Voëtius.* 3 vols. Leyden: Brill, 1893–1914. Registers, 1915.

1141. **Harrison, A.** *The Beginnings of Arminianism.* London: University of London Press, 1926. 408 pages.

1142. **Kaajan, H.** *Das groote Synode von Dordrecht in 1618–1619.* Amsterdam: De Standard, 1918. 234 pages. (Bibliography.)

1143. **Knight, W.** *The Life and Work of H. Grotius.* London: Sweet & Maxwell, 1925. 304 pages.

1144. **Lettenhove, K.** *Les Huguénots et les Gueux.* 6 vols. Brouges: Beyaert-Storie, 1883–85.

1145. **Moronier, J. H.** *Jacobus Arminius.* Amsterdam: Rogge, 1905. 368 pages.

1146. **Schlüter, J.** *Die Theologie des Hugo Grotius.* Göttingen: Vandenhoeck & Ruprecht, 1919. 120 pages.

FRANCE AND SPAIN
JANSENISM

1147. **Baird, H. M.** *The Huguenots and the Revocation of the Edict of Nantes.* 2 vols. New York: Scribner's, 1895.

1148. **Dézert, G. M.** *Desdevisses des.* *L'Espagne de l' ancien régime.* 3 vols. Paris: Société française d'imprimerie et de librairie, 1897–99.

1149. **Dudon, P.** *Le quiétiste espagnol Michel Molinos (1628–1696).* Paris: Beauchesne, 1921. xxi+315 pages.

1150. **Gazier, A.** *Histoire générale du mouvement janséniste depuis ses origines jusqu' à nos jours.* 2 vols. Paris: Champion, 1922.

1151. **Honigsheim, P.** *Die Staats- und Soziallehren der französischen Jansenisten im 17. Jahrhundert.* Heidelberg dissertation. Heidelberg: Pfeffer, 1914. 226 pages.

1152. **Lafitau, P. T.** *Histoire de la Constitution Unigenitus.* 3 vols. Avignon: Lekens, 1737.

1153. **Sainte-Beuve, C.** *Port Royale,* 4th ed. 7 vols. Paris: Hachette, 1878.

PASCAL

1154. **Bornhausen, K.** *Pascal.* Basel: Reinhardt, 1920. 286 pages.

1155. **Boutroux, E.** *Pascal.* Paris: Hachette, 1900. 205 pages.

1156. **Soltau, R.** *Pascal: the Man and His Message.* London: Blackie, 1927. 216 pages.

1157. **Strowsky, F.** *Histoire du sentiment religieux en France au xviiᵉ siècle. Pascal et son temps.* 3 vols. Paris: Plon, 1907–8.

FRANCIS OF SALES

1158. **Strowski, F.** *Saint François de Sales. Introduction à l'usage du sentiment religieux en France au XVIIᵉ siècle.* 2d ed. Paris: Plon, 1928. 311 pages.

THE CHURCH IN THE EIGHTEENTH CENTURY
GENERAL

1159. **Stephan, H.** *Kirchengeschichte der Neuzeit.* (See Item 55.) xii+300 pages.

1160. **McGiffert, A. C.** *Protestant Thought before Kant.* New York: Scribner's, 1911. 261 pages.

1161. ———. *The Rise of Modern Religious Ideas.* New York: Scribner's, 1915. 315 pages.

1162. **Soldau-Heppe, W. G.** *Geschichte der Hexenprozesse.* 2 vols. (New edition by Bauer.) Munich: Müller, 1912.

1163. **Schlosser, F. C.** *Geschichte des 18. Jahrhunderts.* 4th ed. 6 vols. Heidelberg: Mohr, 1853–57.

1164. **Veit, L. A.** *Die Kirche im Zeitalter des Individualismus. 1648–1800.* (See Item 54.) 528 pages.

PIETISM

1165. **Bornkamm, H.** *Mystik, Spiritualismus und die Anfänge des Pietismus.* Giessen: Töpelmann, 1926. 27 pages. (Bibliography.)

1166 **Grünberg, P.** *Philipp Jacob Spener.* 3 Vols. Göttingen: Vandenhoeck & Ruprecht, 1893–1906.

1167. **Heppe, H.** *Geschichte des Pietismus und der Mystik in der reformierten Kirche, namentlich der Niederlande.* Leiden: Brill, 1879. 503 pages.

1168. **Herpel, O.** *Zinzendorf,* Schlüchtern: Neuwerk-Verlag, 1930. 131 pages. (Extracts from his writings.)

1169. **Kramer, G.** *August Hermann Francke.* 2 vols. Halle: Waisenhaus, 1880–82.

1170. **Lamm, M.** *Swedenborg. En studie öfver hans utveckling till mystiker och andeskädare.* Stockholm: Geber, 1915. 334 pages.

1171. **Ritschl, A.** *Geschichte des Pietismus.* 3 vols. Bonn: Marcus, 1880–86.

1172. **Seeberg, E.** *Gottfried Arnold.* (See Item 86.)

1173. **Spangenberg, A. G.** *Leben des Herrn Nicolaus Ludwig, Grafen und Herrn von Zinzendorf.* 8 parts. Barby, 1772–75.

1174. **Trobridge, G.** *A Life of E. Swedenborg.* London: Warne, 1912. 337 pages.

THE ENLIGHTENMENT
GENERAL (SEE ITEMS 270, 276, 278, 1528–33)

1175. **Bartholmèss,** *Histoire critique des doctrines religieuses et de la philosophie.* 2 vols. Prais: Meyrueis, 1855.

1176. **Bauer, B.** *Geschichte der Politik, Kultur und Aufklärung des 18. Jahrhunderts.* 2 vols. Charlottenburg: E. Bauer, 1843–45.

1177. **Cairns, J.** *Unbelief in the Eighteenth Century.* Edinburgh: Black, 1881. 309 pages.

1178. **Findel, G.** *Geschichte der Freimaurerei. Von der Zeit ihres Entstehens bis auf die Gegenwart.* 7th ed. Leipzig: Findel, 1900. viii+350 pages.

1179. **Hoffmann, H.** *Die Aufklärung.* ("Religionsgeschichtliche Volksbücher.") Tübingen: Mohr, 1912. 48 pages.

1180. **Hurst, J. F.** *History of Rationalism.* New York: Eaton & Maines, 1901. 633 pages.

1181. **Lecky, W.** *History of the Rise and Influence of the Spirit of Rationalism in Europe.* 2 vols. London: Longmans, 1866.

1182. **Mauthner, F.** *Der Atheismus und seine Geschichte im Abendlande.* 4 vols. Stuttgart: Deutsche Verlagsanstalt, 1920–23.

1183. **Pfleiderer, O.** *The Philosophy of Religion on the Basis of Its History.* 4 vols. London: Williams & Norgate, 1886–88.

1184. **Robertson, J. M.** *A Short History of Freethought.* 2 vols. 3d ed. New York: Putnam, 1930.

1185. **Schlatter, A.** *Die philosophische Arbeit seit Cartesius in ihrem ethischen und religiösen Ertrag.* 3d ed. Gütersloh: Bertelsmann: 1923, 287 pages.

1186. **Wolfstieg, A.** *Werden und Wesen der Freimaurerei.* 5 vols. Berlin: A. Unger, 1923.

1187. **Wolfstieg, A.** *Bibliographie der freimaurerischen Literatur.* 2d ed. by B. Beyer. 4 vols. Leipzig: Hiersemann, 1923–26.

GERMANY

1188. **Aner, K.** *Der Aufklärer Friedrich Nicolai.* Giessen: Töpelmann, 1912. 196 pages.

1189. ———. *Theologie der Lessingzeit.* Halle: Niemeyer, 1929. xi+376 pages.

1190. **Grützmacher, R. H.** *Alt- und Neuprotestantismus. Eine geistesgeschichtliche und theologie-geschichtliche Untersuchung.* Leipzig: Deichert, 1920. 119 pages.

1191. **Hagenbach, K. R.** *German Rationalism in Its Rise, Progress and Decline.* Edinburgh: Clark, 1865. xix+405 pages.

1192. **Merkle, G.** *Die kirchliche Aufklärung im katholischen Deutschland.* Berlin: Reichl, 1910. xvi+210 pages.

1193. **Petersen, P.** *Geschichte der aristotelischen Philosophie im protestantischen Deutschland.* Leipzig: Meiner, 1921. 542 pages.

1194. **Saintes, F. A.** *Critical History of Rationalism in Germany.* London: Simpkin, 1849. 2d ed., 1860.

1195. **Weiser, C.** *Shaftesbury und das deutsche Geistesleben.* Leipzig: Teubner, 1916. 564 pages.

FRANCE

1196. **Desnoiresterres, G.** *Voltaire et la société française au 18ᵉ siècle.* 8 vols. Paris: Didier, 1867–77.

1197. **Lanfrey, P.** *L'église et les philosophes au dix-huitième siècle.* Paris: Leçon, 1855. 372 pages.

1198. **Morley, J.** *Diderot and the Encyclopaedists.* 2 vols. London: Chapman & Hall, 1878. (Macmillan, 1923.)

1199. ———. *Rousseau and His Era.* 2 vols. London: Macmillan, 1923.

1200. ———. *Voltaire.* London: Macmillan, 1923. xiii+365 pages.

1201. **Parton, J.** *Life of Voltaire.* 2 vols. New York: Houghton Mifflin, 1909.

1202. **Torrey, N. L.** *Voltaire and the English Deists.* New Haven: Yale University Press, 1930. 224 pages. (Bibliography.)

The French Revolution

1203. **Aulard, A.** *Christianity and the French Revolution.* Translated from French. London: Bouverie House, 1927. xi+ 164 pages.

1204. **Durand, C.** *Histoire du Protestantisme française pendant la révolution et l'empire.* Paris: Fischbacher, 1902. 235 pages.

1205. **Gorce, P. de la.** *Histoire religieuse de la révolution française.* 4 vols. Paris: Plon, 1909——.

1206. **Groethuysen, B.** *Die Entstehung der bürgerlichen Welt- und Lebensanschauung in Frankreich.* 2 vols. Halle: Niemeyer, 1928–30.

1207. **Jervis, W.** *The Gallican Church and the Revolution.* London: Kegan Paul, 1882. 524 pages.

1208. **Roustan, M.** *Pioneers of the French Revolution.* Boston: Little, Brown, 1926. 302 pages.

1209. **Sloane, W.** *The French Revolution and Religious Reform. 1789–1804.* New York: Scribner's, 1901. 333 pages.

1210. **Sorel, A.** *L'Europe et la révolution française.* 8 vols. Paris: Plon, 1885–1904.

1211. **Taine, H.** *Les origines de la France contemporaine.* 6 vols. 28th ed. Paris: Hachette, 1920. (English translation: *The Origines of Contemporary France.* New York: Holt, 1878–94. Since then in many new printings.)

The Netherlands

1212. **Hubert, E.** *Notes et documents sur l'histoire religieuse des pays-bas autrichiens au XVIIIᵉ siècle.* Bruxelles: Lamertin, 1924. 142 pages.

1213. **Knappert, L.** *Geschiedenis der Nederlandsche Hervormde Kerk gedurende de 18ᵉ en 19ᵉ Eeuw.* Amsterdam: Meulenhoff, 1912. viii+367 pages.

Switzerland

1214. **Müller, K.** *Die katholische Kirche in der Schweiz seit dem Ausgang des 18. Jahrhunderts.* Einsiedeln: Benzinger, 1928. 341 pages.

1215. **Wernle, P.** *Der schweizerische Protestantismus im 18. Jahrhundert.* 3 vols. Tübingen: Mohr, 1923–25.

CHRISTIANITY IN THE NINETEENTH CENTURY

POLITICAL AND CULTURAL HISTORY

1216. **Abbot, W. C.** *The Expansion of Europe.* 2 vols. New York: Holt, 1918.

1217. **Merz, J. T.** *History of European Thought in the Nineteenth Century.* 4 vols. Edinburgh: Blackwood, 1903.

1218. **Seignobos, C.** *Histoire politique de l'Europe contemporaine. 1814–1914.* 7th ed. Paris: Colin, 1924.

GENERAL CHURCH HISTORY

1219. **Hirsch, E.** *Staat und Kirche im 19. und 20. Jahrhundert.* Göttingen: Vandenhoeck & Ruprecht, 1930. 72 pages.

1220. **Holmquist, H.** *Ur Kristendomens historia mellan världskrigen 1814–1914.* Upsala: Kristliga Studentrörelsen, 1918. 403 pages.

1221. **Moore, E. C.** *An Outline of the History of Christian Thought since Kant.* New York: Scribner's, 1912. 243 pages

1222. ———. *West and East. The Expansion of Christendom and the Naturalization of Christianity in the Orient in the Nineteenth Century.* New York: Scribner's, 1920. 421 pages.

1223. **Nippold, F.** *Handbuch der neuesten Kirchengeschichte.* 5 (6) vols. 3d ed. Elberfeld: Friederichs, 1880–1906.

PROTESTANTISM

GERMANY

1224. **Dilthey, W.** *Leben Schleiermachers.* Vol. I. Edited by H. Mulert. Berlin: Gruyter, 1922. xxxii+879 pages.

1225. **Hirsch, E.** *Die idealistische Philosophie und das Christentum.* Gütersloh: Bertelsmann, 1926. 312 pages.

1226. **Kattenbusch, F.** *Die deutsche evangelische Theologie seit Schleiermacher.* 5th ed. Giessen: Töpelmann, 1928. 124 pages.

1227. **Kissling, J. B.** *Der deutsche Protestantismus 1817–1917.* 2 vols. Münster: Aschendorff, 1917, 1918. (Catholic.)

1228. **Lütgert, W.** *Die Religion des deutschen Idealismus und ihr Ende.* 4 vols. Gütersloh: Bertelsmann, 1925–31.

1229. **Pfleiderer, O.** *The Development of Theology in Germany since Kant, and Its progress in Great Britain since 1825.* (Translated from German.) 1890. 3d ed. New York: Macmillan, 1909. 403 pages.

1230. **Seeberg, R.** *Die Kirche Deutschlands im 19. Jahrhundert.* 4th ed. Leipzig: Hinrichs: 1904. 398 pages.

1231. **Tischhauser, C.** *Geschichte der evangelischen Kirche Deutschlands in der ersten Hälfte des 19. Jahrhunderts.* Basel: Reich, 1900. 711 pages.

SCANDINAVIA

1232. **Bohlin, T.** *Sören Kierkegaard.* Stockholm: Sv. Kyrk. Diakonist. Bokf, 1919. 176 pages.

1233. **Geismar, E.** *Sören Kierkegaard. Seine Lebensentwicklung und seine Wirksamkeit als Schriftsteller.* (Translated from Danish). Göttingen: Vandenhoeck & Ruprecht, 1929. vi+ 672 pages.

1234. **Günther, V. H.** *Hans Nielsen Hauge.* Neumünster: Christophorus-Verlag, 1928. (Bibliography.)

1235. **Roenning, F.** *U.F.S. Grundtvig.* 4 vols. Copenhagen: Schoenberg, 1907–14.

ROMAN CATHOLICISM
GENERAL

1236. **Bury, J. B.** *History of the Papacy in the Nineteenth Century.* London: Macmillan, 1930. vi+175 pages.

1237 **MacCaffrey, J.** *History of the Catholic Church in the Nineteenth Century. 1789–1908.* 2 vols. St. Louis, Mo.: Herder, 1910.

1238. **Nielsen, F.** *The History of the Papacy in the Nineteenth Century.* 2 vols. (Translated from Danish.) New York: Dutton, 1906.

1239. **Schrörs, H.** *Deutscher und französischer Katholizismus in den letzten Jahrzehnten.* Freiburg: Herder, 1917. 228 pages.

1240. **Sell, K.** *Die Entwicklung der katholischen Kirche im 19. Jahrhundert.* Tübingen: Mohr, 1898. 112 pages.

VATICAN COUNCIL

1241. *Acta et decreta ss. oecum. concil. Vaticani.* Freiburg: Herder, 1890.

1242. **Butler, C.** *The Vatican Council.* 2 vols. New York: Longmans, 1930.

1243. **Friedrich, J.** *Geschichte des vatikanischen Konzils.* 3 vols. Bonn: Neusser, 1877–87.

1244. **Granderath-Kirch, J.** *Geschichte des vatikanischen Konzils von seiner ersten Ankündigung bis zu seiner Vertagung.* 3 vols. Freiburg: Herder, 1903–6.

MODERNISM

1245. **Houtin, A.** *Histoire du modernisme catholique.* Paris (private printing), 1913. 458 pages.

1246. *The Programme of Modernism.* Translated from Italian by G. Tyrrell. New York: Putnam, 1908. xvii+245 pages.

1247. **Sabatier, P.** *Modernism.* ("The Jowett Lectures.") London: Fisher Unwin, 1908. 351 pages.

GERMANY

1248. **Goyau, G.** *L'Allemagne religieuse: Le Catholicisme: 1800–1870.* 4 vols. Paris: Perrin, 1909–10.

1249. ———. *Bismarck et l'Eglise: Le Culturkampf 1870–87.* 4 vols. Paris: Perrin, 1911–13.

1250. **Kissling, J. B.** *Geschichte des Kulturkampfes im Deutschen Reiche.* 3 vols. Freiburg: Herder, 1911–18.

FRANCE

1251. **Barbier, E.** *Histoire du Catholicisme libéral et du Catholicisme social en France, du Concile de Vatican à l'avènement de S. S. Benoît XV (1870–1914).* 5 vols. Bordeaux: Delmas, 1923.

1252. **Bourgain, L.** *L'église de France et l'état au XIX⁵ siècle.* 2 vols. Paris: Douniol, 1910.

1253. **Brémond, H., and Others.** *Manuel illustré de la littérature catholique en France de 1870 à nos jours.* Paris: Spes, 1925. 225 pages.

1254. **Briand, A.** *La séparation des églises et de l'état à la chambre des députés.* Paris: Cornély, 1905.

1255. **Collins, R. W.** *Catholicism and the Second French Republic.* New York: Columbia University Press, 1923. 360 pages.

1256. **Lavisse, E.** *Histoire de la France contemporaine depuis la Révolution jusqu'à la paix de 1919.* 10 vols. Paris: Hachette, 1919–22.

1257. Lüttge, W. *Die Trennung von Staat und Kirche in Frankreich und der französische Protestantismus.* Tübingen: Mohr, 1912. xii+208 pages.

1258. Phillips, C. S. *The Church in France, 1789–1848.* London: Mowbray, 1929. 316 pages. (Bibliography.)

1259. Weill, G. *Histoire du catholicisme libéral en France. 1828–1908.* Paris: Alcan, 1909. 312 pages.

CHAPTER VI

CHRISTIANITY IN THE BRITISH ISLES

Under the heading "The Celtic Church" are included titles for Christianity in Wales to about 870, when the influence of Canterbury first became dominant in the Welsh church; in Scotland to the coming of Queen Margaret, 1068; and in Ireland to the Synod of Cashel, 1172. The Celtic element in Anglo-Saxon Christianity is included chiefly under the history of the Church of England. As indicated by the references, some of the general works and sources listed under "The Church of England: General" are of use for Scotland and Ireland as well as England. Other source and reference works are cited in the sections for which they are primarily useful. The special works for the Church of England are grouped for periods divided by the years 1066, 1509, 1603, 1689— dates familiar to every student of the national history.

CELTIC CHRISTIANITY IN BRITAIN AND IRELAND
(SEE ITEMS 562, 596, 619, 708, 809, 825, 1283, 1296–1303, 1469, 1488, 1489, 1491, 1493)

For the numerous periodicals and serial publications not here listed, see Kenney (Item 1263), pp. 71 f., 93 f.

1260. **Anderson, A. O.** *Early Sources of Scottish History. A.D. 500–1286. Collected and Translated, etc.* 2 vols. Edinburgh and London: Oliver, 1922.

1261. **Bury, J. B.** *The Life of St. Patrick and His Place in History.* New York: Macmillan, 1905. xv+404 pages. (Outstanding.)

1262. **Gougaud, L.** *Les chrétientés celtiques.* Paris: Lecoffre, 1911. xxxv+410 pages. (By a Benedictine. The best general study.)

1263. **Kenney, J. F.** *The Sources for the Early History of Ireland.* Vol. I, *Ecclesiastical.* ("Columbia University Records of Civilization Series.") New York: Columbia University Press, 1929. xvi+807 pages. (Comprehensive and authoritative guide to the sources and literature of Irish Christianity to the twelfth century.)

1264. **Lawlor, H. J.** (translator). *St. Bernard of Clairvaux's Life of St. Malachy of Armagh.* London: Society for Promoting Christian Knowledge, 1920. (Valuable Introduction and notes.)

1265. **McNeill, J. T.** *The Celtic Penitentials and Their Influence on Continental Christianity.* Paris: Champion, 1923. (Only 100 copies. The first four of the six chapters in *Revue celtique* [Item 1269], XXXIX [1922], 257–300, and XL [1923], 51–103, 320–41).

1266. **O'Hanlon, J.** *Lives of the Irish Saints.* Dublin: Duffy, 1875–1903. Nine volumes and part of Volume 10. (From the sources, but treating them rather credulously. Arranged by saint's days, and comprising January 1 to October 21.)

1267. **Plummer, C.** *Vitae sanctorum Hiberniae partim hactenus ineditae.* 2 vols. Oxford: Clarendon Press, 1910. (Valuable historical introduction and notes.)

1268. **Reeves, W.** *The Life of St. Columba.* Dublin, 1857. lxxx+497 pages. 2d ed., W. F. Skene, 1874. (Text of Adamnan's *Life* with abundant critical notes.)

1269. *Revue celtique.* Paris: Champion, 1879——. (Quarterly, though somewhat irregular since 1914. While the articles of this periodical are largely on language and culture, its reviews cover all aspects of Celtic church history.)

1270. **Simpson, W. D.** *The Historical St. Columba.* Aberdeen: Milne, 1927. xiii+177 pages. (A revision of the common view, indicating the extent of pre-Columban Christianity in Scotland.)

1271. **Stokes, G. T.** *Ireland and the Celtic Church, a History of Ireland from St. Patrick to the English Conquest in 1172.*

6th ed., edited by Hugh J. Lawlor. London: Society for Promoting Christian Knowledge, 1776. (Lawlor's notes render doubly valuable the somewhat defective work of Stokes.)

1272. *Studies, an Irish Quarterly Review.* . . . . Dublin: Educational Co. of Ireland, 1912——.

1273. **Williams, H.** *Christianity in Early Britain.* Oxford: Clarendon Press, 1912. vii+484 pages. (A scholarly work mainly on the period before the Anglo-Saxon conquest.)

1274. ——. *Gildas: The Ruin of Britain* in "Cymmrodorion Record Series," Vol. III. London, 1899. (Edition and translation.)

THE CHURCH OF ENGLAND: GENERAL

GENERAL HISTORIES

1275. **Carpenter, W. B.** *A Popular History of the Church of England.* New York: Dutton, 1905. xvi+517 pages.

1276. **Collier, J.** *An Ecclesiastical History of Great Britain, Chiefly of England.* 9 vols. 2d ed., edited by T. Lathbury. London: Straker, 1852. (Based on source materials. Brings the history to 1685. The author was a Nonjuror.)

1277. **Fuller, T.** *The Church History of Britain . . . . to 1648.* 6 vols. London: 1655; new ed., Oxford: University Press, 1845. (Marked by a quaint drollery of style and also by solid erudition and common sense.)

1278. **Gwatkin, H. M.** *Church and State in England to the Death of Queen Anne.* New York: Longmans, 1917. viii+416 pages. (Interesting to the general student and generally reliable.)

1279. **Makower, F.** *The Constitutional History and Constitution of the Church of England.* London: Sonnenschein, 1895. x+545 pages. (Translated from the German, with some alterations by the author. Important.)

1280. **Patterson, M. W.** *A History of the Church of England.* New York: Longmans, 1909; 2d ed., 1925. viii+457 pages. (A well-written sketch.)

1281. **Perry, G. G.** *A History of the English Church.* 3 vols. London: Murray, 1890–1903. (Volume II [1509–1717] reached the 6th edition, 1900.)

1282. **Spence, H. D. M.** *The Church of England; A History for the People.* 4 vols. 2d ed. London: Cassell, 1904–5.

1283. **Stephens, W. R. W., and Hunt, W.** *A History of the English Church.* London: Macmillan, 1899–1910. A series of eight works of which all but the last are single volumes. The authors and periods covered are as follows: Vol. I, to 1066, by W. Hunt; Vol. II, 1066–1299, by W. R. W. Stephens; Vol. III, 1299–1509, by W. Capes; Vol. IV, 1509–58, by J. Gairdner; Vol. V, 1558–1625, by W. H. Frere; Vol. VI, 1625–1714, by W. H. Hutton; Vol. VII, 1714–1800, by J. H. Overton and F. Relton; Vol. VIII, in 2 volumes, 1800–1900, by F. W. Cornish. (A scholarly series.)

SOURCE COLLECTIONS AND SELECTIONS (SEE ITEMS 595–606)

1284. **Cheyney, E. P.** *Readings in English History Drawn from the Original Sources.* (1908.) New ed., Boston: Ginn, 1922. xxxix+849 pages.

1285. **Gee, H., and Hardy, W. J.** *Documents Illustrative of English Church History.* New York: Macmillan, 1896. xii+670 pages.

1286. *Rerum Britannicarum medii aevi scriptores. Chronicles and Memorials of Great Britain and Ireland during the Middle Ages.* London: published under direction of the Master of the Rolls, 1858. (For the list of titles in this vast and important series of sources, see Gross [Item 1292], pp. 93 and 704 ff.)

1287. **Stevenson, J.** *Church Historians of England.* 22 vols. London: Seeley, 1853–58. (Translations of medieval historical writings, with an edition of Foxe's *Acts and Monuments.*)

1288. **Stubbs, W.** *Select Charters and Other Illustrations of English Constitutional History from the Earliest Times to the Reign of Edward I.* 9th ed., edited by H. W. C. Davis. Oxford: Clarendon Press, 1913. xx+528 pages.

1289. **Wilkins, D.** *Concilia Magnae Britanniae et Hiberniae. A.D. 446–1718.* 4 vols. London: Gosling, 1737. (A source work for the decisions of councils.)

REFERENCE WORKS (SEE ITEMS 1263, 1387)

1290. *The Cambridge History of English Literature.* Edited by A. W. Ward and A. K. Waller. 15 vols. Cambridge: University Press; New York: Putnam's, 1912–29. (Volumes I–XII for the Middle Ages.)

1291. *The Dictionary of National Biography.* 63 vols. London: Smith, Elder, 1885–1901; new ed., Oxford: University Press, 1921–22, 22 vols. Various supplements, 1901–27.

1292. **Gross, C.** *Sources and Literature of English History . . . . to 1485.* London: Longmans, 1900. 2d ed., 1915. xxiii+820 pages.

1293. **Hunt, W., and Poole, R. L.** *The Political History of England.* 12 vols. New York: Longmans, 1906–29. (By various writers. An ample and scholarly work for the entire period.)

1294. **Ollard, S. L., and Crosse, G.** *A Dictionary of English Church History.* London: Mowbray, 1912; 2d ed., 1919. xviii+677 pages.

THE RISE AND DEVELOPMENT OF THE ANGLO-SAXON CHURCH
(SEE ITEMS 486, 612, 616, 617, 619)

1295. **Allison, T.** *English Religious Life in the Eighth Century.* London: Society for Promoting Christian Knowledge, 1929. viii+154 pages. (Based on the correspondence of leading ecclesiastics.)

1296. *Bedae opera historica, with an English Translation* by J. E. King. 2 vols. London: Heinemann, 1930. ("Loeb Classical Library." T. Stapleton's translation, 1565, is used for the Ecclesiastical History.) There is an annotated translation of Bede's *Ecclesiastical History* by A. M. Sellar (London: Bell, 1907; xiii+439 pages) and one without notes is furnished in the "Everyman Series" (London: Dent, 1913; xxxiv+370 pages). The latter includes also the *Life of St. Cuthbert* and has an Introduction by Vida D. Scudder.

1297. ———. *Historia Ecclesiastica Gentis Anglorum.* Edited by C. Plummer. 2 vols. Oxford: Clarendon Press, 1896. (Edition of the principal source for English church history to 731, with full critical apparatus.)

1298. **Bright, W.** *Chapters in Early English Church History.* Oxford: Clarendon Press, 1878; 3d ed., 1897. xx+525 pages. (A scholarly work showing the development of church organization to the death of Wilfrid, 709.)

1299. **Haddan, A. W., and Stubbs, W.** *Councils and Ecclesiastical Documents Relating to Great Britain and Ireland.* Oxford: Clarendon Press, Vol. I, 1869; Vol. III, 1871; Vol. II, Part I, 1873. The remainder of Vol. II as projected was never published. (Excellent editions of the chief documents for British and Irish Christianity from *ca.* 200 to 1295.)

1300. **Howorth, H.** *The Golden Days of the English Church.* 3 vols. London: Murray, 1917. (Covers in detail the period from 665 to 735. Informing but not always accurate.)

1301. **Liebermann, F.** *Die Gesetze der Angelsachsen.* 3 vols. Halle a.S. 1903–16. (Best edition of Anglo-Saxon law codes, which illustrate the relations of the church and the secular power.)

1302. **Oakley, T. P.** *The Penitentials and Anglo-Saxon Law.* New York: Columbia University Press, 1923. 227 pages. (Social influence of the church penance system. Well documented.)

1303. **Plummer, A.** *The Churches in Britain before A.D. 1000.* 2 vols. London: Scott, 1911–12.

1304. **Robinson, J. A.** *The Times of St. Dunstan.* Oxford: Clarendon Press, 1923. 188 pages.

THE CHURCH OF ENGLAND, 1066–1509
THE POLITICAL, SOCIAL, AND CULTURAL CONDITIONS

1305. **Abram, A.** *Social England in the Fifteenth Century.* London: Routledge, 1909. xvi+243 pages.

1306. **Addy, S. O.** *Church and Manor: A Study in English Economic History.* London: Allen, 1913. 504 pages.

1307. **Chambers, R. W.** *England before the Norman Conquest.* New York: Longmans, 1926. xxv+334 pages. (Source documents in translation, with introductions.)

1308. **Coulton, G. G.** *Chaucer and His England.* London: Methuen, 1908. xii+321 pages.

1309. ———. *Social Life in Britain from the Conquest to the Reformation.* Cambridge: University Press, 1918. 540 pages. (Mainly source materials.)

1310. **Cruttwell, C. T.** *The Saxon Church and the Norman Conquest.* London: Methuen, 1909. xvi+208 pages.

1311. **Davies, R. T.** *Documents Illustrating the History of Civilization in Medieval England (1066–1500).* London: Methuen, 1926. x+413 pages.

1312. **Salzmann, L. F.** *English Life in the Middle Ages.* London: Milford, 1926. 287 pages.

1313. **Trevelyan, G. M.** *England in the Age of Wyclif.* London: Longmans, 1899; 3d ed., 1909. Frequently reprinted. xvi+380 pages. (A work of distinction, specially illuminating on the social and economic changes of the period.)

CHURCH ORGANIZATIONS, INSTITUTIONS, AND WORSHIP

1314. **Abbot, E. A.** *St. Thomas of Canterbury; His Death and Miracles.* 2 vols. London: Black, 1898.

1315. **Bond, F.** *Dedications and Patron Saints of the English Churches; Ecclesiastical Symbolism; Saints and Their Emblems.* Oxford: University Press; London: Milford, 1914. xvi+343 pages.

1316. **Bridgett, T. E.** *History of the Holy Eucharist in Great Britain.* 2d ed. London: Burns, 1908. xix+324 pages.

1317. **Cutts, E. L.** *Parish Priests and Their People in the Middle Ages in England.* London: Society for Promoting Christian Knowledge, 1898. xvii+579 pages.

1318. **Gasquet, F. A.** *Henry III and the Church. A Study of His Ecclesiastical Policy and of the Relations between England and Rome.* London: Bell, 1905. xvi+446 pages.

1319. ———. *Parish Life in Medieval England.* New York: Benziger, 1906. xix+279 pages. (A favorable portrayal.)

1320. **Hill, G.** *English Dioceses; a History of Their Limits.* . . . . London: Stock, 1900. 426 pages. (Entire period.)

1321. **Hook, W. F.** *Lives of the Archbishops of Canterbury.* 12 vols. London: Bentley, 1860–76; Vols. I–II, 3d ed., and Vol. XII, 2d ed., 1884.

1322. **Jennings, A. C.** *The Medieval Church and the Papacy.* London: Methuen, 1909. xiv+277 pages. (Covers the period *ca.* 1250–1529.)

1323. **Lathbury, T.** *A History of the Convocation of the Church of England.* 2d ed. London: Leslie, 1853. xii+538 pages. (To 1742.)

1324. **Owst, G. R.** *Preaching in Medieval England . . . . 1350–1450.* Cambridge: University Press, 1926. xviii+381 pages.

1325. **Powicke, F. M.** *Stephen Langton.* Oxford: Clarendon Press, 1928. viii+227 pages.

1326. **Powis, A. R.** *The English Parish Church.* New York: Longmans, 1930. xix+165 pages.

1327. **Thompson, A. H.** *Cathedral Churches of England.* London: Society for Promoting Christian Knowledge, 1925. New York: Macmillan, 1925. xvi+235 pages.

1328. **Westlake, H. F.** *The Parish Gilds of Medieval England.* London: Society for Promoting Christian Knowledge, 1919. viii+242 pages.

1329. **Wordsworth, J.** *The Ornaments of the Church and Its Ministers.* London: Society for Promoting Christian Knowledge, 1908. 120 pages. (While specially concerned with the questions of Anglican ceremonial, has general historical sections.)

1330. **Wordsworth, W., and Littlehales, H.** *The Old Service-Books of the English Church.* 2d ed. London: Methuen, 1910. xv+319 pages.

MONASTICISM AND THE DEVOTIONAL LIFE

1331. **Brewer, J. S.** *Monumenta Franciscana.* 2 vols. London: Longmans, 1858–82. ("Rolls Series") (Critical edition of thirteenth- to fifteenth-century sources for English Franciscans.)

1332. **Clay, R. M.** *The Hermits and Anchorites of England.* London: Methuen, 1914. xx+272 pages.

1333. **Cooke, A. M.** "The Settlement of the Cistercians in England," *EHR* (Item 24) VIII (1893), 625–76.

1334. **Cranage, H. S.** *The Home of the Monk: An Account of English Monastic Life and Buildings in the Middle Ages.* London: Cambridge Press, 1926. 135 pages. (A book of scientific popularization.)

1335. **Dugdale, W.** *Monasticon Anglicanum.* This work was originally published under the names Roger Dodsworth and Sir

William Dugdale, London, 1655–73, 3 vols. Two volumes were added by John Stearns, London, 1722–23, who also issued an abridged translation in 1718. The best edition is that by John Caley and others, London: Bohn, 1817–30, 6 vols. in 8. (A treasury of materials on English and Welsh, and related Scottish, Irish, and French monasteries.)

1336. **Gasquet, F. A.** *Monastic Life in the Middle Ages.* London: Bell, 1922. vii+342 pages.

1337. **Graham, R.** *English Ecclesiastical Studies.* London: Society for Promoting Christian Knowledge; New York: Macmillan, 1929. xiii+463 pages.

1338. ———. *St. Gilbert of Sempringham and the Gilbertines.* London: Stock, 1901; reprinted 1903. xi+240 pages.

1339. **Hutton, E.** *The Franciscans in England, 1224–1538.* London: Constable, 1926. 326 pages.

1340. **Hutton, W. H.** *The Influence of Christianity upon National Character Illustrated by the Lives and Legends of the English Saints.* New York: Dutton, 1903. xiv+385 pages.

1341. **Jarrett, B.** *The English Dominicans.* London: Burns, 1921. xi+236 pages.

1342. **Jessop, A.** *The Coming of the Friars and Other Essays.* 5th ed. London: Allen, 1888. iv+344 pages; 14th impression 1906. (Additional essays on village life, monastic life, Black Death, etc.)

1343. **Power, E. E.** *Medieval English Nunneries.* Cambridge: University Press, 1922. *ca.* 1250–1535.)

1344. **Snape, R. H.** *English Monastic Finances in the Later Middle Ages.* Cambridge: University Press, 1926. ix+190 pages.

1345. **Taunton, E. L.** *The English Black Monks of St. Benedict from St. Augustine to the Present Day.* 2 vols. London: Nimms, 1898.

1346. **Thompson, E. M.** *The Carthusian Order in England.* London: Society for Promoting Christian Knowledge, 1930. x+550 pages.

1347. **Ward, S. H.** *The Canterbury Pilgrimages.* 2d ed. London: Black, 1927. 320 pages.

DECADENCE AND THE ADVOCACY OF REFORM
(SEE ITEMS 880, 882, 894, 904)

1348. **Arrowsmith, R. W.** *The Prelude to the Reformation.* London: Society for Promoting Christian Knowledge, 1923. xii+226 pages.

1349. **Deansley, M.** *The Lollard Bible and Other Medieval Biblical Versions.* Cambridge: University Press, 1920. xx+483 pages.

1350. **Lechler, J.** *John Wycliffe and His English Precursors.* Translated from German by P. Lorimer. New ed. London: Religious Tract Society, 1884. xxii+512 pages.

1351. **Leube, H.** *Reformation und Humanismus in England.* Leipzig: Scholl, 1930. 38 pages. (Well annotated.)

1352. **Lupton, J. H.** *A Life of John Colet.* . . . . London: Bell, 1887. xiv+323 pages.

1353. **Manning, B. L.** *The People's Faith in the Time of Wyclif.* Cambridge: University Press, 1919. xvi+196 pages. (An objective treatment of fourteenth-century religious conditions.)

1354. **Seebohm, F.** *The Oxford Reformers. 1867.* Rev. ed., 1869. London: Dent, 1914; xi+331 pages.

1355. **Stevenson, F. S.** *Robert Grosseteste, Bishop of Lincoln.* . . . . New York: Macmillan, 1899. xvi+348 pages.

1356. **Workman, H. B.** *John Wyclif, a Study of the English Medieval Church.* 2 vols. Oxford: Clarendon Press, 1926. (Scholarly and ample study of Wyclif, with much information on the English church and its leaders in the fourteenth century.)

THE CHURCH OF ENGLAND IN THE PERIOD OF REFORMATION, 1509–1603
(SEE ITEMS 932–35, 956–60)
POLITICAL AND SOCIAL CONDITIONS

1357. **Brewer, J.** *The Reign of Henry VIII from His Accession to the Death of Wolsey.* Edited by J. Gairdner. 2 vols. London: Murray, 1884.

1358. **Marti, O. A.** *Economic Causes of the Reformation in England.* New York: Macmillan, 1929. xxi+254 pages.

1359. **Salzmann, L. F.** *England in Tudor Times.* London: Batsford, 1926. vi+143 pages.

GENERAL WORKS ON THE REFORMATION IN ENGLAND

1360. **Burnet, G.** (d. 1715). *The History of the Reformation of the Church of England.* Edited by N. Pocock. 7 vols. Oxford: Clarendon Press, 1865. (Contains many documents.)

1361. **Carter, C. S.** *The English Church and the Reformation.* New York: Longmans, 1912; 2d ed. (much enlarged), 1925. xii+273 pages. (Scholarly and sympathetic.)

1362. **Child, G. W.** *Church and State under the Tudors.* London: Longmans, 1890. xix+428 pages.

1363. **Collins, W. E.** *The English Reformation and Its Consequences (1898).* 2d ed. London: Society for Promoting Christian Knowledge, 1901. vi+314 pages.

1364. **Dixon, R. W.** *History of the Church of England from the Abolition of the Roman Jurisdiction.* 6 vols. Oxford: University Press, 1891-1902. (Some volumes revised. Covers the period 1529-70 in detail. Generally fair and reliable, but rather narrowly ecclesiastical.)

1365. **Foxe, J.** (d. 1587). *The Acts and Monuments of John Foxe.* Edited by S. R. Cattley. 8 vols. London: Seeley, 1837-41. (An important source. Foxe was a strong partisan of the Reformation, but in general does not misstate facts.)

1366. **Gairdner, J.** *Lollardy and the Reformation in England.* 4 vols. London: Macmillan, 1908-13. (Mainly on the sixteenth century. Unsympathetic to Protestantism.)

1367. **Gee, H.** *The Reformation Period.* London: Methuen, 1909. x+267 pages.

1368. **Lewis, J.** *The Reformation Settlement 1509-1666.* Cambridge: Deighton, 1885. 504 pages. (Documents.)

1369. *Parker Society Publications.* 56 vols. Cambridge: University Press, 1841-55. (Editions of the works and correspondence of leaders of the English Reformation. A fundamental source.)

1370. **Sanders, N.** (d. 1581). *Rise and Growth of the Anglican Schism.* . . . . Translated with Introduction and Notes, by

D. Lewis. London: Burns, 1877. cxlvii+380 pages. (A Roman Catholic interpretation.)

1371. **Strype, J.** (d. 1737). *Historical and Biographical Works.* 19 vols. Oxford: Clarendon Press, 1812–24. (An Index by R. F. Lawrence was added in 1828, 2 volumes. This set contains editions of Strype's entire contribution to church history. His work is of first-rate importance. Some specially valuable titles of works by Strype are given in Volume III.)

1372. **Trésal, M. J.** *Les origines du schisme anglican (1509–71).* Paris: Lecofire, 1908. xxiii+460 pages.

WORKS ON SHORTER PERIODS

1373. **Pollard, A. F.** *Thomas Cranmer and the English Reformation, 1489–1556.* New York: Putnam's, 1904. xv+339 pages.

1374. ———. *Wolsey.* New York: Longmans, 1929. xvi+393 pages.

1375. **Smyth, C. H.** *Cranmer and the Reformation under Edward VI.* Cambridge: University Press, 1926. 315 pages.

1376. **Strype, J.** *Annals of the Reformation . . . . during Queen Elizabeth's Happy Reign. 1731–1735.* New 4th ed. Oxford: Clarendon Press, 1824. 4 (7) vols.

1377. ———. *Ecclesiastical Memorials. . . . . The Church of England under King Henry VIII, King Edward VI, and Queen Mary I. 1721.* 3 (6) vols. Oxford: Clarendon Press, 1822.

1378. ———. *Memorials of Thomas Cranmer, Archbishop of Canterbury, 1694.* 3d ed., edited by P. E. Barnes. 2 vols. London: Routledge, 1853.

SPECIAL PHASES OF TUDOR ANGLICANISM

1379. **Barkerville, G.** "The Dispossessed Religions after the Suppression of the Monasteries," in *Essays . . . . Presented to Reginald Lane Poole.* Edited by H. W. C. Davis. Oxford: Clarendon Press, 1927. xiv+483 pages. (Pp. 436–65.)

1380. **Brightman, F. E.** *The English Rite.* 2 vols. London: Rivington, 1915; rev. ed., 1921. (Sources and revisions of the Prayer Book.)

1381. **Cardwell, E.** *Synodalia. A Collection of Articles of Religion, Canons and Proceedings of Convocations, 1547–1717.* 2 vols. Oxford: University Press, 1842.

1382. **Carter, C. S.** *The Anglican Via Media, being Studies in the Elizabethan Religious Settlement and in the Teaching of the Caroline Divines.* London: Thynne, 1927. x+201 pages.

1383. **Cox, G. C., and Harvey, A.** *English Church Furniture.* London: Methuen, 1907. xvi+397 pages. (Chiefly for the post-Reformation Anglican church.)

1384. **Dowden, J.** *Theological Literature of the Church of England.* London: Society for Promoting Christian Knowledge, 1897. vi+214 pages. (A useful handbook.)

1385. **Fletcher, J. S.** *The Reformation in Northern England.* London: Allen, 1925. 191 pages.

1386. **Gibson, E.** *Codex juris ecclesiastici anglicani, or the Statutes of the Church of England Methodically Digested under their Proper Heads, with a Commentary, etc.* 2 vols. London: Baskett, 1713; 2d ed., Oxford: Clarendon Press, 1761.

1387. **Gillett, C. R.** *Catalogue of the McAlphin Collection of British History and Theology.* 5 vols. New York: Union Theological Seminary, 1927–30. (Publications of the period 1500–1700.)

1388. **Green, E. T.** *The Thirty-nine Articles and the Age of the Reformation.* London: Gardner, 1896. xiv+456 pages. (Historical exposition of each article.)

1389. **Hooker, R.** (d. 1600). *Of the Laws of Ecclesiastical Polity. Eight Books.* For the early editions see Keble's Introduction in *The Works of Rev. Richard Hooker.* 3 vols. Oxford: Clarendon Press; 7th ed., 1888. (This is the best edition.)

1390. **Jacobs, H. E.** *The Lutheran Movement in England during the Reign of Henry VIII and Edward VI.* Philadelphia: Frederick, 1894. xv+376 pages.

1391. **Janelle, P.** *Obedience in Church and State; Three Political Tracts by Stephen Gardiner.* Cambridge: University Press, 1930. lxx+221 pages. (Edited with translation and notes.)

1392. **Lacey, T. A.** *The Reformation and the People.* New York: Longmans, 1929. vi+120 pages.

1393. **Phillimore, R.** *The Ecclesiastical Law of the Church of England.* 2d ed., edited by W. G. F. Phillimore, and C. F. Jennett. 2 vols. London: Sweet & Maxwell, 1895.

1394. **Pollard, A. F.** *Tudor Tracts. 1532–1588.* Westminster: Constable, 1903. xxxvi+520 pages.

1395. **Procter, F., and Frere, W. H.** *A New History of the Book of Common Prayer.* London: Macmillan, 1902. xxxiv+699 pages.

1396. **Smithen, F. J.** *Continental Protestantism and the English Reformation.* London: Clarke, 1927. 256 pages.

THE RISE OF PURITANISM TO 1603

1397. **Burrage, C.** *The Early English Dissenters in the Light of Recent Research (1550–1641).* 2 vols. Cambridge: University Press, 1912.

1398. **Frere, W. H., and Douglas, C. C.** *Puritan Manifestoes.* London: Society for Promoting Christian Knowledge, 1907. xxxi+155 pages. (Notable early Puritan documents.)

1399. **Hinds, A. B.** *The Making of the England of Elizabeth.* New York: Macmillan, 1895. ix+152 pages. (For the Marian Exiles.)

1400. **Lorimer, P.** *John Knox and the Church of England.* London: King, 1875. xii+317 pages. (On the origins of Puritanism.)

1401. **Martin, C.** *Les Protestants anglais refugiés a Genève au temps de Calvin.* Geneva: Jullien, 1915. xv+352 pages.

1402. **Pauck, W.** *Das Reich Gottes auf Erden: Utopie und Wirklichkeit.* Berlin: De Gruyter, 1928. 208 pages. (Bucer's work in England.)

1403. **Pearson, A. F. S.** *Thomas Cartwright and Elizabethan Puritanism, 1535–1603.* Cambridge: University Press, 1925. xvi+511 pages.

THE PURITAN AGE, 1603–89
(SEE ITEMS 1863–72, 1893, 1894, 1902)
WORKS ON THE ENTIRE PERIOD

1404. **Blaxland, B.** *The Struggle with Puritanism.* London: Methuen, 1910. xii+233 pages.

1405. **Brown, J.** *The English Puritans.* Cambridge: University Press, 1910. vi+160 pages.

1406. **Clark, H. W.** *History of English Nonconformity.* 2 vols. London: Chapman & Hall, 1911–13. (Entire history from Wyclif.)·

1407. **Henson, H. H.** *Puritanism in England.* New York: Hodder, 1912. viii+294 pages. (A penetrating appreciation by an Anglican.)

1408. **Neal, Daniel.** *The History of the Puritans.* . . . . 2 vols. London: Buckland, 1732; 2d ed., 1754. Edited by J. Toulmin, 1811, and by J. O. Charles, 1844. New York: Harper, 1855.

1409. **Plummer, A.** *English Church History from the Death of Charles I to the Death of William III.* Edinburgh: Clark, 1907. xi+187 pages.

1410. **Stoughton, J.** *History of Religion in England.* 5 parts in 9 vols. London, 1867–78. New and rev. ed., New York: Armstrong, 1882, 6 vols. (Covers the period 1640–1760.)

1411. **Trevelyan, G. M.** *England under the Stuarts.* London: Methuen, 1904. xvi+566 pages.

1412. **Wakeman, H. O.** *The Church and the Puritans, 1570–1660.* 5th ed. New York: Longmans, 1907. x+208 pages.

SHORTER PERIODS AND SPECIAL PHASES (SEE ITEM 1387)

1413. **Aitken, G.** (editor). *Later Stuart Tracts.* Westminster: Constable, 1903. xxix+404 pages.

1414. **Barclay, Robert.** *The Inner Life of the Religious Societies of the Commonwealth.* London: Hodder & Stoughton, 1876. xxxi+700 pages. (Valuable for Quakers and other small groups.)

1415. **Burnet, G.** *History of My Own Time.* Edited by O. Airy. 2 vols. Oxford: Clarendon Press, 1897, with Supplement edited by H. C. Foxcraft, 1902. (Later Stuarts.)

1416. **Calamy, E.** *The Nonconformist's Memorial.* 2d ed. 3 vols. London: Button, 1802–3. 3 vols. (On the lives and writings of the ejected ministers of 1662.)

1417. **Crouch, J.** *Puritanism and Art: an Inquiry into a Popular Fallacy.* London: Cassell, 1910. xiv+381 pages. (Holds that the Puritans were not unfavorable to art.)

1418. **Dearmer, P.** *Religious Pamphlets.* New York: Holt, 1898. 380 pages. (Selected pamphlets from Wyclif to Newman.)

1419. **Emmott, E. B.** *A Short History of Quakerism.* New York: Doran, 1923. 352 pages.

1420. **Flynn, J. S.** *The Influence of Puritanism on the Political and Religious Thought of the English.* London: Murray, 1920. xii+257 pages.

1421. **Foster, H. D.** *Collected Papers of Herbert D. Foster.* Hanover, New Hampshire: Privately printed, 1929. xv+249 pages. (Reprints of valuable articles on Calvinism and Puritanism.)

1422. **Froude, J. A.** *Short Studies in Great Subjects.* 1st to 4th Series. 4 vols. New York: Scribner's, 1900–1901. 1st and 2d Series, "Everyman Library." 2 vols. London: Dent, 1915.

1423. **Gardiner, S. R.** *History of the Commonwealth and Protectorate, 1649–1696.* New ed. 4 vols. New York: Longmans, 1903.

1424. **Hanbury, B.** *Historical Memorials Relating to the Independents, or Congregationalists.* 3 vols. London: Congregational Union of England and Wales, 1839–44.

1425. **Henson, H. H.** *Studies in English Religion in the Seventeenth Century.* London: Murray, 1903. xvii+265 pages.

1426. **Hetherington, W.** *History of the Westminster Assembly.* 5th ed. edited by R. Williamson. Edinburgh: Gemmell, 1890. xix+479 pages.

1427. **Milton, J.** *The Prose Works.* Edited by J. A. St. John. 5 vols. London: Bell, 1909–14.

1428. **Pawson, G. P. H.** *The Cambridge Platonists.* London: Society for Promoting Christian Knowledge, 1930. 95 pages.

1429. **Pease, T. C.** *The Leveller Movement.* Washington: American Historical Association, 1916. ix+406 pages.

1430. **Richardson, C. F.** *English Preachers and Preaching, 1640–70.* New York: Macmillan, 1928. xii+359 pages.

1431. **Salmon, N.** *The Lives of the English Bishops from the Restoration to the Revolution.* London: Roberts, 1723. ii+402 pages.

1432. **Seaton, A. A.** *The Theory of Toleration under the Later Stuarts.* Cambridge: University Press, 1911. vii+364 pages.

1433. **Shaw, W. A.** *A History of the English Church during the Civil War and under the Commonwealth, 1640–1660.* 2 vols. New York: Longmans, 1900. (Comprehensive and objective.)

1434. **Tatham, G. B.** *The Puritans in Power . . . . 1640–1660.* Cambridge: University Press, 1913. vi+282 pages.

1435. **Tawney, R. H.** *Religion and the Rise of Capitalism.* New York: Harcourt, 1926. x+337 pages.

1436. **Tulloch, J.** *Rational Theology and Christian Philosophy in England in the Seventeenth Century.* 2 vols. Edinburgh: Blackwood, 1872. Vol. I, *Liberal Churchmen.* Vol. II, *The Cambridge Platonists.*

1437. **Usher, R. G.** *The Reconstruction of the English Church.* 2 vols. London: Appleton, 1910. (A scholarly study of the early years of James I. Anglican viewpoint.)

1438. **Weber, M.** *The Protestant Ethic and the Spirit of Capitalism.* Translated from the revised German edition [1920], by T. Parsons. London: Allen, 1930. xi+292 pages. First published 1904–5. (Important for the economic ethics of Puritanism.)

Works Mainly Biographical

1439. **Brook, B.** *The Lives of the Puritans.* 3 vols. London: Black, 1813. (Leaders of the period 1558–1662.)

1440. **Collins, W. E.** *Typical English Churchmen from Parker to Maurice.* London: Society for Promoting Christian Knowledge, 1902. xvi+369 pages.

1441. **Duncan-Jones, A. L.** *Archbishop Laud.* London: Macmillan, 1927. x+273 pages.

1442. **Fox, G.** *The Journal of George Fox.* Edited by N. Penny. London: Dent, 1924. xxii+359 pages.

1443. **Gardiner, S. R.** *Oliver Cromwell.* 2d ed. London: Longmans, 1901. iv+319 pages; reprinted 1925.

1444. **Gosse, E. W.** *Jeremy Taylor.* New York: Macmillan, 1904. xi+234 pages.

1445. **Kittel, H.** *Oliver Cromwell: seine Religion und seine Sendung.* Berlin: De Gruyter, 1928. ix+262 pages.

1446. **Masson, D.** *The Life of John Milton: Narrated in Connection with the Political, Ecclesiastical and Literary History of the Time.* 7 vols. London: Macmillan, 1859–94. (A work of high value for the religious history.)

1447. **Powicke, F. J.** *A Life of the Reverend Richard Baxter*, and *Rev. Richard Baxter under the Cross.* 2 vols. London: Cape, 1924–27.

1448. **Speight, H. E. B.** *The Life and Writings of John Bunyan.* New York: Harper, 1928. xxii+224 pages.

1449. **Stephen, Sir J.** *Essays in Ecclesiastical Biography (1849).* 2 vols. London: Longmans, 1907. (Includes Baxter, Wilberforce, the Clapham sect.)

1450. **Wordsworth, C.** (editor). *Ecclesiastical Biography . . . . from the . . . . Reformation to the Revolution.* 6 vols. London: Rivington, 1810. New ed. 4 vols. London: Rivington, 1853.

CHRISTIANITY IN SCOTLAND, 1093–1689

General Works on Scottish Church History

1451. **Blaikie, W. G.** *The Preachers of Scotland from the Sixth to the Nineteenth Century.* (Cunningham Lectures.) Edinburgh: Clark, 1888. xviii+350 pages.

1452. **Clark, I. M.** *A History of Church Discipline in Scotland.* Aberdeen: Lindsay, 1929. viii+235 pages.

1453. **Cunningham, J.** *The Church History of Scotland from the Commencement of the Christian Era to the Present Century.* 2 vols. Edinburgh: Black, 1859; 2d ed., 1882. (Volume I treats the history to 1603; Vol. II, from 1603 to 1631. Long the best general work; now largely superseded.)

1454. **MacEwan, A. R.** *A History of the Church of Scotland.* New York: Hodder, Vol. I (397–1546), 1913. 2d edition, 1915. Vol. II (1546–1560), 1918. (The outstanding work for the period covered.)

Works on the Period 1068–1547 (See Items 1451–54, 1461, 1469)

1455. **Dowden, J.** *The Medieval Church in Scotland; Its Constitution, Organization and Law.* Glasgow: Maclehose, 1910.

xlviii+352 pages. (A substantial work by a bishop in the Scottish Episcopal church.)

1456. **Mackie, J. D.** *Margaret, Queen and Saint.* Edinburgh: Oliphant, 1905. 77 pages.

1457. **Patrick, D.** *Statutes of the Scottish Church 1225–1559. Being a Translation of Concilia Scotiae,* .... Edinburgh: Constable, 1907. cxiv+311 pages. ("Scottish History Society Publications," No. 54.)

1458. **Robertson, J.** *Concilia Scotiae. Ecclesiae Scotticanae statuta tam provincialia quam synodalia quae supersunt. MCCXXV–MDLIX.* 2 vols. Edinburgh: Bannatyne Club, 1866. (Records of the synods held in Scotland in the later Middle Ages, with a long historical preface in English.)

Works on the Period 1547–1689

1459. **Balfour of Burleigh, Lord.** *An Historical Account of the Rise and Development of Presbyterianism in Scotland.* Cambridge: University Press; New York: Putnam's, 1911. vii+172 pages. (Useful elementary textbook for the period from about 1547 to 1910.)

1460. **Brown, P. H.** *John Knox: a Biography.* 2 vols. London: Black, 1895.

1461. **Calderwood, D.** *The History of the Kirk of Scotland.* Edited by T. Thomson. 8 vols. Edinburgh: Wodrow Society, 1842–49. (Treats in detail the period 1514–1625, using much source material. Strongly opposed to episcopacy.)

1462. **Dunlop, W.** *A Collection of the Confessions . . . . of Public Authority in the Church of Scotland.* 2 vols. Edinburgh, 1719–20.

1463. **Fleming, D. H.** *The Scottish Reformation; Causes, Characteristics, Consequences.* London: Blackwood, 1900. xliv+318 pages.

1464. **Hewison, J. K.** *The Covenanters. A History of the Church in Scotland from the Reformation to the Revolution.* 2 vols. Glasgow: J. Smith & Son, 1908; 2d rev. ed. 1913.

1465. **Johnston, J. C.** *The Treasury of the Covenant.* Edinburgh: Elliot, 1887. 672 pages. (Contains a selection of documents

and an extensive bibliographical section. Well indexed. Still
a useful reference work.)

1466. **Kinloch, M. G. F.** *Studies in Scottish Ecclesiastical History
in the Seventeenth and Eighteenth Centuries.* London: Simpkin, 1898. xi+348 pages. (A Roman Catholic view.)

1467. **Knox, John.** *Works of John Knox.* Edited by David Laing.
6 (7) vols. Edinburgh: printed for the Bannatyne Club,
1846–64. (Critical edition.)

1468. **Macmillan, D.** *The Aberdeen Doctors, a Notable Group of
Scottish Theologians of the First Episcopal Period, 1610–
1638, etc.* London: Hodder & Stoughton, 1909. x+320
pages.

1469. **Macpherson, G.** *A History of the Church in Scotland.* London: Gardner, 1901. viii+458 pages.

1470. **Mathieson, W. L.** *Politics and Religion: a Study in Scottish
History from the Reformation to the Revolution.* 2 vols. Glasgow: Maclehose, 1902.

1471. **McCrie, C. G.** *The Confessions of the Church of Scotland.*
Edinburgh: MacNiven, 1907. vii+318 pages. (History of
confessions and theology.)

1472. **McNeill, J. T.** "John Knox, Destroyer and Builder," *Canadian Journal of Religious Thought,* II (1925), 380–92.

1473. **Mitchell, A. F., and Struthers, J.** *Minutes of the Sessions of
the Westminster Assembly . . . . November 1644—March
1649.* Edinburgh: Blackwood, 1874. lxxxvii+556 pages.

1474. **Scott, H.** *Fasti Ecclesiae Scotticanae, 1866–68.* Revised and
continued by W. S. Crockett and others (a committee of the
General Assembly of the Church of Scotland). 7 vols. Edinburgh: Oliver, 1915–29. (Short accounts of Church of Scotland ministers since the Reformation. Arranged by synods.
Last volume includes "The Church of Scotland Overseas."
Each volume has extensive bibliography.)

1475. *Scottish Divines, 1505-1872.* (St. Giles Lectures, No. III.)
Edinburgh: MacNiven, 1883. viii+460 pages. (Lectures on
twelve Scottish church leaders by various authors.)

ROMAN CATHOLICISM IN GREAT BRITAIN SINCE THE REFORMATION

1476. **Brady, W. M.** *The Episcopal Succession in England, Scotland and Ireland, 1400–1875.* 3 vols. Rome, 1876–77.

1477. **Butler, C.** *Historical Memorials Regarding the English, Irish and Scottish Catholics from the Reformation.* 4 vols. London, 1819–21. New (3d) ed., London: Murray, 1822.

1478. **Gillow, J.** *Biographical and Bibliographical Dictionary of the English Catholics.* 5 vols. London: Burns, 1902.

1479. **Haile, M.** *Life of Reginald Pole.* New York: Longmans, 1910. xiii+554 pages.

1480. **Hughes, P.** *The Catholic Question, 1688–1829.* New York: Benziger, 1929. 334 pages.

1481. **Hyland, G. K.** *A Century of Persecution under Tudor and Stuart Sovereigns from Contemporary Records.* London: Kegan Paul, 1920. xvi+494 pages.

1482. **Leith, W. F.** *Memoirs of the Scottish Catholics.* 2 vols. London: Longmans, 1909. (1627–1793.)

1483. **Muller, J. A.** *Stephen Gardiner and the Tudor Reaction.* London: Society for Promoting Christian Knowledge, 1926. (New York: Macmillan.) xvi+429 pages.

1484. **Pollen, J. H.** *The English Catholics in the Reign of Queen Elizabeth. . . . .* New York: Longmans, 1920. xi+387 pages.

1485. **Taunton, E. L.** *The History of the Jesuits in England, 1580–1773.* London: Methuen, 1901. xii+513 pages.

1486. **Trappes-Lomax, R.** *The English Franciscan Nuns, 1619–1821, and the Friars Minor . . . . 1618–1761.* Catholic Record Society XXIV, 1922. viii+339 pages. London: privately printed by Pollard in Exeter.

1487. **Ward, B. N.** *The Eve of Catholic Emancipation.* 3 vols. New York: Longmans, 1911–12.

CHRISTIANITY IN IRELAND SINCE 1172

1488. **Bellesheim, A.** *Geschichte der katholischen Kirche in Irland.* 3 vols. Mainz: Kirchheim, 1890–91. (Volume I to 1509.)

1489. **Heron, J.** *The Celtic Church in Ireland, the Story of Ireland and Irish Christianity from Before the Time of St. Patrick to* *the Reformation.* London: Service, 1898. x+429 pages. (Presbyterian viewpoint.)

1490. **Holloway, H.** *The Reformation in Ireland.* London: Society for Promoting Christian Knowledge; New York: Macmillan, 1919. 240 pages.

1491. **Killen, W. D.** *The Ecclesiastical History of Ireland from the Earliest Period to the Present Times.* 2 vols. London: Macmillan, 1875.

1492. **Marti, O. A.** "Passive Resistance of the Scotch-Irish Presbyterians during the Period of the Restoration 1660–72." *Journal of Religion* (Item 150), VIII (1928), 581–602.

1493. **Olden, T.** *The Church of Ireland.* London: Gardner, 1892. x+439 pages. (Entire history to 1870. Anglican.)

1494. **Ronan, M. V.** *The Reformation in Dublin, 1536–1558.* New York: Longmans, 1926. xxxii+543 pages. (By a Roman Catholic scholar.)

1495. ———. *The Reformation in Ireland under Elizabeth. 1558–1580.* New York: Longmans, 1930. xxxii+678 pages. (Well documented.)

1496. **Seymour, J. D.** *The Puritans in Ireland, 1647–61.* Oxford: Clarendon Press, 1921. xiv+240 pages.

1497. **Stokes, G. T.** *Ireland and the Anglo-Norman Church.* London: Hodder & Stoughton, 1889. xvi+391 pages; 2d ed., 1892.

CHRISTIANITY IN GREAT BRITAIN SINCE 1689

(SEE ITEMS 1159–61, 1216–23, 1237–39)

PRINCIPAL RELIGIOUS MOVEMENTS IN ENGLAND

MOVEMENTS IN ANGLICANISM

1498. **Balleine, G. R.** *A History of the Evangelical Party in the Church of England.* New York: Longmans, 1909. xi+338 pages.

1499. **Brilioth, Y. T.** *The Anglican Revival. Studies in the Oxford Movement.* New York: Longmans, 1925. xv+357 pages. (A penetrating study by a Swedish Lutheran.)

1500. **Foakes-Jackson, F. J.** *Anglican Church Principles.* New York: Macmillan, 1924. xii+232 pages.

1501. **Headlam, A. C.** *The Church of England.* New York: Longmans, 1924. xiii+296 pages.
1502. **Henson, H. H.** *Anglicanism. Lectures delivered . . . . in Upsala . . . . 1920.* London, Macmillan, 1921. xliii+267 pages.
1503. **Lacey, T. A.** *A Roman Diary and Other Documents Relating to the Papal Inquiry into English Ordinations.* London: Longmans, 1910. xvi+420 pages.
1504. **Legg, J. W.** *English Church Life, 1660–1833.* London: Longmans, 1914. xix+428 pages.
1505. **Mathieson, W. L.** *English Church Reform, 1815–1840.* London: Longmans, 1923. x+180 pages.
1506. **May, G. L.** *Some Eighteenth Century Churchmen.* London: Society for Promoting Christian Knowledge; New York: Macmillan, 1920. 224 pages.
1507. **Overton, J. H.** *The Non-jurors.* London: Smith, 1902. vi+503 pages.
1508. **Portus, G. V.** *Caritas Anglicana, or an Historical Inquiry into Those Religious and Philosophical Societies . . . . 1678–1740.* London: Mowbray, 1912. 302 pages.
1509. **Stewart, H. L.** *A Century of Anglo-Catholicism.* London: Dent, 1929. xvii+404 pages.
1510. *Tracts for the Times by Members of the University of Oxford.* Newman, Keble, Palmer, Froude, and others. 6 (5) vols. London: Rivington, 1834–40.

METHODISM AND NONCONFORMITY (SEE ITEMS 1405, 1406, 1408, 1421 F., 1424; ALSO ARTICLE "UNITARIANISM" IN *ERE* [ITEM 120], XII, 519–27)

1511. **Bogue, D., and Bennett, J.** *A History of the Dissenters from the Revolution in 1688 to the year 1808.* 4 vols. London: printed for the authors, 1808–12.
1512. **Colligan, J. H.** *Eighteenth Century Nonconformity.* New York: Longmans, 1915. vii+143 pages.
1513. **Dimond, S. G.** *The Psychology of the Methodist Revival.* Oxford: University Press, 1926. xv+296 pages.
1514. **Drysdale, A. H.** *A History of the Presbyterians in England.* London: Presbyterian Church of England, 1889. xi+644

pages. (Condensed in a popular booklet *The English Presbyterians*, 1891. 198 pages.)

1515. **Eayrs, G.** *John Wesley, Christian Philosopher and Church Founder.* London: Epworth Press, 1926. 288 pages.

1516. **Gow, H.** *The Unitarians.* Garden City, New York: Doubleday, 1928. xii+180 pages.

1517. **Horne, C. S.** (editor). *Eras of Nonconformity.* 13 volumes by various writers. London: National Council of Free Churches, 1904-7. (The series includes a volume each on the Lollards, the Anabaptists, the Friends, Foreign Missions [Vol. XII], and Scotland's Struggle for Religious Liberty [Vol. VIII]. Methodism is treated in two volumes. There is no documentation except a Bibliography in Volume XII.)

1518. **Lunn, A. H. M.** *John Wesley.* London: Longmans; New York: MacVeagh, 1929. xix+371 pages.

1519. *The Methodist Magazine,* 1928——. London: Epworth Press (monthly). In continuation with the *Arminian Magazine,* 1778-97, the *Methodist Magazine,* 1797-1822, the *Wesleyan Magazine,* 1822-1914, and the *Magazine of the Wesleyan Methodist Church,* 1914-28. (Much historical material.)

1520. **Parker, I.** *Dissenting Academies in England.* Cambridge: University Press, 1914. xii+168 pages.

1521. **Selbie, W. B.** *Congregationalism.* London: Methuen, 1927. xi+199 pages.

1522. ——. *Nonconformity, Its Origin and Progress.* London: Williams & Norgate, 1912. 256 pages.

1523. **Simon, J. S.** *The Revival of Religion in England in the Eighteenth Century.* London: Culley, 1907. 331 pages.

1524. **Smiles, S.** *The Huguenots . . . . in England and Ireland.* Rev. ed. London: Murray, 1881. xv+448 pages.

1525. **Townsend, W. J.; Workman, H. B.; Eayrs, G.** (editors). *A New History of Methodism.* 2 vols. London: Hodder, 1909. ("Authorities" at beginning of chapters.)

1526. **Wesley, J.** *Journal of John Wesley.* Edited by N. Curnock. 8 vols. London: Culley, 1909-16.

1527. **Whitley, W. T.** *A History of the British Baptists.* London: Griffin, 1923. xii+381 pages.

DEISM, LIBERALISM, AND THEOLOGY (SEE ITEMS
1177, 1179–87, 1195–1202)

1528. **Farrar, A. S.** *A Critical History of Freethought in Reference to the Christian Religion.* New York: Appleton, 1894. xlvi+ 487 pages.

1529. **Leland, John.** *A View of the Principal Deistic Writers.* . . . . 5th ed. 2 vols. London: Cadell, 1798.

1530. **Pattison, M.** "Tendencies of Religious Thought in England, 1688–1750," in *Essays and Reviews*, pp. 254–329. 9th ed. London: Longmans, 1861. 433 pages. (The whole work is a source for the rise of modern liberal and critical thought in England.)

1531. **Sorley, W. R.** *A History of English Philosophy.* Cambridge: University Press, 1920. xvi+380 pages.

1532. **Stephen, L.** *History of English Thought in the Eighteenth Century.* 2 vols. New York: Putnam's, 1876; 3d ed., 1902.

1533. **Storr, V. F.** *The Development of English Theology in the Nineteenth Century.* London, New York, etc.: Longmans, 1913. viii+486 pages. (Only one of the two volumes projected appeared. Treats the period 1800–1860.)

SCOTTISH CHURCHES

1534. **Cowan, H.** *The Influence of the Scottish Church in Christendom.* London: Black, 1896. xvii+294 pages.

1535. **Fleming, J. R.** *A History of the Church in Scotland, 1843– 1874.* Edinburgh: Clark, 1927. x+276 pages. (Comprehensive and scholarly. Contains lists of authorities by chapters.)

1536. **Innes, A.** *The Law of Creeds in Scotland.* Edinburgh and London: Blackwell, 1902. xiii+390 pages. (A study of the legal basis of the relations of church and state in Scotland, and of law cases and decisions affecting those relations. Chiefly useful for the nineteenth century.)

1537. **Logan, R.** *The United Free Church, an Historical Review of the Hundred and Twenty-five Years, 1681–1906.* Edinburgh: Macniven, 1906. xii+272 pages. (A useful sketch.)

1538. **MacKay, G.** *The Church in the Highlands.* London: Hodder & Stoughton, 1914. vii+280 pages.

1539. **Macpherson, H.** *The Intellectual Development of Scotland.*
New York and London: Hodder & Stoughton, 1911. vi+
223 pages. (Discusses chiefly the revival of intellectual and
scientific activity in eighteenth-century Scotland. Valuable
for the church-history student.)

1540. **McKerrow, J.** *History of the Secession Church,* 1839. 2 vols.
Rev. ed. Glasgow: Fullerton, 1841. Several times reprinted.
Edinburgh: Oliphant, 1889.

MISSIONS, CHURCH UNITY, AND SOCIAL REFORM (SEE
ITEMS 939, 946, 965, 1516, 2174, 2183)

1541. **Allen, W. O. B., and McClure, E.** *The History of the Society
for Promoting Christian Knowledge.* London: Society for
Promoting Christian Knowledge, 1898. vii+551 pages.

1542. **Bell, G. K. A.** *Documents on Christian Unity, 1920–1924.*
London: Oxford University Press, 1924. xv+382 pages. 2d
ser., 1924–30, bound with the foregoing, same publisher,
1931. 636 pages.

1543. **Davidson, R.** *The Six Lambeth Conferences, 1867–1920,
Compiled under the Direction of the Most Reverend Lord
Davidson of Lambeth, Archbishop of Canterbury, 1908–1928.*
London: Society for Promoting Christian Knowledge, 1929.
xi+446 pages with Appendix, xiv+161 pages. (Narrative
and documents.)

1544. **Findlay, G. G., and Holdsworth, W. W.** *The History of the
Wesleyan Methodist Missionary Society.* 5 vols. London:
Epworth Press, 1921–24.

1545. **Fleming, J. R.** *The Story of Church Union in Scotland . . . .
1560–1929.* London: Clarke, 1930. 175 pages.

1546. **Foakes-Jackson, F. J.** *Social Life in England, 1750–1850.*
New York: Macmillan, 1916. ix+338 pages.

1547. **Hall, T. C.** *The Social Meaning of Modern Religious Movements in England.* New York: Scribner's, 1900. xv+283
pages. (Social results of the Evangelical Revival and subsequent movements.)

1548. **Holl, K.** "Thomas Chalmers und die Anfänge der kirchlich-
sozialen Bewegung," pp. 404–36 of Holl's *Gesammelte Aufsätze,* Vol. III. Tübingen; Mohr, 1928. xiii+602 pages.

1549. **Lovett, R.** *The History of the London Missionary Society, 1795–1895.* 2 vols. London: Froude, 1899. See also Item 2281.

1550. **MacKichan, D.** *The Missionary Ideal in the Scottish Church.* London: Hodder & Stoughton, 1927. 238 pages.

1551. **Martin, H.** *Christian Social Reformers of the Nineteenth Century.* London: Student Christian Movement, 1927. 242 pages. (Representative leaders of various churches.)

1552. **Pascoe, C. S.** *An Historical Account of the Society for the Propagation of the Gospel.* London: Society for Propagation of the Gospel, 1901. xli+1429 pages.

1553. **Stock, E.** *History of the Church Missionary Society.* 3 vols. London: Church Missionary Society, 1899.

1554. **Vedder, H. C.** *A Short History of Baptist Missions.* Philadelphia: Judson Press, 1927. vii+559 pages.

1555. **Wagner, D. O.** *The Church of England and Social Reform since 1854.* New York: Columbia University Press, 1930. 341 pages.

CHAPTER VII

HISTORY OF EASTERN CHRISTIANITY

This chapter deals with the history of the Orthodox, Separated, Uniate, Roman Catholic, and Protestant racial and national groups comprised in Eastern Europe, parts of Asia and Africa. Geographically delimited, the field of study comprises the territories east of Germany, Austria, and Italy as far as Europe is concerned; those parts of Asia which have been affected by Christianity prior to the era of modern missions; and finally, Egypt and Ethiopia in Africa. Because of the heterogeneous nature of the subject, both racially and ecclesiastically, it will be studied by separate groups where a more inclusive method is not possible.

Definite nomenclature regarding the various groups has not as yet gained general acceptance. It is necessary, therefore, to define some of the terms used. Those groups which, for non-acceptance of the decrees of some general council, either have been excluded or have separated themselves from the dominant church in the Eastern Empire, and which are often designated as "heterodox" or "non-Orthodox," are termed "Separated." They include the so-called "Nestorians," the Monophysites, and the Armenians.

In the selection of literature, preference was given to English, French, and German works, not because these are the best, but because they are likely to prove most useful to the majority of students and scholars. Since this is not an exhaustive bibliography, the rich literature in the vernacular of the particular countries studied (especially Russian, Czech, Polish, and Greek) had to be, to a large extent, omitted. This is regrettable in view of the fact that bibliography on the history of Eastern Christianity is not readily accessible, but the limits of this work make such curtailment imperative.

GENERAL HISTORY OF THE EASTERN ORTHODOX AND THE SEPARATED CHURCHES

GENERAL TEXTBOOKS (SEE ITEMS 54, 101)

1556. **Adeney, W. F.** *The Greek and Eastern Churches.* New York: Scribner's, 1908. xiv+634 pages. (Written from the Protestant point of view; some parts, especially the Slavic section, are not adequately or reliably treated.)

1557. **Fortescue, A.** *The Orthodox Eastern Church.* London: Catholic Truth Society, 1920. xxxiii+451 pages. (Written by a Roman Catholic scholar with a marked pro-Roman bias.)

1558. **Kidd, B. J.** *The Churches of Eastern Christendom.* London: Faith Press, 1927. 541 pages. (General treatment satisfactory except for the most recent period.)

PERIODICALS (SEE ITEMS 25, 26, 149, 150, 151, 154, 161, 163, 164)

1559. *Byzantinische Zeitschrift.* Leipzig: Teubner, 1892——.

1560. *Échos d'orient.* Paris: La Bonne Presse, 1897——. (Edited by the Augustinians of the Assumption in Constantinople; contains very useful section entitled "Chronique des Églises.")

1561. *Oriens Christianus.* Leipzig: Otto Harrassowitz, 1901——. (Founded by the German Priestly College Campo Santo in Rome.)

1562. *Orient und Occident.* Blätter für Theologie, Ethic und Soziologie. Leipzig: Hinrichs, 1929——. (Devoted largely

to Russian religious life.   N. Berdyaev is one of the co-
workers.)

1563. *Orientalia christiana*. Rome: Pontificio Istituto Orientale,
1920——.

1564. *Slavonic Review*. London: The School of Slavonic Studies in
the University of London, King's College, 1921——. (Much
valuable material dealing with Slavic religious history.)

ORTHODOX CHURCHES

SOURCES (SEE ITEMS 313, 315, 316, 318, 321, 325, 328, 329, 331,
332, SERIES I)

REFERENCE WORKS (SEE ITEMS 112, 115, 120, 123, 124, 125,
127, 129, 135, 136, 347, 349, 353, 355, 356, 589, 590, 591)

1565. **Langford-James, R. L.** *A Dictionary of the Eastern Orthodox
Church*. London: Faith Press, 1923. xiv+144 pages.

DOGMATIC DEVELOPMENT (SEE ITEMS 248, 249, 251,
447, 503, 505, 506, 508, 509)

1566. **Gavin, F.** *Some Aspects of Contemporary Greek Orthodox
Thought*. Milwaukee: Morehouse, 1923. xxxiv+430 pages.

1567. **Jugie, M.** *Theologia dogmatica christianorum orientalium*.
3 vols. (Incomplete.) Paris: Letouzey, 1926——.

CREEDS AND CONFESSIONS (SEE ITEMS 193, 195, 267, 269)

1568. **Kattenbusch, F.** *Lehrbuch der vergleichenden Konfessions-
kunde*. Freiburg: Mohr, 1892. Vol. I, *Die orthodoxe ana-
tolische Kirche*. (Good bibliography.)

1569. **Michalcescu, J.** *Die Bekenntnisse und die wichtigsten Glau-
benszeugnisse der griechisch-orientalischen Kirche*. Leipzig:
Hinrichs, 1904. iv+314 pages. (Greek only.)

ORGANIZATION, WORSHIP, AND RELIGIOUS LIFE (SEE
ITEMS 496, 499, 500, 502, 522, 787)

1570. **Arseniew, N.** *Mysticism and the Eastern Church*. Translated
from German. London: Student Christian Movement, 1926.
173 pages.

1571. **Brightman, F. E.** *Liturgies Eastern and Western*. Vol. I,
Eastern Liturgies. Oxford: Clarendon Press, 1896. civ+

603 pages. (This includes not only the Orthodox liturgies but also those of the separated communions.)

1572. **Cole, F. G.** *Mother of All Churches.* London: Skeffington, 1908. ix+234 pages. (An elementary introduction to the study of the worship and dogmas of the Eastern churches.)

1573. **Nilles, N.** *Kalendarium manuale utriusque ecclesiae, orientalis et occidentalis.* 2 vols. 2d ed. Innsbruck: Rauch, 1896–97.

1574. **Zankov, S.** *The Eastern Orthodox Church.* Translated from German. Milwaukee: Morehouse, 1929. 168 pages. (Although elementary in its treatment, this work is an excellent introduction to the study of the Eastern doctrinal and sacramental systems.)

Canon Law (See Items 126, 198, 202, 487)

1575. **Бердниковъ, И. С.** Краткій курсь церковнаго права православной церкви. 2d ed. Kazan: Imperial University, 1903. xx+342 pages.

1576. **Milasch, N.** *Das Kirchenrecht der morgenländischen Kirche.* Translated from Serbian. 2d ed. Mostar: Pacher & Kisić, 1905. xv+742 pages. (A comprehensive and authoritative treatment of the subject. Based upon original sources.)

Separated Churches

1577. **Assemanus, J. S.** *Bibliotheca orientalis Clementino-Vaticana, in qua manuscriptos codices Syriacos, Arabicos, Persicos, Turcicos, Hebraicos, Samaritanos, Armenicos, Aethiopicos, Graecos, Aegyptiacos, Ibericos, et Malabaricos....recensuit.* 3(4) vols. Rome: Sacred Congregation for the Propagation of Faith, 1719–28.

1578. **Chabot, J. B., and Others** (editors). *Corpus scriptorum christianorum orientalium.* Paris, Rome, and Leipzig: Imprimerie National, 1903——. (Ninety-one volumes published, comprising the original text and Latin translation of Ethiopic, Arabic, Coptic, and Syriac sources.)

1579. **Fortescue, A.** *The Lesser Eastern Churches.* London: Catholic Truth Society, 1913. xv+468 pages.

CHRISTIANITY IN THE EASTERN ROMAN EMPIRE

GENERAL WORKS ON THE POLITICAL AND
CULTURAL BACKGROUND

SOURCES

1580. **Niebuhr, B. G., and Others** (editors). *Corpus scriptorum historiae byzantinae.* 50 vols. Bonn: Weber, 1828–97.

TEXTBOOKS AND MONOGRAPHS (SEE ITEMS 90, 562
[VOL. IV], 564, 801, 822, 824)

1581. **Bréhier, L.** *L'art byzantin.* Paris: Laurens, 1924. 203 pages.

1582. **Byron, R.** *The Byzantine Achievement, A.D. 330–1453.* London: Routledge, 1929. xiii+346 pages. (Summarizes the Byzantine contribution to modern culture.)

1583. **Diehl, C.** *History of the Byzantine Empire.* Translated from French. Princeton: University Press, 1925. 199 pages.

1584. ———. *The Byzantine Portraits.* New York: Knopf, 1927. vii+342 pages. (Biographical sketches, the most important of which are those dealing with Theodora, Irene, and the Blessed Theodora.)

1585. ———. *Byzance, grandeur et décadence.* Paris: Flammarion, 1920. 342 pages.

1586. **Krumbacher, K.** *Geschichte der byzantinischen Literatur (527–1453).* 2d ed. Munich: Beck, 1897, xx+1193 pages. (The chief authority on the subject.)

1587. **Vasiliev, A. A.** *History of the Byzantine Empire.* Translated from Russian. 2 vols. Madison, Wisconsin: University of Wisconsin, 1928–29. (The author ranks among the chief Byzantinists.)

THE PROCESS OF ALIENATION FROM THE LATIN WEST ON THE PART OF THE EASTERN PATRIARCHATES (TO 1054). (SEE ITEMS 363, 366, 368, 445, 456, 458, 459, 462, 471, 474, 475, 476, 477, 478, 479, 480, 481, 483, 537, 538, 539, 545, 546, 547, 552, 553, 554, 558)

MONASTICISM (SEE ITEMS 527 f., 530 f., 533–35)

DEVELOPMENT OF THE ANTI-BYZANTINE NATIONAL CHURCHES

1588. **Pargoire, P. J.** *L'église byzantine de 527 à 847.* Paris: Le-coffre, 1905. xx+405 pages. (A very successful presentation

of the conflicts, theological and nationalistic, which led to
the separation of the Nestorians and the Monophysites.)

1589. **Wigram, W. A.** *The Separation of the Monophysites*. London:
Faith Press, 1923. xviii+210 pages. (An excellent study.)

The Struggle for Supremacy between the State and the Church

1590. **Bréhier, L.** *La querelle des images (viiie–ixe siècles)*. Paris:
Bloud, 1904. 64 pages.

1591. **Bury, J. B.** *History of the Eastern Roman Empire from the Fall of Irene to the Accession of Basil I (802–867)*. London:
Macmillan, 1912. xv+530 pages.

1592. **Diehl, C.** *Justinien et la civilisation byzantine au vi^e siècle*.
Paris: Leroux, 1901. xl+695 pages.

1593. **Gardner, A.** *Theodore of Studium, his Life and Times*. London: Arnold, 1905. xiii+284 pages.

1594. **Holmes, W. G.** *The Age of Justinian and Theodora*. 2 vols.
London: Bell, 1905–7.

1595. **Hutton, W. H.** *The Church of the Sixth Century*. New York:
Longmans, 1897. xx+314 pages.

1596. **Martin, E. J.** *A History of the Iconoclastic Controversy*. London: Society for Promoting Christian Knowledge, 1930. 296
pages.

1597. **Tougard, A.** "La persécution iconoclaste d'après la correspondence de saint Théodore Studite," *Revue des questions historiques* (Paris: Bureaux de la Revue), N.S., VI (1891), 80–118.

Expansion of the Ecumenical Patriarchate and the Great Schism

1598. **Bréhier, L.** *Le schisme oriental du xie siècle*. Paris: Leroux,
1899. xxix+312 pages. (Still important.)

1599. **Brückner, A.** *Die Wahrheit über die Slavenapostel*. Tübingen:
Mohr, 1913. iii+127 pages. (Brilliant but erratic.)

1600. **Dvorník, F.** *Les Slaves, Byzance et Rome au ixe siècle*. Paris:
Champion, 1926. v+360 pages. (Christianization of the
Moravians and the Balkan Slavs.)

1601. **Hergenröther, J.** *Photius, Patriarch von Constantinopel.* 3 vols. Regensburg: G. J. Manz, 1867–69. (Still the most authoritative treatment of the subject.)

1602. **Παπαδόπουλος, Χ.** Τὸ πρωτεῖον τοῦ ἐπισκόπου Ῥώμης. Ἱστορικὴ καὶ κριτικὴ μελέτη. Athens: Anaplasis, 1930. xvi+337 pages. (A scholarly presentation of the Eastern Orthodox version of the causes of the Great Schism; written by the present archbishop of Athens.)

1603. **Schlumberger, G. L.** *L'épopée byzantine à la fin du dixième siècle.* 3 vols. Paris: Hachette, 1896–1905. (From 969 to 1057; very important.)

1604. **Scott, S. H.** *The Eastern Churches and the Papacy.* London: Sheed & Ward, 1928. iv+404 pages. (Prior to the schism of the ninth century. Inaccurate, pro-papal.)

1605. **Jagić, V.** "Conversion of the Slavs," *CMH* (Item 562), Vol. IV, chap. vii(B), pp. 215–29.

1606. **Spinka, M.** "Conversion of Russia," *JR* (Item 150), VI (1926), 41–57. (A critical study, based on Golubinsky.)

1607. **Теодоровъ-Балановъ, А.** Кириль и Методи. Vol. I. Sofia: Governmental Press, 1920. 178 pages. (Source materials in Church-Slavonic.)

1608. **Zlatarski, V. N.** "The Making of the Bulgarian Nation," *Slavonic Review* (Item 1564), IV (1925), 362–83, and IV (1926), 629–44. (A critical treatment of the conversion of Boris and of Bulgaria.)

Struggle for Self-Preservation

Rise of the Mohammedan Power and the Crusades
(See Items 647, 648, 651)

1609. **Bevan, A. A.** "Mohamet and Islām," *CMH* (Item 562), Vol. II, chap. x. (Brief and conservative, but still the most satisfactory life of the Prophet.)

1610. **Bréhier, L.** *L'église et l'orient au moyen âge. Les Croisades.* 4th ed. Paris: Lecoffre, Gabalda, 1921. xiii+397 pages. (Includes a good bibliography.)

1611. **Chalandon, F.** *Les Comnènes, études sur l'empire byzantin au xie et au xiie siècles.* Paris: Picard, 1912. lxiii+709 pages.

1612. **Goldziher, I.** *Vorlesungen über den Islam.* 2d ed. Heidelberg: Winter, 1925. xii+406 pages. (Still the best treatment of the subject.)

1613. **Iorga, N.** *Brève histoire des Croisades en Terre Sainte.* Paris: Gamber, 1924. xix+194 pages.

1614. **Krey, A. C.** *The First Crusade.* Princeton: University Press, 1921. viii+299 pages. (Consists of translations from the sources.)

1615. **Norden, W.** *Das Papstum und Byzanz; die Trennung der beiden Mächte und das Problem ihrer Wiedervereinigung bis zum Untergange des byzantinischen Reichs.* Berlin: Behr, 1903. xix+764 pages.

1616. **Pears, E.** *The Fall of Constantinople: Being the Story of the Fourth Crusade.* New York: Harper, 1886. xvi+422 pages. (Good.)

1617. **Schlumberger, G. L.** *Byzance et Croisades.* Paris: Geuthner, 1927. 366 pages.

1618. **Stevenson, W. B.** *The Crusaders in the East.* Cambridge: University Press, 1907. xi+387 pages. (The writer conceives of the Crusades as part of the history of the Moslem East.)

ATTEMPTS AT REUNION WITH THE LATIN WEST TO THE FALL OF THE BYZANTINE EMPIRE (SEE ITEM 895)

1619. **Chapman, C.** *Michel Paléologue, restaurateur de l'empire byzantin (1261–1282).* Paris: Figuière, 1926. 204 pages. (Useful.)

1620. **Miller, W.** *The Latins in the Levant; A History of Frankish Greece (1204–1566).* London: Murray, 1908. vii+675 pages. (Enlarged translation of a Greek word of Lambros.)

1621. **Παπαμιχαὴλ, Γ.** Ὁ ἅγιος Γρηγόριος Παλαμᾶς, ἀρχιεπίσκοπος Θεσσαλονίκης. Alexandria, 1911. (A good treatment of the mystical movements of the fourteenth century.)

1622. **Pears, E.** *The Destruction of the Greek Empire.* New York: Longmans, 1903. xxiv+476 pages.

CHRISTIANITY AMONG RACIAL OR NATIONAL GROUPS INFLUENCED PREDOMINANTLY BY EASTERN ORTHODOXY

The extremely heterogeneous character of the history of Eastern Christianity makes it difficult to find logical divisions of the subject. The most satisfactory principle is that of classifying each racial or national group by the predominant form of Christianity prevalent among its members, i.e., either Eastern Orthodox, or Roman Catholic and Protestant. Under these main divisions, the various separate units are arranged geographically. Hence different autocephalous or autonomous Orthodox, Separated, and Uniate (Melchite and Maronite) communions are dealt with conjointly wherever common land makes them members of the same group.

GENERAL WORKS—RELIGIOUS, POLITICAL, AND CULTURAL

1623. **Beth, K.** *Die orientalische Christenheit der Mittelmeerländer.* Berlin: Schwetschke, 1902. xvi+427 pages. (A valuable contribution to the history, statistics, and constitutional development of the Greek, Armenian, and Coptic churches. Much of the material is out of date.)

1624. **Janin, R.** *Les églises orientales et les rites orientaux.* 2d ed. Paris: La Bonne Presse, 1925. xii+653 pages. (A good survey of the post-war status written from the point of view of a Roman Catholic missionary.)

1625. ———. *Les églises séparées d'orient.* Paris: Bloud, 1930. 198 pages.

1626. **Kohn, H.** *A History of Nationalism in the East.* Translated from German. New York: Harcourt, Brace, 1929. xi+476 pages. (Important for the political and cultural movements in Egypt, Turkey, and Arabia.)

1627. .**Kyriakos, A.** *Geschichte der orientalischen Kirchen von 1453–1898.* Translated from Greek. Leipzig: Deichert, 1902. x+280 pages. (A good treatment of the Greek but not of the Slavic churches.)

1628. **Máchal, J.** *Slovanské Literatury.* 3 vols. Praha: Matice Česká, 1922–29. (An excellent handbook of Slavic national literatures.)

PATRIARCHATES IN GENERAL: WORKS ON RELIGIOUS,
POLITICAL, OR CULTURAL HISTORY

1629. **Gelzer, H. K. G.** *Geistliches und weltliches aus dem türkisch-griechischen Orient.* Leipzig: Teubner, 1900. 253 pages.

1630. **Meyer, P.** *Die theologische Litteratur der griechischen Kirche im sechzehnten Jahrhundert.* Leipzig: Dietrichs, 1899. xii + 179 pages.

1631. **Le Quien, M.** *Oriens christianus in quatuor patriarchatus digestus.* 3 vols. Paris: Typographia Regia, 1740. (A standard work for the period treated.)

1632. **Sidarouss, S.** *Des patriarcats: les patriarcats dans l'empire Ottoman et spécialement en Égypte.* Paris: Rousseau, 1906, xvii + 534 pages. (Contains sections dealing with the Uniates.)

PATRIARCHATE OF CONSTANTINOPLE (AFTER 1453)

1633. **Cobham, C. D.** *The Patriarchs of Constantinople.* Cambridge: University Press, 1911. 106 pages. (A summary of M. T. Gedeon, Πατριαρχικοὶ Πίνακες. Constantinople, *ca.* 1887.)

1634. **Hoffmann, G.** "Griechische Patriarchen und römische Päpste, II¹, Patriarch K. Lukaris." *Orientalia christiana,* Vol. V, xv, 52. 114 pages.

1635. **Miklosich, F., and Müller, J.** *Acta et diplomata graeca medii aevi sacra et profana.* Vols. I–II, *Acta patriarchatus Constantinopolitani.* Vienna, 1860–62.

CHURCHES OF EGYPT: PATRIARCHATE OF ALEXANDRIA
AND THE COPTIC CHURCH

1636. **Butcher, E. L.** *The Story of the Church of Egypt.* 2 vols. London: Smith, Elder, 1897.

1637. **Butler, A. J.** *The Ancient Coptic Churches in Egypt.* 2 vols. Oxford: Clarendon Press, 1884.

1638. **Charles, R. H.** (translator). *The Chronicle of John, Bishop of Nikiu.* London and Oxford: Williams & Norgate, 1916. xii + 216 pages.

1639. **Graf, G.** *Ein Reformversuch innerhalb der koptischen Kirche im zwölften Jahrhundert.* Paderborn: Schöningh, 1923. xiv +208 pages.

1640. **Maspero, J.** *Histoire des patriarches d'Alexandrie (518–616).* Paris: Champion, 1923. xv+429 pages.

THE ETHIOPIAN CHURCH

1641. **Budge, E. A. W.** (translator). *The Book of the Saints of the Ethiopian Church.* 4 vols. Cambridge: University Press, 1928.

1642. ———. *A History of Ethiopia, Nubia, and Abyssinia.* 2 vols. London: Methuen, 1928. (A monumental work; based throughout on Ethiopian chronicles and other sources.)

1643. **Hyatt, H. M.** *The Church of Abyssinia.* London: Luzac, 1928. 302 pages. (An excellent account of certain ecclesiastical practices of the Ethiopian church.)

1644. **Rey, C. F.** *The Romance of the Portuguese in Abyssinia.* London: Witherby, 1929. 319 pages. (Based upon hitherto unused Portuguese sources, it deals with the attempt to convert Abyssinia to Roman Catholicism.)

1645. **Strothmann, R.** "Die koptischen Metropoliten der abessinischen Kirche," **Theologische Blätter** (Leipzig: Hinrichs), IX (1930), 225–33.

PATRIARCHATE OF JERUSALEM AND ANTIOCH

1646. **Bauer, K.** *Antiochia in der ältesten Kirchengeschichte.* Tübingen: Mohr, 1919. iv+47 pages.

1647. **Bertram, A., and Luke, H. C.** *The Orthodox Patriarchate of Jerusalem, Report of the Commission.* Oxford: University Press, 1921. vi+336 pages. (A commission appointed by the government of Palestine to inquire into the affairs of the patriarchate of Jerusalem, included in its report much information of historical character.)

1648. **Bertram, A., and Young, J. W. A.** *The Orthodox Patriarchate of Jerusalem, Report of the Commission.* Oxford: University Press, 1926. viii+379 pages. (Contains a great deal of valuable material for the present status of the church.)

1649. **Duckworth, H. T. F.** *The Church of the Holy Sepulchre.* London: Hodder & Stoughton, 1922. 299 pages.

1650. **Luke, H. C.** *Prophets, Priests and Patriarchs.* London: Faith Press, 1927. ix+129 pages.

1651. **Παπαδοπούλος, Χ.** Ἱστορία τῆς Ἐκκλησίας Ἱερουσαλύμων. Jerusalem and Alexandria, 1910. (Written by the present archbishop of Athens.)

1652. **Neal, J. M.** *A History of the Holy Eastern Church: the Patriarchate of Antioch.* London: Rivington, 1873. ix+229 pages.

THE CHURCH OF CYPRUS

1653. **Hackett, J.** *A History of the Orthodox Church of Cyprus.* London: Methuen, 1901. xviii+720 pages. (A comprehensive work, based partly upon original research but mainly upon secondary sources not easily accessible.)

THE GREEK CHURCH

1654. **Kephala, E.** *The Church of the Greek People, Past and Present.* London: Williams & Norgate, 1930. 128 pages. (This is a good elementary work dealing with the history, doctrines, and the sacramental practices of the Greek church. It is based upon Greek authorities.)

1655. **Miller, W.** *A History of the Greek People (1821–1921).* New York: Dutton, 1923. x+184 pages.

THE ARMENIAN CHURCH

1656. **Abrahamian, A.** *The Church and Faith of Armenia.* London: Faith Press, 1920. 75 pages. (Deals largely with the organization and the theological position of the Armenian church.)

1657. **Arpee, L.** *The Armenian Awakening.* Chicago: University of Chicago Press, 1909. xi+235 pages. (A valuable contribution to the history of the Armenian church, covering the years between 1820 and 1860, by an Armenian Protestant.)

1658. **Ormanian, M.** *Azkabadum.* 3 vols. Vols. I–II. Constantinople: Ter-Nersessian, 1913–14. Vol. III. Jerusalem: St. Hagopian's Publishing House, 1927. (A comprehensive work dealing with the history of the Armenian people as well as their church, written by the former Armenian patriarch of Constantinople, an outstanding scholar.)

1659. ———. *The Church of Armenia*. Translated from French. London: Mowbray, *ca.* 1912. xxxii+271 pages.

1660. **Weber, S.** (editor). *Ausgewählte Schriften der armenischen Kirchenväter*. 2 vols. (See Item 303.)

THE MELCHITE GROUP

1661. **Bacel, P.** "Une période troublée de l'histoire de l'église melkite," *Échos d'orient* (Item 1560), XIV (1911), 340 ff.

1662. *Die Christen des Ostens und ihre Beziehungen zu Rom in 18. Jahrhundert*. (See Item 54, Vol. IV, Part 1, Book III, chap. ii.)

1663. **Dib, P.** "Les conciles de l'église maronite de 1557 à 1644," *Revue des sciences religieuses*, IV (1924), 193–220, 421–39.

1664. **Fortescue, A.** *The Uniate Eastern Churches*. New York: Benziger, 1923. xxiii+244 pages. (This posthumous work supplies information on the Uniate churches of Italy, Sicily, Syria, and Egypt.)

1665. **Karalevsky, C.** *Histoire des patriarcats melkites (Alexandrie, Antioche, Jerusalem)*. 3 vols. Rome: Imprimerie du Sénat, 1909–11. (The third volume deals with the liturgy, hierarchy, organization, and statistics.)

THE NEAR-EAST GROUP

THE BALKANS (GENERAL POLITICAL AND CULTURAL BACKGROUND)

1666. **Murko, M.** *Geschichte der ältesten südslavischen Literaturen*. ("Die Literaturen des Ostens," Vol. V, 2 parts.) Leipzig: Amelang, 1908. 248 pages. (Good for MSS bibliography.)

1667. **Schevill, F.** *The Balkan Peninsula and the Near East*. New York: Harcourt, Brace, 1922. vii+558 pages.

1668. **Seton-Watson, R. W.** *The Rise of Nationality in the Balkans*. London: Constable, 1917. 308 pages.

1669. **Zeiller, J.** *Les origines chrétiennes dans les provinces danubiennes de l'Empire romain*. Paris: Boccard, 1918. iv+667 pages. (Noricum, Pannonia, and Moesia.)

THE BULGARIAN NATIONAL ORTHODOX CHURCH (SEE ITEM 862)

1670. **Avril, A. d'.** "La Bulgarie chrétienne," *Revue de l'orient chrétien* (Paris), 1897, Nos. 1–4.

1671. **Gelzer, H. K. G.** *Der Patriarchat von Achrida; Geschichte und Urkunden.* ("Abhandl. d. k. sächs. Ges. d. Wissensch., phil.-hist. Cl.," Vol. XXIV.) Leipzig: Teubner, 1902. 231 pages.

1672. **Hajek, A.** *Bulgarien unter der Türkenherrschaft.* Berlin und Leipzig: Stuttgart, 1925. 330 pages. (Especially chap. vii, "Der Kampf um die Unabhängigkeit der bulgarischen orthodoxen Kirche"; and chap. x, "Die Festsetzung des Kampfes um die kirchliche Unabhängigkeit.")

1673. **Mach, R.** *The Bulgarian Exarchate: Its History and the Extent of Its Authority in Turkey.* Translated from German. London: Fisher Unwin, 1907, 105 pages.

1674. **Runciman, S.** *A History of the First Bulgarian Empire.* London: Bell, 1920. xii+337 pages.

1675. **Sharenkoff, V. N.** *A Study of Manichaeism in Bulgaria with Special Reference to the Bogomils.* New York: Author, 1927. xxv+83 pages.

1676. **Slatarski, W. N.** (=Zlatarski, V. N.) *Geschichte der Bulgaren,* Vol. I. Leipzig: Iwan Parlapanoff, 1918. x+182 pages. (From 679 to 1396. The author is the outstanding Bulgarian historian of today.)

1677. **Staneff, N.** *Geschichte der Bulgaren.* Vol. II, *Vom Beginn der Türkenzeit bis zur Gegenwart.* Leipzig: Parlapanoff, 1917. viii+192 pages. (Continuation of Slatarski.)

1678. **Цухлевъ, Д.** История на Българската църква. Vol. I. Sofia: Sv. Sofia, 1910. 1,153 pages. (A detailed and authoritative treatment of the period·from 864 to 1186.)

1679. **Златарски, В. Н.** История на Българската Държава прѣзъ срѣднитѣ вѣкове. Vol. I, Part 2. Sofia: Governmental Press, 1927. xvi+893 pages (An authoritative treatment of the period from 852 to 1018.)

Yugoslav Churches

1680. **Avril, A. d'.** *La Serbie chrétienne; étude historique.* Paris: Leroux, 1897. 134 pages. (Reprint from *Revue de l'orient chrétien.*)

1681. **Evans, A. J.** *Through Bosnia and Herzegovina on Foot.* 2d ed. London: Longmans, 1877. 435 pages. (A fair account of the Bogomil movement; based on Rački.)

1682. **Hudal, A.** *Die serbisch-orthodoxe Nationalkirche.* Graz: Moser, 1922. vii+126 pages. (Written by a Roman Catholic priest; somewhat antagonistic to the Orthodox.)

1683. **Ilwof, L.** *Der Protestantismus in Steiermark, Kärnten und Krain vom xvi. Jahrhundert bis die Gegenwart.* Graz: Leykam, 1900. 300 pages.

1684. **Jireček, K.** *Geschichte der Serben.* 2 vols. Gotha: Perthes, 1911–18. (To 1537; no more published.)

1685. **Klaic, V.** *Geschichte Bosniens von den ältesten Zeiten bis zum Verfalle des Königreiches.* Leipzig: Friedrich, 1885. 464 pages. (From the Serbo-Croatian; the author was an outstanding authority on the Serbo-Croatian history.)

1686. **Lazarovic-Hrebelianović, S. L. E. and E. C.** *The Servian People, Their Past Glory and Their Destiny.* 2 vols. New York: Scribner's, 1910.

1687. **Loserth, J.** *Die Reformation und Gegenreformation in den innerösterreichischen Ländern im 16. Jahrhundert.* Stuttgart: Cotta, 1898. viii+614 pages.

1688. **Yanich, V., and Hankey, C. P.** *Lives of the Serbian Saints.* London: Society for Promoting Christian Knowledge, 1921. xx+108 pages. (A collection of medieval legends.)

1689. **Zeiller, J.** *Les origines chrétienne dans la province romaine de Dalmatie.* Paris: Champion, 1906. 188 pages.

ROUMANIAN CHURCHES

1690. **Institute für Grenz- und Auslanddeutschtum an der Universität Marburg.** *Die evang. Landeskirche a.b. in Siebenbürgen mit den angeschlossenen evang. Kirchenverbänden Altrumänien, Banat, Bessarabien, Bukowina, Ungarisches Dekanat.* Jena: Fischer, 1923. vi+140 pages.

1691. **Iorga, N.** *Istoria Bisericii Românești.* 2 vols. Bucureşti: Editura ministeriului de culte; Vol. I, ed. 2, 1928; Vol. II, ed. 1, 1909.

1692. ———. *A History of Roumania.* New York: Dodd, Mead, 1926. Translated from the second French edition. xii+284 pages.

1693. **Кургановъ, Ф.** Наъроски и очерки изъ новѣйшей исторіи Румынской Церкви. Published serially in Ученый записки

Казанскаго Университѣта, 1899–1904. (A valuable contribution to the history of the Roumanian church in the second half of the nineteenth century.)

1694. **Nistor, I.** *Istoria Bisericii din Bucovina.* Bucureşti: Carol Göbl, 1916. xi+298 pages.

1695. **Schullerus, A.** *Luthers Sprache in Siebenbürgen. Forschungen zur siebenbürgischen Geistes- und Sprachgeschichte im Zeitalter der Reformation.* 2(1) vols. Hermannstadt: Krafft, 1923–28.

1696. **Tichner, H. M.** *Roumania and Her Religious Minorities.* London: Philpot, 1925. 100 pages. (Considerably pro-Roumanian.)

THE ALBANIAN ORTHODOX CHURCH

1697. **Swire, J.** *Albania.* New York: R. R. Smith, 1930. xxiv+560 pages.

THE GEORGIAN ORTHODOX CHURCH

1698. **Kekelidse, K.** *Die Bekehrung Georgiens zum Christentum.* Leipzig: Hinrichs, 1928. (In *Morgenland*, Heft 18.) 51 pages. (An excellent monograph, reconstructing on the basis of original material the traditional account of the beginnings of Christianity in Georgia.)

1699. **Peradse, G.** "Die Anfänge des Mönchtums in Georgien," *ZK* (Item 161), XLVI (1927), 34–74.

THE EASTERN SYRIAN CHURCH (SEE ITEMS 542, 543, 629)

THE ASSYRIANS

1700. **Barthold, W.** *Zur Geschichte des Christentums in Mittel-Asien bis zur mongolischen Eroberung.* Nach dem Russischen. Tübingen: Mohr, 1901. 74 pages.

1701. **Mingana, A.** *The Early Spread of Christianity in Central Asia and the Far East: a New Document.* Manchester: University Press, 1925. 80 pages.

1702. **Stewart, J.** *Nestorian Missionary Enterprise; the Story of a Church on Fire.* Edinburgh: Clark, 1928. xxxiv+351 pages.

1703. **Wigram, W. A.** *The Assyrians and Their Neighbors.* London: Bell, 1929. xvi+242 pages.

1704. ———. *An Introduction to the History of the Assyrian Church, 100–640 A.D.* London: Society for Promoting Christian Knowledge, 1910. xviii+318 pages.

1705. **Yohannan, A.** *The Death of a Nation.* New York: Putnam's, 1916. xx+170 pages.

THE CHURCHES OF THE MALABAR COAST

1706. **Anantakrishna-Ayyar, L. K.** *Anthropology of the Syrian Christians.* Ernakulam: Cochin Government Press, 1926. xvii+338 pages. (The historical part is not critical; the sociological and anthropological is helpful.)

1707. **Farquhar, J. N.** *The Apostle Thomas in South India.* Manchester: University Press, 1927. 33 pages.

1708. **Germann, W.** *Die Kirche der Thomaschristen.* Gütersloh: Bertelsmann, 1877. 792 pages.

1709. **Mingana, A.** *The Early Spread of Christianity in India.* Manchester: University Press, 1926. 82 pages.

1710. **Panjikaran, J. C.** "Christianity in Malabar, with Special Reference to the St. Thomas Christians of the Syro-Malabar Rite," *Orientalia christiana*, Vol. VI², No. 23. 136 pages.

THE RUSSIAN CHURCH AND THE SECTS

The section includes the entire territory of the present Union of Socialist Soviet Republics.

POLITICAL AND CULTURAL BACKGROUND (SEE ITEM 1629)

1711. **Grushevsky, M.** *Geschichte des ukrainischen (ruthenischen) Volkes.* Vol. I. Leipzig: Teubner, 1906. 753 pages. (No more published.)

1712. **Kluchevsky, V. O.** *A History of Russia.* 4 vols. New York: Dutton, 1911–26. (A standard general history, written from the social point of view. The fourth volume ends with the reign of Tsar Peter III.)

1713. **Kornilov, A.** *Modern Russian History.* 2 vols. New York: Knopf, 1916. (From the death of Catherine the Great to 1916.)

1714. **Leger, L.** (translator and editor). *Chronique dite de Nestor.* (*Publications de l'École des langues orientales vivantes.* 2ᵉ ser., Vol. XIII.) Paris: Leroux, 1884. xxviii+399 pages.

1715. **Masaryk, T. G.** *The Spirit of Russia.* Translated from the German edition. 2 vols. London: Allen & Unwin, 1919. (The best work in English on the philosophical and literary movements of the nineteenth century.)

1716. **Pares, B.** *A History of Russia.* New York: Knopf, 1926. xxiii+558 pages. (A good general history, based on Russian sources.)

General Works on the Russian Church History

1717. **Frere, W. H.** *Some Links in the Chain of Russian Church History.* London: Faith Press, 1918. xvi+200 pages. (Fragmentary, but on the whole a satisfactory treatment.)

1718. **Голуъинскiй, Е. Е.** Исторiя Русской Церкви. 2(3) vols. Moscow: University Press, 1900–1904. (The most comprehensive and critical treatment of the period down to 1563. Reprints source materials.)

1719. **Howe, S. E.** *Some Russian Heroes, Saints, and Sinners.* London: Williams & Norgate, 1916. xvi+370 pages.

1720. **Palmieri, P. A.** *La chiesa russa.* Firenze: Fiorentina, 1908. v+759 pages.

1721. **Philaret, Metropolitan** (Gumilevsky, D. G.). *Geschichte der Kirche Russlands.* Translated from the Russian. 2 vols. Frankfurt a.M.: Baer, Sotheran & Co., 1872. (Although antiquated, it is still useful for discriminating students.)

1722. **Reyburn, H. Y.** *The Story of the Russian Church.* London: Andrew Melrose, 1924. vii+323 pages. (Based entirely upon non-Russian secondary sources. Nor reliable.)

1723. **Знаменскiй, П.** Руководство къ Русской Церковной Исторiи. 2d ed. Kazan: University Press, 1876. vi+482 pages.

Monographs on Particular Periods to the Revolution

1724. **Baumgarten, N.** "Chronologie ecclésiastique des terres Russes du xe au xiiie siècle," *Orientalia christiana* (Item 1563), Vol. XVII (1930) No. 58. 176 pages.

1725. **Goetz, L. K.** *Staat und Kirche in Altrussland; Kiever periode 988–1240.* Berlin: Duncker, 1908. 214 pages.

1726. **Знаменскiй, П.** Приходское духовенство въ Россiи со времени реформы Петра. Kazan: University Press, 1873. 850 pages.

The Post-Revolutionary Period

1727. "L'église orthodoxe panukrainienne créée en 1921," *Orientalia christiana* (Item 1563), I (1923), Nos. 3–4, 73–220.

1728. Гидулянов, П. В. Отделение Церкви от государства в С.С.С.Р. 3d ed. Moscow: Juridical Publishing Department of the National Commissariat of Justice, 1926. 712 pages. (A collection of Soviet laws concerning religion.)

1729. Hecker, J. F. *Religion under the Soviets*. New York: Vanguard, 1927. xvii+207 pages.

1730. Koch, H. "Die orthodox-autokephale Kirche der Ukraina," *Osteuropa*, September 1928, pp. 833–46.

1731. "La législation soviétique contre la religion," *Orientalia christiana* (Item 1563), Vol. V¹ (1925), No. 18. 135 pages.

1732. Schweigl, J. "Die Hierarchien der getrennten Orthodoxie in Sowjetrussland," *Orientalia christiana* (Item 1563), XIII (1928), No. 46, 1–76, and XV (1929), No. 54, 279–378.

1733. Spinka, M. *The Church and the Russian Revolution*. New York: Macmillan, 1927. xiii+330 pages. (Bibliography on the post-revolutionary period.)

The Slavophil Theologians and Their Successors; Worship

1734. Berdjajew (=Berdyaev), N. A. *Die Philosophie des freien Geistes, Problematik und Apologie des Christentums*. From the Russian. Tübingen: Mohr, 1930. 412 pages. (The author is probably the most distinguished Russian religious philosopher of today.)

1735. ———. *Die Weltanschauung Dostojewskijs*. From the Russian. Munich: Beck, 1925. viii+208 pages.

1736. Бердяевъ, Н. Ал. С. Хомяковъ. Moscow: 1912. viii+251 pages. (Khomyakov is regarded as "the father of the Russian theology.")

1737. Ehrenberg, H., und Bubnoff, N. *Oestliches Christentum; Dokumente*. 2 vols. Munich: Beck, 1923–25. 372+411 pages. (Translations of representative treatises of Russian Slavophil and religio-philosophical thinkers.)

1738. Hapgood, I. F. (translator). *Service Book of the Holy Orthodox Catholic Apostolic Church*. Rev. ed. New York: Association Press, 1922. xl+615 pages.

1739. **Herbigny, M. d'.** *Vladimir Soloviev, a Russian Newman (1853–1900).* Translated from French. London: Washbourne, 1918. 267 pages. (The author, a distinguished Jesuit, is pronouncedly biased.)

1740. **Soloviev·** (= Solov'ev), **V.** *War, Progress, and the End of History.* Translated from Russian. London: University of London Press, 1915. xxxiv+228 pages.

1741. ———. *The Justification of the Good.* Translated from Russian. London: Constable, 1918. lxiii+475 pages. (Solov'ev was the greatest of Russian religious philosophers.)

Russian Sectarians

1742. **Conybeare, F. C.** *Russian Dissenters.* Cambridge: Harvard University Press, 1921. x+370 pages. (A good monograph, based upon Russian secondary sources, although not an original investigation.)

1743. **Dalton, H.** *Beiträge zur Geschichte der evangelischen Kirche in Russland.* 4(3) vols. Gotha: Perthes, 1887–1903.

1744. **Grass, K. K.** *Die russischen Sekten,* 2 vols. Leipzig: Hinrichs, 1907–14. (A comprehensive treatment.)

1745. **Пругавинъ, А. С.** Религіозные отщепенцы. 2(1) vols. Moscow: Posrednik, 1906.

1746. **Séverac, J. B.** *La secte russe des hommes-de-dieu.* Paris: Cornely, 1906. 255 pages.

Relation to the Roman Catholic Church

1747. **Koncevičius, J. B.** *Russia's Attitude toward Union with Rome (Ninth to Sixteenth Centuries).* Washington: Catholic University of America, 1927. xxix+197 pages. (Well documented.)

1748. **Šmurlo, E.** *Le Saint Siège et l'orient orthodox Russe, 1609–1654.* Prague: Orbis, 1928. viii+256 pages. (Russian text with a French translation; an excellent monograph.)

CHRISTIANITY AMONG RACIAL AND NATIONAL GROUPS INFLUENCED PREDOMINANTLY BY ROMAN CATHOLICISM AND PROTESTANTISM

CZECHOSLOVAKIA

GENERAL AND CULTURAL HISTORY

1749. **Denis, E.** *Fin de l'indépendance bohême.* 2 vols. Paris: Colin, 1890. (Also in Czech, *Konec samostatnosti české* 2, vols. Praha: Šimáček, 1909.)

1750. ————. *La Bohême depuis la Montagne-Blanche.* 2 vols. Paris: Leroux, 1903. (Also in Czech: *Čechy po Bílé Hoře*, 2 vols. in 5, 2d ed. Praha: Šimáček, 1911.)

1751. **Heyberger, A.** *Jean Amos Comenius (Komenský).* Paris: Champion, 1928. ix+280 pages. (A good résumé of the present state of knowledge of Comeniana.)

1752. **Lützow, F. v.** *Bohemia, an Historical Sketch.* ("Everyman's Library.") London: Dent; and New York: Dutton, 1909. xvi+359 pages.

1753. **Novotný, V.** *České Dějiny.* (In process of publication.) Praha: Laichter, 1912————. Vol. I (in 2 parts); Vol. III (in 3 parts; written by R. Urbánek). (Largely supersedes Palacký; the most comprehensive and critical work on the subject.)

1754. **Palacký, F.** *Geschichte von Böhmen (bis 1526).* 5 vols. 3d ed. Prague: Kronberger & Řiwnač, 1844–67.

RELIGIOUS HISTORY (SEE ITEMS 1056, 1066, 1067)

1755. **Bartos, F. M.** *Literární činnost M. Jakoubka ze Stříbra.* Praha: Česká Akademie věd a umění, 1925. 72 pages.

1756. ————. *Do čtyř Pražských artykulů.* Praha: Greger, 1925. 111 pages.

1757. **Bidlo, J.** *Akty Jednoty Bratrské.* 2 vols. Brno: Matice Moravská, 1915–23. (Sources for the Unity of Brethren.)

1758. **Czerwenka, B.** *Geschichte der evangelischen Kirche in Böhmen.* 2(1) vols. Bielefeld und Leipzig: Velhagen & Klasing, 1869–70.

1759. **Flajšhans, W.** *Mag. Joannis Hus Opera omnia.* 3 vols. Prag: J. R. Vilímek, 1903——. (The publication has not been completed.)

1760. **Goll, J.** *Chelčický a Jednota v xv. století.* Praha: Historický Klub, 1916. xxx+325 pages.

1761. **Grigorić, V.** *Pravoslavná církev v republice československé.* Praha: Politika, 1928. 176 pages.

1762. **Kitts, E. J.** *Pope John xxiii and Master John Hus of Bohemia.* London: Constable, 1910. xxxi+446 pages.

1763. **Kýbal, V.** "Étude sur les origines du mouvement hussite en Bohême, Matthias de Janov," *RH* (Item 26), CIII (1910), 1–31.

1764. **Lützow, F. v.** *The Life and Times of Master John Hus.* London: Dent, 1909. xiv+398 pages.

1765. ——. *The Hussite Wars.* London: Dutton; 1914. 384 pages.

1766. **Müller, J. Th.** *Geschichte der böhmischen Brüder.* 2 vols. Herrnhut: Missionsbuchhandlung, 1922–31. (Incomplete. Based throughout upon documentary sources. The Czech edition of Vol. I, *Dějiny Jednoty Bratrské*, was augmented by notes of the translator, F. M. Bartoš. Prague: Jednota Bratrská, 1923.)

1767. **Müller, L.** *Der Kommunismus der mährischen Wiedertäufer* (see Item 978), Vol. XLV (1927), No. 142. 123 pages.

1768. **Novotný, V., and Kýbal, V.** *M. Jan Hus, život a učení.* 2 vols. in 5 parts. Praha: Laichter, 1919–30.

1769. **Novotný, V., and Urbánek, R.** *Sborník Blahoslavův (1523–1923).* Přerov: Obzov, 1923. 216 pages. (A collection of articles.)

1770. **Palacký, F.** (editor). *Documenta magistri Joannis Hus vitam, doctrinam, causam in Constantiensi concilio actam et controversias de religione in Bohemia annis 1403–18 motas illustrantia.* Prague: Tempsky, 1869. 768 pages.

1771. **Schweinitz, E. de.** *The History of the Church Known as The Unitas Fratrum.* Bethlehem, Pennsylvania: Moravian Publishing Office, 1885. 693 pages. (No longer adequate.)

1772. **Spinka, M.** "Religious Movements in Czechoslovakia," *JR* (Item 150), III (1923), 616–631.

1773. **Toman, H.** *Žizkův duch, povaha a listy.* 2d ed. Praha: Státní nakladatelství, 1924. 85 pages.

POLAND (SEE ITEMS 958, 960, 1074, 1075, 1130)

1774. **Dalton, H.** *Lasciana nebst den ältesten evang. Synodalprotokollen Polens, 1555–61.* (In "Beiträge zur Geschichte der ev. Kirche in Russland," Vol. III.) Berlin: Reuther & Reichard, 1898.

1775. **Dreszer, Z.** "L'expansion catholique et l'église orthodoxe en Pologne," *L'est européen* (Warsaw), VI (1926), 207–61.

1776. **Fox, P.** *The Reformation in Poland; Some Social and Economic Aspects.* Baltimore: Johns Hopkins Press, 1924. viii+153 pages.

1777. **Kirsch, J. P.** (Item 54.) Vol. IV, Part 1, Book I, chap x, "Die Kirche in Polen," and Book III, chap. iv, "Das Schisma in Polen."

1778. **Korzok, A.** *Die griechisch-katholische Kirche in Galizien.* Leipzig and Berlin: Teubner, 1921. xi+162 pages.

1779. **Kostka, E.** "La christianisation de la Pologne," *Congres d'histoire du christianisme* (Paris: Rieder), III (1928), 109–17.

1780. **Krasiński, V.** *Historical Sketch of the Rise and Progress and Decline of the Reformation in Poland.* 2 vols. London: Murray, 1838–40. (The Polish translation, *Zarys dziejów reformacji w Polsce* [Warsaw, 1903–5; 3 vols.], contains notes which bring the original text up to date. Strongly Protestant and anti-Socinian.)

1781. **Kurnatowski, G.** "L'archevêque Jean Łaski," *Le monde Slave* (Paris: Alcan), N.S., V (1928), 369–94.

1782. **Lescœur, L.** *L'église catholique en Pologne sous le gouvernement russe, depuis le premier partage jusqu'à nos jours (1772–1875).* 2 vols. 3d ed. Paris: Plon, 1876.

1783. **Likowski, E.** *Geschichte des allmaeligen Verfalls der unierten ruthenischen Kirche im xviii. und xix. Jahrh. unter polnischem und russischem Scepter.* 2(1) vols. Posen: Jolowicz, 1885–87.

1784. ————. *Die ruthenisch-römische Kirchenvereinigung, genannt Union zu Brest.* Freiburg: Herder, 1904. 365 pages. (A second edition published in Polish, *Unia Brzeska.* Warsaw: Gebethner & Wolff, 1907.)

1785. **Morawski, S.** *Arjanie Polscy.* Lwow: privately published, 1906. xxx+564 pages. (A good study of Arianism and Socinianism in Poland.)

1786. **Völker, K.** *Kirchengeschichte Polens.* Berlin: De Gruyter, 1930. xii+337 pages. (Good bibliographies; an excellent short history.)

1787. ————. *Der Protestantismus in Polen auf Grund der einheimischen Geschichtschreibung.* Leipzig: Hinrichs, 1910. viii+238 pages.

1788. **Wotschke, T.** *Geschichte der Reformation in Polen.* Leipzig: Verein für Reformationsgeschichte, 1911. xii+316 pages.

HUNGARY

1789. **Bod, P.** *Historia Hungariorum Ecclesiastica.* 3 vols. Leyden: Brill, 1888–90. (A well-documented work.)

1790. **Borbis, J.** *Die evangelisch-lutherische Kirche Ungarns in ihrer geschichtlichen Entwickelung.* Nördlingen, 1861. 522 pages.

1791. *History of the Protestant Church in Hungary, from the Beginning of the Reformation to 1850.* Boston: Sampson, 1854. xxix+559 pages.

1792. **Lencz, G.** *Der Aufstand Bocskays und der Wiener Friede.* Debreczen: Hegedüs & Sandor, 1917. 296 pages.

THE BALTIC STATES: LITHUANIA, LATVIA, ESTONIA, AND FINLAND (SEE ITEMS 626, 628)

1793. **Adamovics, L.** "Le rôle particulier de la communauté des frères moraves de Hernhute dans la vie religieuse, spirituelle et sociale du peuple letton," *Congres d'histoire du christianisme* (Paris: Rieder), III (1928), 169–79.

1794. **Eck, S.** *Die kirchliche Lage in den baltischen Provinzen Russlands.* Darmstadt: Waitz, 1891. 47 pages.

1795. **Lelewel, J.** *Histoire de la Lithuanie et de la Ruthenie jusqu'à leur union définitive avec la Pologne conclue à Lubin en 1569.* Paris and Leipzig: Franck, 1861.

1796. **Lukaszewicz, J.** *Geschichte der reformierten Kirchen in Lithauen.* 2(1) vols. Leipzig: Dyk, 1848–50.

1797. **Naperskij, J. G. L.** *Beiträge zur Geschichte der Kirchen und Prediger in Livland.* 4 vols. Riga and Mitau, 1843–52.

1798. **Pohrt, O.** *Zur Frömmigkeitsgeschichte Livlands zu Beginn der Reformationszeit.* Riga: Löffler, 1925. 37 pages.

1799. ————. *Reformationsgeschichte Livlands* (see Item 978), Vol. XLVI (1928), No. 145. viii+134 pages.

1800. **Wiegand, F.** *Siebenhundert Jahre baltischer Kirchengeschichte.* Gütersloh: Bertelsmann, 1921. 67 pages.

CHAPTER VIII

CHRISTIANITY IN THE AMERICAS

CANADA, NEWFOUNDLAND, AND BERMUDA

1801. **Audet, F. J.** *Canadian Historical Dates and Events, 1492–1915.* Ottawa: Beauregard, 1917. vii+239 pages. (Contains statistical data of ecclesiastical as well as secular history.)

1802. **Bill, I. E.** *Fifty Years with the Baptist Ministers and Churches of the Maritime Provinces of Canada.* St. John: Barnes, 1880. xii+778 pages.

1803. **Dorland, A. G.** *A History of the Society of Friends (Quakers) in Canada.* Toronto: Macmillan, 1927. xiii+343 pages.

1804. **Eastman, M.** *Church and State in Early Canada.* Edinburgh: Constable, 1915. ix+301 pages. Deals with the chief issues in which church and state were jointly interested, to the end of the French régime.)

1805. **Fitch, E. R.** *The Baptists of Canada—A History of Their Progress and Achievements.* Toronto: Standard Publishing Co., 1911. 304 pages. (Prepared as a handbook for the Baptist Young People's Union.)

1806. **Gosselin, A. H.** *L'église du Canada depuis Monseigneur de Laval jusqu'à la conquête.* 3 vols. Quebec: Laflamme, 1911–14. *L'église du Canada après la conquête.* 2 vols. Quebec: Laflamme, 1916–17. (These two works comprise a full account of the Roman Catholic church in Canada to 1789.)

1807. **Gregg, W.** *History of the Presbyterian Church in the Dominion of Canada, from the Earliest Times to 1834, with a Chronological Table of Events to the Present Time, and Map.* Toronto: Presbyterian Printing & Publishing Co., 1885. 646 pages. (Cites much source material.)

1808. **Hawkins, E.** *Historical Notices of the Missions of the Church of England in the North American Colonies Previous to the Independence of the United States.* London: Fellowes, 1845.

xix+447 pages. (Based on the Society for Propagation of the Gospel manuscript records.)

1809. **Howley, F. M.** *Ecclesiastical History of Newfoundland.* Boston: Doyle, 1888. 426 pages. (Roman Catholic church to 1850.)

1810. **Kenton, E.** (editor). *Jesuit Relations and Allied Documents . . . . Selected and Edited. . . . .* New York: Boni, 1925. liv+527 pages.

1811. **Kilpatrick, T. B.** *Our Common Faith, and a Brief History of the Church Union Movement in Canada by Kenneth H. Cousland.* Toronto: Ryerson, 1928. vii+216 pages. (For fuller information on the union movement and the United church the student may see the yearbooks of the United Church of Canada and the records of the General Council. R. J. Wilson, *Church Union in Canada after Three Years* [1929, 54 pages], and S. D. Chown, *Story of Church Union in Canada* [1930, xv+156 pages], may also be consulted. All of these are published by the United Church Publishing House, Toronto. See also Items 1815, 1818, 1819.)

1812. **Langtry, J.** *History of the Church in Eastern Canada and Newfoundland.* London: Society for Promoting Christian Knowledge, 1892. vi+256 pages.

1813. **Lindsey, C.** *Rome in Canada: the Ultramontane Struggle for Supremacy over the Civil Authority.* Toronto: Lovell Bros., 1877. 398 pages. (A well-informed controversial work against Roman Catholicism, with special reference to Quebec.)

1814. **Mackinnon, I. F.** *Settlement and Churches in Nova Scotia, 1749-1779.* Halifax: Allen, 1930. 111 pages.

1815. **McNeill, J. T.** *The Presbyterian Church in Canada, 1875-1925.* Toronto: United Church Publishing House, 1925. xi+276 pages.

1816. ———. "Religious and Moral Conditions among the Canadian Pioneers," *ASCH* (Item 348), VIII (1928), 65-122. (With Bibliography.)

1817. **Morice, A. G.** *History of the Catholic Church in Western Canada from Lake Superior to the Pacific, 1655-1895.* 2 vols. Toronto: Musson, 1910. Also a French edition. (An ample historical work by a member of the Order of Mary Immaculate which has been prominent in Western Roman Catholic missions.)

1818. **Morrow, E. L.** *Church Union in Canada, Its History, Motives, Doctrine and Government.* Toronto: Allen, 1923. 450 pages. (By an opponent of union.)

1819. **Oliver, E. H.** *The Winning of the Frontier.* Toronto: The United Church Publishing House, 1929. xii+271 pages. (A general sketch stressing the frontier as the determining factor in Canadian church history.)

1820. **Parkman, F.** *The Jesuits in North America in the Seventeenth Century.* Boston: Little, 1902; reprinted 1925. xvii+586 pages. (First published in 1867. Many editions and reprints.)

1821. **Prowse, D. W.** *A History of Newfoundland.* 2d ed. London: Eyre, 1896. x+634 pages.

1822. **Robertson, J.** *History of the Mission of the Secession Church to Nova Scotia and Prince Edward Island from 1765.* London: Johnstone, 1847. 292 pages. (Brings the narrative approximately to date of publication.)

1823. **Sanderson, J. E.** *The First Century of Methodism in Canada.* Vol. I (1775–1839); Toronto: Briggs, 1908.

1824. **Shortt, A., and Doughty, A. G.** *Canada and Its Provinces. A History of the Canadian People and Their Institutions by One Hundred Associates.* 23 vols. Toronto: Glasgow, Brook & Co. (Volume XI [1914] of this valuable work contains articles by various writers on the missions and expansion of the churches. See also the Bibliography for this subject given in XXIII [1917], 264–70.)

1825. **Smith, T. W.** *History of the Methodist Church . . . . in the Late Conference of Eastern British America.* 2 vols. Vol. I, Halifax: Methodist Book Room, 1877. Vol. II, Halifax: Huestis, n.d. (Maritime Provinces, Newfoundland, Bermuda.)

1826. **Sutherland, A.** *Methodism in Canada, Its Work and Its Story.* London: Kelley, 1903. iii+350 pages.

1827. **Têtu, H.** *Les évêques de Quebec.* Quebec: Hardy, 1889. 692 pages. (Biographical and historical account of the bishops of Quebec to the time of writing.)

1828. **Thwaites, R. G.** (editor.) *Jesuit Relations and Allied Documents, 1610–1791*. 73 vols. Cleveland: Clark, 1896–1901. (The last two volumes are indexes.)

1829. **Vernon, C. W.** *The Old Church in the New Dominion*. London: Society for Promoting Christian Knowledge, 1929. viii+215 pages. (A brief sketch of the entire history of the Anglican church in Canada.)

1830. **Wittke, C.** *A History of Canada*. New York: Knopf, 1928. xiv+397 pages. (Useful for political and economic development. Bibliographies by chapters.)

1831. **Wood, J.** *Memoir of Henry Wilkes, His Life and Times*. Montreal, 1887. London: Hodder & Stoughton, 1888. 280 pages. (Valuable for Congregationalism.)

UNITED STATES

American church history as a special field of interest is relatively new, and for that reason little has been done to furnish adequate guides for its study. There have been few students of the entire field of American religious history, and therefore the writing of American church history has been very largely the work of the denominational historian. Too often these denominational histories have been written in such a manner as to take little account of the general economic, social, and political forces, to say nothing of the other religious bodies existing alongside of their own church. For this reason it is thought advisable to list a number of general American histories and bibliographies so that the student may always have at hand such materials as will aid him in relating his study of religion to the other forces at work at any given time. The organization of the bibliography is not denominational, but topical; and it is hoped that the student who follows this outline may be able to visualize the sum total of the religious forces at work in the several periods of American history.

BIBLIOGRAPHICAL AND GENERAL
AMERICAN HISTORY—GENERAL WORKS AND BIBLIOGRAPHY

1832. **Beard, C. A., and Mary R.** *Rise of American Civilization*. 2 (1) vols. New York: Macmillan, 1926. (Brilliant interpretation of American development.)

1833. **Channing, E.** *A History of the United States.* 7 vols. New York: Macmillan, 1905–31. (Most recent and best comprehensive account of the entire history of the United States.)

1834. **Channing, E.; Hart, A. B.; and Turner, E. R.** *Guide to the Study and Reading of American History.* Boston: Ginn, 1912. 650 pages. (The most satisfactory bibliography of American history.)

1835. *Dictionary of American Biography.* New York: Scribner's, 1928——. (To be complete in twelve volumes.)

1836. **Hart, A. B.** (editor). *American History Told by Contemporaries.* 5 vols. New York: Macmillan, 1897–1929. (A comprehensive collection of sources with considerable material bearing on religion.)

1837. **Johnson, A.** (editor). *Chronicles of American Series.* 50 vols. New Haven: Yale University Press, 1918–19. (Volumes by separate authors, told in "story-telling" manner, with brief bibliographies in each volume.)

BRIEF MANUALS—CHURCH HISTORY

1838. **Hargraves, J. R., and Others.** *Community Religion and the Denominational Heritage.* New York: Harper, 1930. viii+ 150 pages. (A brief interpretation of the principles of the chief Protestant denominations.)

1839. **Phelan, M.** *The New Handbook of All Denominations,* 6th ed. Nashville: Cokesbury Press, 1930. 314 pages. (Largely statistical.)

1840. **Rowe, H. K.** *The History of Religion in the United States.* New York: Macmillan, 1928; first published in 1924 and reprinted without revision. 213 pages. (Largely interpretative, and useful after a fair factual knowledge has been secured.)

1841. **Sweet, W. W.** *Our American Churches.* New York: The Methodist Book Concern, 1924. 135 pages. (A brief historical account of the principal denominations; intended for young people.)

LARGER WORKS—GENERAL AND BIBLIOGRAPHICAL

1842. **Allison, W. H.** *Inventory of Unpublished Material for American Religious History in Protestant Archives and Other Re-*

positories. Washington: Carnegie Institution, 1910. 254 pages.

1843. "American Church History Series" consisting of a series of denominational histories published under the auspices of the American Society of Church History. 13 vols. by separate authors. New York: Christian Literature Co., 1893–95.

1844. **Bacon, L. W.** *A History of American Christianity*. New York: Scribner's, 1927. 429 pages. (Volume XIII of the "American Church History Series," first printed in 1897 and here reprinted without revision.)

1845. **Dorchester, D.** *Christianity in the United States*. New York: The Methodist Book Concern, 1890. 799 pages. (A storehouse of useful facts, but long out of date.)

1846. **Fry, C. L.** *The United States Looks at Its Churches*. New York: Institute of Social and Religious Research, 1930. xiv+183 pages. (A study of the facts revealed by the 1926 federal census of religious bodies.)

1847. **Jackson, S. M.** *Bibliography of American Church History, 1820–1893*. ("American Church History Series," XII, 441–513.) (See Item 1843.) (The first attempt to compile a bibliography for religious history in the United States.)

1848. **Mode, P. G.** *Source Book and Bibliographical Guide for American Church History*. Menasha, Wisconsin: Banta Publishing Co., 1921. xxiv+735 pages. (The most complete bibliography yet compiled.)

1849. *Religious Bodies, 1926*. 2 vols. Washington: Government Printing Office, 1930. (Official returns of the last federal census of religious bodies in the United States.)

1850. **Sweet, W. W.** *The Story of Religions in America*. New York: Harper, 1930. 571 pages. (The most recent survey and interpretation of the entire field of American church history. (Contains also a selected bibliography)

1851. **Weigle, L. A.** *American Idealism*. ("The Pageant of America Series," Vol. X.) New Haven: Yale University Press, 1928. 356 pages. (A successful attempt at picturing the religious and educational development of the United States.)

PERIODICALS AND HISTORICAL SOCIETY PUBLICATIONS

1852. *Anglican Theological Review.* Evanston, Illinois, 1919——.
(A Protestant Episcopal publication.)

1853. *Crozer Quarterly.* Philadelphia: Judson Press, 1924——.
(A Baptist review.)

1854. *Lutheran Church Quarterly.* Continuing the *Lutheran Quarterly* and the *Lutheran Church Review.* Gettysburg and Philadelphia, 1928——.

1855. *Mennonite Quarterly Review.* Goshen, Indiana: Goshen College, 1927. (Contains materials on American Mennonites and their European background.)

1856. *Methodist Review.* New York: The Methodist Book Concern, 1818–1930. (The organ of the Methodist Episcopal church.)

1857. *Methodist Quarterly Review.* Nashville, Tennessee: Cokesbury Press, 1845–1930. (The organ of the Methodist Episcopal church, South.)

1858. *Mid-America: An Historical Review.* Chicago: Illinois Catholic Historical Society, 1918——. (Devoted to Catholic history in the Mississippi Valley.)

1859. *Mississippi Valley Historical Review:* Lincoln, Nebraska: Historical Association, prints occasional articles on American church history.)

1860. *Journal of Negro History.* Washington: The Association for the Study of Negro Life and History, 1916——. (Has occasional articles on negro religion and their churches.)

1861. *New England Quarterly: An Historical Review of New England Life and Letters.* Portland, Maine: Southworth Press, 1928.

1862. *Journal of the Department of History,* continuing the *Journal of the Presbyterian Historical Society.* Philadelphia: Presbyterian Historical Society, 1917——.

1863. Numerous historical societies throughout the United States publish historical magazines or transactions or both. The most important of these societies, with their publications, are: American Antiquarian Society, *Transactions* and *Collections,* Boston, 1813——; American Society of Church History, *Papers*, Series I, Vols. I–VIII, and Series II, Vols. I–VIII; American Catholic Historical Association, *Historical Records and Studies*, New York, 1885——; Illinois State Historical Society, *Collections*, and also *Journal of the Illinois State Historical Society*, Springfield, 1908——; Indiana Historical Society, *Collections*, and also *Indiana Magazine of History*, Indianapolis, 1905——; State Historical Society of Iowa, *Annals* and *Historical Quarterly*, Iowa City, 1869——; Massachusetts Historical Society, *Proceedings*, Boston, 1791——; Pioneer and Historical Society of Michigan, *Collections*, Detroit, 1874——; Ohio State Archaeological and Historical Society, *Publications*, Columbus, 1887——; Historical Society of Pennsylvania, *Memoirs*, 1826–95, and *Collections*, 1853——; Virginia Historical Society, *Collections*, also *Virginia Magazine of History and Biography*, Richmond, 1894——; State Historical Society of Wisconsin, *Collections*, 1855——; and also the *Wisconsin Magazine of History*, Madison, 1918——.

EUROPEAN BACKGROUND

American Christianity sprang from a European background, and a comprehensive understanding of this background is therefore a necessity. The books listed below are intended to give an adequate basis for an understanding of the Old-World beginnings of religion in America.

1864. **Baird, C. W.** *The Huguenot Emigration to America.* 2 vols. New York: Dodd Mead, 1885.

1865. **Bolton, H. E., and Marshall, T. M.** *Colonization of North America, 1492–1783.* New York: Macmillan, 1920. xvi+609 pages. (Excellent for international background of colonization.)

1866. **Braithwaite, W. C.** *The Beginnings of Quakerism.* London: Macmillan, 1912. xliv+562 pages.

1867. **Cheyney, E. P.** *European Background of American History. 1300–1600.* ("The American Nation Series," Vol. I.) New York: Harper, 1904. xxviii+343 pages. (An excellent book for beginners.)

1868. **Cross, A. L.** *History of England and Greater Britain.* New York: Macmillan, 1914. xiii+1,165 pages. (Chapters xxvi and xxxv are devoted to a description of Elizabethan England.)

1869. **Eggleston, E.** *Beginnings of a Nation.* New York: Appleton, 1896. 377 pages. (Particularly good for the new sects arising in England.)

1870. **Faust, A. B.** *The German Element in the United States.* 2 (1) vols. New York: The Steuben Society of America, 1927.

1871. **Hall, T. C.** *The Religious Background of American Culture.* Boston: Little, Brown, 1930. xiv+348 pages. (Part I deals with the English background and advances a new viewpoint.)

1872. **Hanna, C. A.** *The Scotch Irish or the Scot in North Britain, North Ireland, and North America.* 2 vols. New York: Putnam's, 1902.

1873. **Thompson, C. L.** *The Religious Foundations of America.* New York: Revell, 1917. 307 pages. See also Items 899, 958, 959.

The Colonial Period
General Works

1874. **Adams, J. T.** *Provincial Society, 1690–1763.* ("A History of American Life," Vol. III.) New York: Macmillan, 1927. 374 pages.

1875. **Andrews, C. M.** *Colonial Folkways.* ("Chronicles of America Series," Vol. IX.) New Haven: Yale University Press, 1918. 255 pages.

1876. **Channing, E.** *A History of the United States.* (Item 1833.) (The first three volumes of this work cover the Colonial period and are considered a leading authority.)

1877. **Doyle, J. A.** *English Colonies in America.* 5 vols. Vol. I, *Virginia, Maryland and the Carolinas;* Vols. II and III, *The Puritan Colonies;* Vol. IV, *The Middle Colonies;* Vol. V, *The Colonies under the House of Hanover.* New York: Henry Holt, 1882–1907.

1878. **Greene, E. B.** *The Foundations of American Nationality.* New York: American Book Co., 1922. x+614+xl pages. (The best single volume on the Colonial period.)

1879. **Jameson, J. F., and Others** (editors). *Original Narratives of Early American History.* 18 vols. New York: Scribner's, 1906–17.

1880. **Jernegan, M. W.** *The American Colonies, 1492–1750.* ("Epochs of American History," Vol. I.) New York: Longmans, Green, 1929. xxxiii+457 pages. (Especially valuable for bibliography on social and religious conditions.)

1881. **Osgood, H. L.** *American Colonies in the Seventeenth Century.* 3 vols. New York: Macmillan, 1904–7.

1882. ———. *American Colonies in the Eighteenth Century.* 4 vols. New York: Columbia University Press, 1924–25. (These volumes deal chiefly with the political and administrative aspects of Colonial history, but some attention is given to economic, social, and religious matters.)

1883. **Parrington, V. L.** *The Colonial Mind, 1620–1800.* ("Main Currents in American Thought," Vol. I. 3 vols. New York: Harcourt, Brace, 1927. xvii+413 pages. (A brilliant interpretation of the outstanding Colonial leaders.)

1884. **Tyler, M. C.** *History of American Literature during the Colonial Period.* 2 vols. New York: Putnam's, 1897. (Valuable for early religious literature.)

1885. **Wertenbaker, T. J.** *The First Americans, 1609–1690.* ("History of American Life," Vol. II.) New York: Macmillan, 1927. 358 pages. (Useful for the early Colonial churches.)

NEW ENGLAND

GENERAL ACCOUNTS

1886. **Adams, J. T.** *Founding of New England.* Boston: Atlantic Monthly Press, 1921. 482 pages. (The most recent general account in the light of modern research.)

1887. **Andrews, C. M.** *Fathers of New England.* (Item 1837.)

1888. **Fiske, J.** *Beginnings of New England.* Boston: Houghton Mifflin, 1889. 296 pages.

1889. **Morison, S. E.** *The Founding of the Bay Colony.* Boston: Houghton Mifflin, 1930. xiv+365 pages.

1890. **Weeden, W. B.** *Economic and Social History of New England.* 2 vols. Boston: Houghton Mifflin, 1890. 964 pages.

THE PURITANS AND CONGREGATIONALISM

1891. **Adams, B.** *The Emancipation of Massachusetts.* 2d ed. Boston: Houghton Mifflin, 1903. vi+382 pages.

1892. **Adams, C. F.** *Three Episodes of Massachusetts History— The Settlement of Boston Bay, The Antinomian Controversy, A Study of Church and Town Government.* 2 vols. Boston: Houghton Mifflin, 1892. 1,067 pages.

1893. **Bradford, W.** *History of Plymouth Plantations.* (In Jameson's series of "Original Narratives of Early American History," edited by W. T. Davis.) New York: Scribner's, 1908. 473 pages.

1894. **Byington, E. H.** *The Puritan in England and New England.* Boston: Houghton Mifflin, 1896. 406 pages.

1895. **Dexter, H. M.** *The Congregationalism of the Last Three Hundred Years as Seen in Its Literature* (with a bibliographical Appendix). New York: Harper, 1880. 326 pages.

1896. **Elson, L. C.** *The History of American Music.* New York: Macmillan, 1915. 387 pages. (Chapter i, "The Religious Beginnings of American Music.")

1897. **Felt, J. B.** *Ecclesiastical History of New England.* 2 vols. Boston: Congregational Library Association, 1855–62.

1898. **Mather, C.** *Magnalia Christi Americana: or the Ecclesiastical History of New England.* 2 vols. Hartford: S. Andrus, 1820.

1899. **Oliver, P.** *The Puritan Commonwealth. An Historical Review of Puritan Government in Massachusetts in Its Civil and Ecclesiastical Relations from Its Rise to the Abrogation of the First Charter.* Boston: Little, Brown, 1865. xii+502 pages.

1900. **Pratt, W. S.** *The Music of the Pilgrims.* Boston: Oliver Ditson, 1921. 80 pages.

1901. **Schneider, H. W.** *The Puritan Mind.* New York: Henry Holt, 1930. 301 pages. (An excellent interpretation.)

1902. **Sewell, S.** *Diary.* (Mark Van Doren, editor.) Abridged ed. New York: Macy Masius, 1927. 272 pages. (Complete *Diary* published in "Massachusetts Historical Society Collections," Series 5, Vols. V–VIII [1878–1882.])

1903. **Walker, W.** *History of the Congregational Churches in the United States.* ("American Church History Series," Vol. III.) New York: Christian Literature Co., 1894. xiii+451 pages. (The best single volume on the subject.)

OTHER CHURCHES OF COLONIAL NEW ENGLAND

1904. **Backus, I.** *A History of New England with Particular Reference to the Denomination of Christians Called Baptists.* 2 vols. Boston: Edward Draper, 1777–96. 2d edition with notes by David Weston, Newton, Mass.: Backus Hist. Society, 1871.

1905. **Beardsley, E. E.** *History of the Episcopal Church in Connecticut, from 1635 to 1865.* 2 vols. 4th ed. New York: Houghton Mifflin, 1883.

1906. **Blaikie, A.** *A History of Presbyterianism in New England.* Boston: A. Moore, 1881. 2 (1) vols., continuous paging. 512 pages.

1907. **Greenwood, F. W. P.** *A History of King's Chapel in Boston, the First Episcopal Church in New England. Comprising Notices of the Introduction of Episcopacy into the Northern Colonies.* Boston: Tichnor, 1833. 215 pages.

WITCHCRAFT DELUSION IN NEW ENGLAND

1908. **Calef, R.** *More Wonders of the Invisible World,* or *The Wonders of the Invisible World,* displayed in five parts. London: Printed for M. Hillar and J. Collyer, 1700. 156 pages. Reprinted in Drake: *Witchcraft Delusion in New England.*

1909. **Drake, S. G.** *Witchcraft Delusion in New England: Its Rise, Progress, and Termination, etc.* 3 vols. Roxbury, Massachusetts: H. E. Woodward, 1866.

1910. **Mather, C.** *Wonders of the Invisible World.* Boston: 1684. Reprinted in Drake, *Witchcraft Delusion in New England.*

1911. **Nevins, W. S.** *Witchcraft in Salem Village in 1692, Together with Some Account of Other Witchcraft Prosecutions in New England and Elsewhere.* Boston: Lee & Shepard, 1892. 273 pages.

1912. **Notestein, W.** *History of Witchcraft in England from 1558 to 1718.* Washington: The American Historical Association, 1911. xiv+442 pages.

1913. **Taylor, J. M.** *Witchcraft Delusion in Colonial Connecticut, 1647–1697.* New York: The Grafton Press, 1908. xv+172 pages.

NEW ENGLAND COLONIAL BIOGRAPHY

1914. **Allen, A. V. G.** *Jonathan Edwards.* Boston: Houghton Mifflin, 1890. (v)+xi+401 pages. (The best life of Edwards.)

1915. **Augur, Helen.** *An American Jezebel: The Life of Anne Hutchinson.* New York: Brentano's, 1930. 320 pages.

1916. **Easton, Emily.** *Roger Williams, Prophet and Pioneer.* Boston: Houghton Mifflin, 1930. 399 pages.

1917. **Murdock, K. B.** *Increase Mather, the Foremost American Puritan.* Cambridge: Harvard University Press, 1925. xv+442 pages. (A thorough treatment, somewhat apologetic.)

1918. **Straus, O. S.** *Roger Williams: the Pioneer of Religious Liberty.* New York: Century Co., 1894. 257 pages.

1919. **Walker,** *Ten New England Leaders.* New York: Silver Burdett, 1901. 471 pages. (Has chapters on William Bradford, John Cotton, John Eliot, Increase Mather, Jonathan Edwards, Charles Chauncy, and Samuel Hopkins.)

THE MIDDLE COLONIES

GENERAL

1920. **Fiske, J.** *The Dutch and Quaker Colonies in America.* 2 vols. Boston: Houghton Mifflin, 1899.

THE DUTCH REFORMED

1921. **Corwin, E. T.** *A History of the Reformed Dutch Church.* ("American Church History Series," Vol. VIII.) New York: The Christian Literature Co.; 1895. xvi+212 pages.

1922. **Putnam, Ruth.** *The Dutch Element in the United States.* American Historical Association reports. Washington: Government Printing Office, 1909. 205+218 pages.

1923. **Zwierlein, F. J.** *Religion in New Netherland.* Rochester: J. P. Smith Printing Co., 1910. vii+365 pages. (A history of the development of the religious conditions in the Province of New Netherland, 1623–1664.)

THE GERMAN REFORMED

1924. **Dubbs, J. H.** *A History of the Reformed Church, German in the United States* (Item 1843), Vol. VIII, 213–423 pages.)

1925. **Harbaugh, H., and Heisler, D. Y.** *The Fathers of the German Reformed Church in Europe and America.* 2 vols. Lancaster and Reading, Pennsylvania: Sprenger & Westhaeffer, 1857.

THE MORAVIANS

1926. **De Schweinitz, E.** *The History of the Church of the Unitas Fratrum.* Bethlehem, Pennsylvania: Moravian Publishing Office, 1885. 693 pages.

1927. **Hamilton, J. T.** *A History of the Church Known as the Moravian Church of the Unitas Fratrum.* Bethlehem, Pennsylvania: Tinner Publishing Co., 1900. 631 pages.

THE DUNKERS OR THE GERMAN BAPTIST BRETHREN

1928. **Brumbaugh, Marion, G.** *A History of the German Baptist Brethren in Europe and America.* 1st ed. Mount Morris, Illinois: Brethren Publishing House, 1899. 559 pages. 2d ed., Elgin, Illinois, 1910.

1929. **Sachse, J. F.** *The German Pietists of Provincial Pennsylvania 1694–1708.* Philadelphia: printed for the author, 1895. xiii+504 pages.

1930. ———. *The German Sectarians of Pennsylvania, 1708–1742.* 2 vols. Philadelphia: printed for the author, 1899. Vol. I, xxi+506 pages. Vol. II, 1742–1800, xvi+535 pages.

1931. **Winger, O.** *History and Doctrines of the Church of the Brethren.* 2d ed. Elgin, Illinois: Brethren Publishing House, 1920, 320 pages.

THE MENNONITES (SEE ITEMS 1058–61, 1064–68)

1932. **Smith, C. H.** *The Mennonites.* (See Item 1071.)

1933. ———. *Mennonite Immigration to Pennsylvania in the Eighteenth Century.* Norristown, Pennsylvania: Pennsylvania German Society, 1929. 412 pages.

LUTHERANS

1934. **Bente, F.** *American Lutheranism.* 2 vols. St. Louis: Concordia Publishing House, 1919. (Volume I covers the Colonial period.)

1935. **Hazelius, E. L.** *History of the American Lutheran Church, from its Commencement in 1685 to the year 1842.* Zanesville, Ohio, 1846. 300 pages. (Contains several useful appendixes.)

1936. **Jacobs, H. E.** *A History of the Evangelical Lutheran Church in the United States.* (Item 1843, Vol. IV.) (Parts I, II, and III deal with the Colonial period.)

1937. **Neve, J. L.** *A Brief History of the Lutheran Church in America.* Burlington, Iowa: German Lutheran Board, 1916. 205 pages.

1938. **Wentz, A. R.** *The Lutheran Church in American History.* Philadelphia: The United Lutheran Publication House, 1923. 355 pages. (Parts I and II cover the Colonial period.)

THE PRESBYTERIANS

1939. **Alexander, A.** *Biographical Sketches of the Founder and the Principal Alumni of the Log College, Together with an Account of the Revivals of Religion under Their Ministry.* Princeton: printed by J. T. Robinson, 1851. 369 pages.

1940. **Briggs, C. A.** *American Presbyterianism: Its Origin and Early History. Together with an Appendix of Letters and Documents, Many of Which Have Recently Been Discovered.* With maps. New York: Scribner's, 1885. xiii+373+cxlii pages.

1941. **Gillett, E. H.** *History of the Presbyterian Church in the United States of America.* 2 vols. Philadelphia: Presbyterian Board of Publication. 1st ed., 1864; rev. ed., 1873. (Volume I covers the Colonial period.)

1942. **Hodge, C.** *The Constitutional History of the Presbyterian Church in the United States of America.* Part I, 1705–41, viii+256 pages. Part II, 1741–88, viii+516 pages. Philadelphia: William S. Martien, 1839–40.

1943. **Nevin, A.** *Churches of the Valley: or An Historical Sketch of the Old Presbyterian Congregations of Cumberland and Franklin Counties in Pennsylvania.* Philadelphia: Joseph M. Wilson, 1852. xix+338 pages.

1944. *Records of the Presbyterian Church in the United States of America Embracing the Minutes of the General Presbytery and General Synod, 1706–1788, Together with an Index and*

*the Minutes of the General Convention for Religious Liberty,
1766–1775.* Philadelphia: Presbyterian Board of Publication, 1904. 582+48 pages.

1945. **Thompson, C. L.** *A History of the Presbyterian Churches in
the United States.* (Item 1843, xxxi+424 pages. (Contains
Bibliography; the first six chapters treat briefly of Colonial
period.)

1946. **Webster, R.** *A History of the Presbyterian Church in
America, from Its Origin until the Year 1760. With Biographical Sketches of Its Early Ministers. With a Memoir of Its
Author by the Rev. C. Van Rensselaer, D.D., and an Historical
Introduction by the Rev. William Blackwood, D.D.* Philadelphia: Joseph M. Wilson, 1857. 720 pages.

THE QUAKERS OR FRIENDS

1947. **Bowden, J.** *History of Friends in America.* 2 vols. London: W. & F. G. Cash, 1850, 1854. (Volume II, Pennsylvania and New Jersey.)

1948. **Gummere, A. M.** (editor). *The Journal and Essays of John
Woolman.* New York: Macmillan, 1922. xvii+643 pages.

1949. **Jones, R. M., assisted by Isaac Sharpless and Amelia M.
Gummere.** *The Quakers in the American Colonies.* London:
Macmillan, 1911. xxxii+603 pages.

1950. ———. *The Faith and Practice of the Quakers.* New York:
Doran, 1927? xi+181 pages.

1951. **Penney, N.** *The Journal of George Fox Edited from the MSS
with an Introduction by T. Edmund Harvey.* (Item 1442.)
2 vols. (Pages 176–258 of Volume II contain the journal
during Fox's American tour.)

1952. **Thomas, A. C. and R. H.** *A History of the Society of Friends
in America.* ("American Church History Series," XII, pp.
163–308.) Item 1843.

THE SOUTHERN COLONIES

THE ESTABLISHED CHURCH OF ENGLAND OR ANGLICAN

1953. **Anderson, J. S.** *History of the Church of England in the
Colonies and Foreign Dependencies of the British Empire.* 3
vols. London: Rivington, 1845. (An old work but still of
great value.)

1954. **Cross, A. L.** *The Anglical Episcopate and the American Colonies.* New York: Longmans, Green, 1902. ix+368 pages.

1955. **Goodwin, E. L.** *The Colonial Church in Virginia.* Milwaukee: Morehouse Publishing Co., 1927. xxiv+342 pages. (A recent work advancing some new conclusions.)

1956. **Hawks, F. L.** *Contributions to the Ecclesiastical History of the United States of America.* Vol. I, *Rise and Progress of the Protestant Episcopal Church in Virginia.* New York: Harper, 1836. Vol. II, *Rise and Progress of the Protestant Episcopal Church in Maryland.* New York: John S. Taylor, 1839.

1957. **Jarratt, D.** *Life of Devereux Jarratt.* Baltimore: Warner & Hanna, 1806. iv+223 pages. (The autobiography of the outstanding evangelical leader in the Anglican church of Virginia.)

1958. **Meade, W.** *Old Churches, Ministers and Families of Virginia.* 2 vols. Philadelphia: Lippincott, 1906. (First edition, 1857.)

1959. **Perry, W. S.** *The History of the American Episcopal Church, 1587–1883.* 2 vols. Vol. I, *The Planting and Growth of the American Colonial Church.* Boston: Osgood, 1885.

1960. ———. *Historical Collections Relating to the American Colonial Church.* Hartford, Connecticut: Church Press, 1870–78. Vol. I, Virginia; Vol. II, Pennsylvania; Vol. III, Massachusetts; Vol. IV, Maryland and Delaware.

DISSENTING CHURCHES IN THE SOUTHERN COLONIES
Baptists (See Item 1073)

1961. **Benedict, D.** *A General History of the Baptist Denomination in America and Other Parts of the World.* 2 vols. Boston: Manning & Loring, 1813. (Volume II deals with the rise of the Baptists in the southern colonies.)

1962. **Semple, R. B.** *A History of the Rise and Progress of the Baptists in Virginia.* Richmond, Virginia: John Lynch, printer, 1810. 446 pages. (This is the classic account of the rise of southern Baptists.)

1963. **Taylor, J. B.** *Virginia Baptist Ministers.* Series I, Philadelphia: Lippincott, 1860; and Series II, Richmond: T. J. Stark, 1860.

Presbyterians

1964. **Davies, S.** *Sermons on Important Subjects.* 7th ed. 4 vols. Philadelphia: 1794; London: W. Baynes, 1815.

1965. **Foote, W. H.** *Sketches of Virginia.* First Series, Philadelphia, W. S. Martien, 1850; Second Series, Philadelphia: 1855. (Good for religious conditions during the Colonial period.)

1966. ———. *Sketches of North Carolina, Historical and Biographical, Illustrative of the Principles of a Portion of Her Early Settlers.* New York: R. Carter, 1846. (ix)+xxxii, (33)+557 pages.

1967. **Howe, G.** *History of the Presbyterian Church in South Carolina.* 2 vols. Columbia, South Carolina: Diffie & Chapman, 1870. (Volume I, the Colonial period.)

Catholics

1968. **Gambrall, T. C.** *Church Life in Colonial Maryland.* Baltimore: G. Lycott, 1855. 309 pages.

1969. **Shea, J. G.** *History of the Roman Catholic Church in the United States.* 4 vols. New York: McBride, 1886. xxix+663 pages. (Volume I, *Colonial Days.* The Thirteen Colonies—the Ottawa and Illinois Country—Louisiana, Florida—Texas—New Mexico and Arizona, 1521–1763.)

Methodists

1970. **Lednum, J.** *A History of the Rise of Methodism in America Containing Sketches of Methodist Itinerant Preachers from 1736 to 1785.* Philadelphia: published by the author, 1859. xx+434 pages. (Contains also account of many of the first members of the American Methodist societies, and chapels.)

1971. **Lee, J.** *A Short History of the Methodists in the United States of America.* Baltimore: Magill & Clime, 1810. 368 pages. (The first history of American Methodism.)

1972. **Stevens, A.** *History of the Methodist Episcopal Church in the United States of America.* 3 vols. Vol. I, *The Planting of American Methodism.* New York: Carlton & Porter, 1864.

Other Bodies

1973. **Bernheim, G. D.** *History of the German Settlements and of the Lutheran Church in North and South Carolina.* Philadelphia: Lutheran Book Store, 1872. xvi+557 pages.

1974. **Hirsch, A. H.** *The Huguenots of Colonial South Carolina.* Durham, North Carolina: Duke University Press, 1928. xv+338 pages. (Also Item 1522.)

BIOGRAPHY

1975. **Belden, A. D.** *George Whitefield: The Awakener. A Modern Study of the Evangelical Revival.* Nashville, Tennessee: Cokesbury Press, 1930. xvii+302 pages.

1976. **Edwards, J.** *Life of Rev. David Brainerd, Chiefly Extracted from His Diary.* . . . . New York: The American Tract Society, 1833. iv+360 pages. (Embracing in the chronological order, Brainerd's public journal of the most successful year of his missionary labor. First edition 1749.)

1977. **Ëekhof, A.** *Jonas Michaëlius, Founder of the Church in New Netherland. His Life and Work, Together with the Facsimile Transcription and English Translation of an Extensive Unknown Autograph Latin Letter, Which He Wrote from Manhattan Island 13 September 1630 Now Published for the First Time.* Leyden: A. W. Sijthoff's Publishing Co., 1926. xii+148 pages.

1978. **Harbaugh, H.** *The Life of Reverend Michael Schlatter: with Full Account of His Travels and Labors among the Germans in Pennsylvania, New Jersey, Maryland and Virginia* . . . . *etc. 1716–1790.* Philadelphia: Lindsay & Blakiston, 1857. xxxi+27+375 pages.

1979. **Mann, W. J.** *Life and Times of Henry Melchior Muhlenberg.* Philadelphia: General Council Publication Board, 1911. xvi+547 pages.

1980. **Tyerman, L.** *The Life of the Rev. George Whitefield.* 2 vols. London: Hodder & Stoughton, 1876–77.

COLONIAL EDUCATION

ELEMENTARY EDUCATION

1981. **Cubberley, E. P.** *Public Education in the United States: A Study and Interpretation of American Educational History, etc.* Boston: Houghton Mifflin, 1919. xv+517 pages.

1982. **Dexter, E. G.** *A History of Education in the United States.* New York: Macmillan, 1922. xxi+656 pages.

1983. **Jernegan, M. W.** "Beginnings of Public Education in New England," *School Review* (University of Chicago), XXIII (1915), 319–30, 361–80.

1984. **Kemp, W. W.** *Support of Schools in Colonial New York by the Society for the Propagation of the Gospel in Foreign Parts.* New York: Teachers College, Columbia University, 1913. 279 pages.

1985. **Kilpatrick, W. H.** *Dutch Schools of New Netherland and Colonial New York.* Washington: Government Printing Office, 1912. 239 pages.

1986. **Meriwether, C.** *Our Colonial Curriculum, 1607–1776.* Washington, D.C.: Capital Publishing Co., 1907. 301 pages.

1987. **Raper, C. L.** *Church and Private Schools in North Carolina.* Greensboro, North Carolina: J. J. Stone, printer, 1898. 247 pages.

1988. **Small, W. H.** *Early New England Schools.* Boston: Ginn, 1914. 401 pages.

1989. **Woody, Thomas.** *Early Quaker Education in Pennsylvania.* New York: Teachers College, Columbia University, 1920. 287 pages.

1990. ———. *History of Quaker Education in the Colony and State of New Jersey.* Philadelphia: published by the author, 1923. 408 pages.

COLLEGES

1991. **Adams, H. B.** *The History of College of William and Mary from Its Foundation, 1693 to 1870.* Baltimore: J. Murphy & Co., 1870. 162 pages.

1992. **Bush, G. G.** *Harvard, the First American University.* Boston: Upham, 1886. v+vi+9+160 pages.

1993. **Chase, F.** *A History of Dartmouth College and the Town of Hanover, New Hampshire.* 2 vols. Cambridge, Massachusetts: J. Wilson & Son, 1901–13.

1994. **Kingsley, W. L.** *Yale College, A Sketch of Its History, with Notices of Its Several Departments, Instructors, and Benefactors, etc.* 2 vols. New York: Holt, 1879.

1995. **Maclean, J.** *History of the College of New Jersey from Its Origin to the Commencement of 1854.* 2 vols. Philadelphia: Lippincott, 1877.

1996. **Montgomery, T. H.** *History of the University of Pennsylvania from Its Foundation to A.D. 1770.* Philadelphia: G. W. Jacobs & Co., 1900. 500 pages.

THE GREAT COLONIAL AWAKENING
IN NEW ENGLAND (SEE ITEMS 1511–21)

1997. **Chauncy, C.** *Some Seasonable Thoughts on the State of Religion in New England.* Boston: S. Eliot, 1743. 424 pages. (Chauncy was the chief opponent of the revival.)

1998. ———. *Enthusiasm Described and Cautioned Against.* Boston, 1742.

1999. **Edwards, J.** *A Faithful Narrative of the Surprising Work of God in the Conversion of Many Hundreds of Souls in Northampton, and Neighboring Towns and Villages of New Hampshire and New England.* London: J. Oswald, 1837. xvi+132 pages.

2000. **Prince, T., Jr.** (editor). *The Christian History.* 2 vols. Boston, 1744. (This was a weekly publication describing the progress of the awakening, and is the best contemporary account.)

2001. **Tracy, J.** *The Great Awakening: A History of the Revival of Religion in the Time of Edwards and Whitefield.* Boston Tappan & Dennet, 1842. xviii+433 pages. (Deals largely with the New England phase of the revival.)

IN THE MIDDLE COLONIES

2002. **Maxson, H.** *The Great Awakening in the Middle Colonies.* Chicago: University of Chicago Press, 1920. vii+158 pages.

IN THE SOUTHERN COLONIES

2003. **Gewehr, W. M.** *The Great Awakening in Virginia.* Durham, North Carolina. Duke University Press, 1930. x+292 pages.

COLONIAL INDIAN MISSIONS AND OTHER BENEVOLENCES
(SEE ITEM 948)

2004. **Brown, W.** *The History of Missions; or the Propagation of Christianity among the Heathen, since the Reformation.* 2 vols. Philadelphia: M'Carty & Davis, 1820.

2005. **DeSchweinitz, E. A.** *The Life and Times of David Zeisberger, the Western Pioneer and Apostle of the Indians.* Philadelphia: Lippincott, 1871. xii+13+747 pages.

2006. **Loskiel, G. H.** *History of the Mission of the United Brethren among the Indians in North America.* Translated from German by Christian I. Latrobe. London: Brethrens Society for the Furtherance of the Gospel, 1794. (Part I, Indians of North America. Missions.)

2007. **Love, W. D.** *Samson Occom and the Christian Indians of New England.* Boston: Pilgrim Press, 1899. xi+379 pages.

2008. "Massachusetts Historical Society Collections." Vol. I, Thomas Cooper, *Fabulous Tradition and Customs of the Indians of Martha's Vineyard.* Boston, 1792; reprinted 1806, 1859. Vol. III, Roger Williams, *Key into the Language of America* (Indians of New England). Boston, 1794; reprinted 1810.

2009. **North, E. M.** *Early Methodist Philanthropy.* New York: Methodist Book Concern, 1914. viii+181 pages. (Chapter iv and Appendixes contain materials on Whitfield's Orphan House.

2010. **Shepard, T.** *The Clear Sunshine of the Gospel Breaking Forth upon the Indians of New England, or an Historicall Narration of Gods Wonderfull Workings upon Sundry of the Indians, Both Chief Governors and Common People, in Bringing Them to a Willing and Desired Submission to the Ordinances of the Gospel, etc.* London: printed by R. Coates for J. Bellamy, 1648. 7+1+38 pages. Reprinted, New York: J. Sabin, 1865. 56 pages.

THE AMERICAN CHURCHES AND THE WAR FOR INDEPENDENCE

2011. **Baldwin, Alice, M.** *The New England Clergy and the American Revolution.* Durham, North Carolina: Duke University Press, 1928. xiii+222 pages.

2012. **Breed, W. P.** *Presbyterians and the Revolution.* Philadelphia: Presbyterian Board of Publication, 1876. 205 pages.

2013. **Cathcart, W.** *The Baptists and the American Revolution.* Philadelphia: S. A. George & Co., 1876. 118 pages.

2014. **Jameson, J. F.** *The American Revolution Considered as a Social Movement.* Princeton: Princeton University Press, 1926. 158 pages. (Chapter iv, entitled "Thought and Feeling," deals with the religious influences.)

2015. **Thornton, J. W.** *The Pulpit of the American Revolution.* Boston: Gould & Lincoln, 1860. 537 pages.

2016. **Van Tyne, C. H.** *The Causes of the War of Independence.* Boston: Houghton Mifflin, 1922. x+499 pages. (Chapter xiii deals especially with the "Religious and Sectarian Forces Which Threatened Imperial Unity.")

THE STRUGGLE FOR RELIGIOUS LIBERTY AND THE SEPARATION OF CHURCH AND STATE

The struggle for the separation of church and state centered in Virginia and New England.

2017. **Cobb, S. H.** *Rise of Religious Liberty in America: A History.* New York: Macmillan, 1902. xx+541 pages.

2018. **Greene, Maria Louise.** *The Development of Religious Liberty in Connecticut.* Boston: Houghton Mifflin, 1905. xiii+552 pages.

2019. **Johnson, T. C.** *Virginia Presbyterianism and Religious Liberty in Colonial and Revolutionary Times.* Richmond: Presbyterian Committee of Publication, 1907. 128 pages.

2020. **Lauer, P. E.** *Church and State in New England.* ("Johns Hopkins University Studies in History and Political Science," Vol. X.) Baltimore: Johns Hopkins University Press, 1892. 106 pages.

2021. **McIlwaine, H. R.** *Religious Toleration in Virginia.* ("Johns Hopkins University Studies in History and Political Science," Vol. XII.) Baltimore: Johns Hopkins University Press, 1894. 67 pages.

2022. **Meyer, J. C.** *Church and State in Massachusetts from 1740 to 1833. A Chapter in the History of the Development of Individual Freedom.* Cleveland: Western Reserve University Press, 1930. viii+276 pages.

2023. **Reed, Susan M.** *Church and State in Massachusetts, 1691–1740.* ("University of Illinois Studies in Social Science," Vol. III, No. 4.) Urbana: University of Illinois, 1914. 208 pages.

2024. **Thom, W. T.** *The Struggle for Religious Freedom in Virginia; The Baptists.* ("Johns Hopkins University Studies in History and Political Science," Series XVIII, Nos. 10, 11,

12.) Baltimore: Johns Hopkins University Press, 1900. 105 pages.)

2025. **Weeks, S. B.** *Church and State in North Carolina.* ("Johns Hopkins University Studies in History and Political Science," Eleventh Series, Nos. V–VI.) Baltimore: Johns Hopkins University Press, 1893. 65 pages.

NATIONALIZING THE AMERICAN CHURCHES

"American Church History Series" (Item 1843):

2026. **Buckley, J. M.** *Methodists,* Vol. V, chap. ix.

2027. **Jacobs, H. E.** Vol. IV, *Lutherans,* chaps. xix, xx.

2028. **O'Gorman, T.** Vol. IX, *Roman Catholics,* chaps. xvii, xix.

2029. **Thompson, R. E.** Vol. VI, *Presbyterians,* chap. vi.

2030. **Tiffany, C. C.** Vol. VII, *Protestant Episcopal,* chaps. xii, xiii.

2031. **Beardsley, E. E.** *Life and Correspondence of the Right Reverend Samuel Seabury, First Bishop of Connecticut, and of the Episcopal Church in the United States.* 1881. 497 pages.

2032. **Fortenbaugh, R.** *The Development of the Synodical Polity of the Lutheran Church in America.* Philadelphia: University of Pennsylvania, 1926. 252 pages.

2033. **Guilday, P.** *Life and Times of John Carroll, Archbishop of Baltimore, 1735–1815.* New York: Encyclopedia Press, 1922. (v)+xiv+864 pages.

2034. **Humphrey, E. F.** *Nationalism and Religion in America, 1774–1789.* Boston: Chipman Law Publishing Co., 1924. viii+536 pages.

2035. **Wilson, B.** *Memoir of the Life of the Right Reverend William White, Bishop of the Protestant Episcopal Church in the State of Pennsylvania.* Philadelphia: James Kay, Jr., & Brother. 430 pages.

THE CHURCH AND THE PROBLEMS OF THE FRONTIER

GENERAL

2036. **Mathews, L. K.** *The Expansion of New England; the Spread of New England Settlement and Institutions to the Mississippi River, 1620–1875.* Boston: Houghton Mifflin, 1909. xiv+303 pages.

2037. **McMaster, J. B.** *History of the People of the United States.* 8 vols. New York: Appleton, 1888–1913. (References to the westward movement of population and to the West will be found especially in Volumes II, III, and IV.)

2038. **Paxson, F. L.** *History of the American Frontier, 1763–1893.* Boston: Houghton Mifflin, 1924. viii+595 pages.

2039. **Reigel, R. E.** *America Moves West.* New York: Holt, 1930. x+595 pages.

2040. **Roosevelt, T.** *The Winning of the West.* 4 vols. New York: Putnam's, 1889. (Other editions published by the Century Co., Scribner's, and Review of Reviews Co.)

2041. **Turner, F. J.** *The Frontier in American History.* New York: Holt, 1921; reprinted 1926, 1928. 4+375 pages.

THE CHURCHES ON THE FRONTIER

2042. **Benedict, D.** *A General History of the Baptist Denomination in America and Other Parts of the World.* 2 vols. Boston: Manning & Loring, 1813. Later edition, New York: Colby & Co., 1848. (Volume II contains much material on Baptist churches in the West obtained through personal visitations of the author.)

2043. **Bishop, R. H.** *An Outline of the History of the Church in the State of Kentucky during a Period of Forty Years: Containing the Memoirs of Reverend David Rice and Sketches of the Origin and Present State of Particular Churches and Lives and Labours of a Number of Men, etc.* Lexington, Kentucky: T. T. Skillman, 1824. xii+422 pages.

2044. **Brunson, A.** *A Western Pioneer or Incidents of the Life and Times of Alfred Brunson.* 2 vols. New York: Methodist Book Concern, 1872. (Brunson was a Methodist preacher and worked in Ohio, Illinois, Wisconsin, and Minnesota.)

2045. **Cartwright, P.** *Autobiography of Peter Cartwright, the Backwoods Preacher.* Edited by W. P. Strickland. New York: Methodist Book Concern, 1856. 525 pages. (Presents one of the best pictures of frontier life.)

2046. **Davidson, R.** *History of the Presbyterian Church in the State of Kentucky.* New York: Robert Carter, 1847. x+371 pages. (An excellent account of religious conditions in Kentucky, with a strong old-school Presbyterian bias.)

2047. **Finley, J. B.** *Autobiography of James B. Finley, or Pioneer Life in the West.* Edited by W. P. Strickland. New York: Methodist Book Concern, 1857. 455 pages.

2048. ———. *Sketches of Western Methodism. Biographical, Historical and Miscellaneous; Illustrative of Pioneer Life.* Edited by W. P. Strickland. New York: Methodist Book Concern, 1854. 551 pages.

2049. **Kennedy, W. S.** *The Plan of Union: Or a History of the Presbyterian and Congregational Churches of the Western Reserve, with Biographical Sketches of the Early Missionaries.* Hudson, Ohio: Pentagon Press, 1856. iv+262 pages.

2050. **Mode, P. G.** *The Frontier Spirit in American Christianity.* New York: Macmillan, 1923. x+196 pages.

2051. **O'Daniel, V. F.** *The Right Reverend Edward Dominic Fenwick: O. P. Founder of the Dominicans in the United States: Pioneer Missionary in Kentucky, Apostle of Ohio: First Bishop of Cincinnati.* Washington, D.C.: The Dominicana, 1920. xiv+473 pages.

2052. **Rusk, R. L.** *The Literature of the Middle-Western Frontier.* 2 vols. New York: Columbia University Press, 1925. (Volume I has chapters on "Cultural Beginnings," "Newspapers and Magazines," "Controversial Writings," and "Scholarly Writings and Schoolbooks" which have more or less material dealing with frontier religion.)

2053. **Smith, J.** *Old Redstone or Historical Sketches of Western Presbyterianism, Its Early Ministers, Its Perilous Times and Its First Records.* Philadelphia: Lippincott, Greenibo & Co., 1854. 429 pages.

2054. **Spencer, J. H.** *A History of Kentucky Baptists, from 1769 to 1885 Including More than 800 Biographical Sketches.* 2 vols. Cincinnati: T. R. Baumes, 1885.

2055. **Sweet, W. W.** *Religion on the American Frontier.* Vol. I, *The Baptists.* New York: Holt, 1931. 640 pages. (A collection of source materials illustrating Baptist work on the frontier.)

2056. ———. *Rise of Methodism in the West.* New York: Methodist Book Concern, 1920. 207 pages. (Contains the Minutes of the Western Conference from 1800 to 1812, with historical introduction.)

2057. **Taylor, J.** *The History of Ten Churches of Which the Author Has Been Alternately a Member; in Which Will Be Seen Something of a Journal of the Author's Life for More than Fifty Years.* Frankfort, Kentucky: J. H. Holeman, 1823. iv+300 pages.

2058. **Tipple, E. S.** *Francis Asbury: The Prophet of the Long Road.* New York: Methodist Book Concern, 1916. 333 pages. (The best life of the pioneer bishop.)

2059. **Webb, B. J.** *The Centenary of Catholicism in Kentucky.* Louisville: G. A. Rogers, 1884. v+544 pages. (Contains details of emigration to the state from 1785 to 1814, with sketches of prominent colonists and missionary priests.)

FRONTIER REVIVALISM

2060. **Cleveland, Catherine C.** *The Great Revival in the West, 1795–1805.* Chicago: University of Chicago Press, 1916. xii+215 pages. (A study based on modern research.)

2061. **Davenport, F. M.** *Primitive Traits in Religious Revivals: A Study in Mental and Social Evolution.* New York: Macmillan, 1905. vii+323 pages.

2062. **McGready, J.** *The Posthumous Works of.* 2 vols. Edited by Reverend James Smith. Louisville, Kentucky: W. W. Worsley, 1831–33.

2063. **McNemar, R.** *The Kentucky Revival: or a Short History of the Late Extraordinary Out-pouring of the Spirit of God in . . . . America . . . . With a Brief Account of Shakerism in Ohio and Kentucky, etc.* Cincinnati: J. W. Browne, 1807. vii+119 pages.

2064. **Speer, W.** *The Great Revival of 1800.* Philadelphia: Presbyterian Board of Publication, 1872. 112 pages.

FRONTIER SCHISMS
DISCIPLES

2065. **Garrison, W. E.** *The Sources of Alexander Campbell's Theology.* St. Louis: Christian Publishing Co., 1900. 302 pages.

2066. **Gates, E.** *The Disciples of Christ.* ("The Story of the Churches Series.") New York: Baker & Taylor Co., 1905. 346 pages.

2067. ———. *The Early Relation and Separation of Baptists and Disciples.* Chicago: R. R. Donnelley & Sons, 1904. 124 pages.

2068. **Rogers, J.** *The Biography of Eld. Barton Warren Stone Written by Himself with Additions and Reflections.* Cincinnati: published for author, 1847. 687 pages.

CUMBERLAND PRESBYTERIANS

2069. **McDonnald, B. W.** *History of the Cumberland Presbyterian Church.* Nashville: Board of Publication Cumberland Presbyterian Church, 1888. xxxi+687 pages.

THE UNITED BRETHREN IN CHRIST

2070. **Drury, A. W.** *History of the Church of the United Brethren in Christ.* Dayton, Ohio: Otterbein Press, 1924. 821 pages.

THE EVANGELICAL CHURCH

2071. **Yeakel, R.** *History of the Evangelical Association.* 2 vols. Cleveland: J. H. Lamb, agent, 1909.

THE RISE OF MODERN MISSIONS AND BEGINNINGS OF MISSIONARY ORGANIZATION (ALSO ITEMS 954, 2275–77, 2280, 2290, 2304–06)

2072. **Bashford, J. W.** *The Oregon Missions: The Story of How the Line Was Run between Canada and the United States.* New York: Abingdon Press, 1918. 311 pages.

2073. **Elsbree, O. W.** *The Rise of the Missionary Spirit in America, 1790–1815.* Williamsport, Pennsylvania: Williamsport Printing Co., 1928. 187 pages.

2074. **Emory, Julia C.** *A Century of Endeavor 1821–1921. A Record of the First Hundred Years of the Domestic and Foreign Missionary Society of the Protestant Episcopal Church in the U.S.A.* New York: Department of Missions, 1921. xiii+466 pages.

2075. **Green, A.** *Historical Sketch of Domestic and Foreign Missions of the Presbyterian Church of the United States.* Philadelphia: Presbyterian Board of Publication, 1838. New edition, with Supplementary Notes by John C. Lowrie, 1855 and 1868. New York: Randolph Co., 1893. xiii+249 pages.

2076. **McCoy, I.** *History of Baptist Indian Missions Embracing Remarks on the Former and Present Conditions of the Aboriginal Tribes: Their Settlement within the Indian Territory, and Their Future Prospects.* Washington: W. M. Morrison; New York: H. and S. Raynor, 1840. 5+621 pages.

2077. **Mills, S. J., and Smith, D.** *Report of a Missionary Tour through That Part of the United States Which Lies West of the Alleghany Mountains Performed under the Direction of the Massachusetts Missionary Society.* Andover: Flagg & Gould, 1915. 64 pages.

2078. **Reid, J. M.** *Missions and Missionary Society of the Methodist Episcopal Church.* 2 vols. New York: Methodist Book Concern, 1879.

2079. **Schermerhorn, J. F.** *Report Respecting the Indians, Inhabiting the Western Parts of the United States.* ("Massachusetts Historical Society Collections," Series 2, Vol. II.) Boston: published by the Society. 1814.

2080. **Strickland, W. P.** *History of the American Bible Society from Its Organization to the Present Time.* New York: Harper, 1856. xxx+512 pages. (With an Introduction by Rev. N. L. Rice.)

2081. **Strong, W. E.** *The Story of the American Board: an Account of the First Hundred Years of the American Board of Commissions for Foreign Missions.* Boston: Pilgrim Press, 1910. xv+523 pages.

2082. **Sweet, W. W.** *Circuit Rider Days along the Ohio.* New York: The Methodist Book Concern, 1923. 299 pages. (Chapter iv, entitled "The Wyandot Mission," brings together the essential facts regarding the beginnings of Methodist missions.)

2083. **Vail, A. L.** *The Morning Hour of American Baptist Missions.* Philadelphia: American Baptist Publication Society, 1907. 477 pages.

THE ERA OF CONTROVERSY, 1815–50

RISE OF UNITARIANISM AND UNIVERSALISM
(SEE ITEMS 1074, 1075, 1523)

2084. **Allen, J. H., and Eddy, R.** *A History of the Unitarians and the Universalists in the United States.* ("American Church History Series," Vol. X.) (Item 1843.)

2085. **Chadwick, J. W.** *William Ellery Channing Minister of Religion.* Boston: Houghton Mifflin, 1903. xvii+463 pages.

2086. **Cooke, G. W.** *Unitarianism in America: A History of Its Origin and Development.* Boston: American Unitarian Association, 1902. xi+463 pages.

2087. **Eddy, R.** *Universalism in America. A History.* 2 vols. Boston: Universalist Publishing House, 1884–86. (Has a useful bibliography.)

2088. **Ware, J.** *Memoirs of the Life of Henry Ware Jr.* 2 vols. Boston: Unitarian Association, 1890.

2089. **Whittemore, T.** *Life of Reverend Hosea Ballou; with Account of His Writings, and Biographical Sketches of His Seniors and Contemporaries in the Universalist Ministry.* 4 vols. Boston: James M. Usher, 1854–55.

Presbyterian Controversy and Schism

2090. **Baird, S. J.** *A History of the New School, and of the Questions Involved in the Disruption of the Presbyterian Church in 1838.* Philadelphia: Claxton, Remsen & Haffelfinger, 1868.

2091. **Beecher, C.** (editor). *Autobiography, Correspondence, etc., of Lyman Beecher.* 2 vols. New York: Harper, 1866.

2092. **Brown, I. V.** *A Historical Vindication of the Abrogation of the Plan of Union by the Presbyterian Church in the United States of America.* Philadelphia: W. S. & S. Mantien, 1854.

2093. **Gillett, E. H.** *History of the Presbyterian Church in the United States of America.* (Item 1941.) (Volume II, chapters xxxvi–xxxviii.)

Lutheran Controversy

2094. **Ferm, V.** *The Crisis in American Lutheran Theology.* New York: Century, 1927. xiii+409 pages.

2095. **Niebuhr, H. R.** *The Social Sources of Denominationalism.* New York: Henry Holt, 1929. x+304 pages. (Especially chapters v, "Nationalism and the Churches," and viii, "The Churches of the Immigrants.")

Protestant Episcopalian Controversy

2096. **McConnell, S. D.** *History of the American Episcopal Church.* 10th ed. Milwaukee: The Young Churchman Co., 1916. xx+468 pages. (Especially chapters vii–x.)

2097. **Wentz, A. R.** *The Lutheran Church in American History.* (Item 1938.) (Especially chapters xiii–xvii.)

ROMAN CATHOLIC CONTROVERSY

2098. **Shea, J. G.** *History of the Catholic Church in the United States.* (Item 1969.) (Volumes III and IV.)

SLAVERY CONTROVERSY AND SLAVERY SCHISMS
(ALSO ITEM 2261)

2099. **Barnes, A.** *An Inquiry into the Scriptural Views of Slavery.* Philadelphia: Perkins & Purvis, 1846; later edition 1855. (A powerful refutation of the scriptural arguments for slavery.)

2100. ———. *The Church and Slavery.* Philadelphia: Perry & McMillan, 1857. 7+196 pages.

2101. **Birney, J. G.** *The American Churches the Bulwarks of American Slavery.* 3d ed. Newburyport, Massachusetts, 1842. Reprinted, Concord, New Hampshire: P. Pillsbury, 1885. 48 pages.

2102. **Dodd, W. E.** *The Cotton Kingdom.* ("The Chronicles of America Series.") (Item 1837.) ix+161 pages.

2103. **Hart, A. B.** *Slavery and Abolition.* ("American Nations Series," Vol. XVI.) New York: Harper, 1906. xiii+360 pages.

2104. **Matlack, L. C.** *The Anti-Slavery Struggle and Triumph in the Methodist Episcopal Church.* New York: The Methodist Book Concern, 1881. (An account of the slavery struggle in the Methodist church by one who took a leading part in it.)

2105. **McNeilly, J. H.** *Religion and Slavery, A Vindication of the Southern Churches.* Nashville: Publishing House, M.E. Church, South, 1911. 88 pages.

2106. **Norwood, J. N.** *The Schism in the Methodist Episcopal Church, 1844. A Study of Slavery and Ecclesiastical Politics.* Alfred, New York: Alfred University Press, 1923. 225 pages.

2107. **Phillips, U. B.** *American Negro Slavery: A Survey of the Supply, Employment and Control of Negro Labor as Determined by the Plantation Régime.* New York: Appleton, 1927. xi+529 pages.

2108. **Stringfellow, F.** *Scriptural and Statistical Views in Favor of Slavery.* 4th ed., with additions. Richmond, Virginia: J. W. Randolph, 1856. 149 pages.

2109. **Swaney, C. B.** *Episcopal Methodism and Slavery, with Sidelights on Ecclesiastical Politics.* Boston: Badger, 1926. (11)+356 pages.

2110. **Thomas, A. C.** *The Attitude of the Society of Friends toward Slavery in the Seventeenth and Eighteenth Centuries.* ("Papers of the American Society of Church History," Series I, Vol. VIII, pp. 263-99.) New York: Putnam's, 1897.

RELIGIOUS MOVEMENTS AND COMMUNISTIC EXPERIMENTS IN THE EIGHTEEN THIRTIES AND FORTIES

MORMONISM

2111. **Bennion, A. S.** *What It Means To Be a Mormon.* Salt Lake City: The Deseret Sunday School Union, 1925. vi+176 pages.

2112. **Linn, W. A.** *The Story of the Mormons from the Date of Their Origin to the Year 1901.* New York: Macmillan, 1902. xxv+637 pages. (The best account covering the whole development of Mormonism.)

2113. **Roberts, B. H.** *A Comprehensive History of the Church of Jesus Christ of Latter-Day Saints.* 6 vols. Salt Lake City: published by the Church, 1930.

2114. **Werner, M. R.** *Brigham Young.* London: Jonathan Cape, 1925. xvi+478 pages. (So far the best life of the great Mormon leader.)

MILLERITE MOVEMENT

2115. **Harkness, R. E. E.** *Social Origins of the Millerite Movement.* Ph.D. thesis MSS, University of Chicago, 1927.

2116. **Sears, Clara E.** *Days of Delusion: A Strange Bit of History.* Boston: Houghton Mifflin Co., 1924. xxvi+264 pages. (Based largely on the recollections of survivors.)

COMMUNISTIC EXPERIMENTS

2117. **Evans, F. W.** *Shakers. Compendium of the Origin, History, Principles, Rules and Regulations, Government and Doctrines of the United Society of Believers in Christ's Second Appear-*

ing. With Biographies of Ann Lee. New York: Appleton, 1859. x+189 pages.

2118. **Hinds, W. A.** *American Communities and Co-operative Colonies.* 2d rev. Chicago: C. H. Kerr & Co., 1908. 608 pages.

2119. **Lockwood, G. B.** *The New Harmony Movement.* New York: Appleton, 1905. xvi+404 pages.

2120. **Nordhoff, C.** *The Communistic Societies of the United States; from Personal Visit and Observation; Including Detailed Accounts of the Economists, Zoarites, Shakers, The Amana, Oneida, Bethel, Aurora, Icarian and Other Existing Societies; Their Religious Creeds, Social Politics, Numbers, Industries, and Present Condition.* New York: Harper, 1875. viii+ (9)+439 pages.

2121. **Noyes, J. H.** *History of American Socialisms.* Philadelphia: Lippincott, 1870. vi+678 pages.

2122. ———. *Religious Experience of Founder of the Oneida Community.* New York: Macmillan, 1923. xiii+416 pages.

2123. **Robinson, C. E.** *A Concise History of the United Society of Believers Called Shakers.* East Canterbury, New Hampshire: H. C. Blum, 1893. ix+134 pages.

2124. **Seldes, G. V.** *The Stammering Century.* New York: John Day Co., 1928. xviii+414 pages. (A record of cults and manias in America during the nineteenth century.)

2125. **Shambaugh, Bertha M.** *Amana the Community of True Inspiration.* Iowa City, Iowa: State Historical Society of Iowa, 1908. 414 pages.

2126. **Shaw, A.** *Icara, a Chapter in the History of Communism.* New York: Putnam's, 1884. ix+219 pages.

2127. **Stewart, I. D.** *The History of the Freewill Baptists, for Half a Century.* Vol. I, *From the Year 1780 to 1830.* Dover, New Hampshire: Freewill Baptist Printing Establishment, 1862. xii+479 pages.

2128. **Swift, L.** *Brook Farm; Its Members, Scholars, and Visitors.* New York: Macmillan, 1900. x+300 pages.

2129. **Warfield, B. B.** *John Humphrey Noyes and His Bible Commonwealth.* ("Bibliotheca Sacre," Vol. LXXVIII.) Oberlin,

Ohio; since 1920, St. Louis: Bibliotheca Sacre Co., 1921. (Pages 37–72, 172–200, 319–75.)

PRE-CIVIL WAR REVIVALISM AND COUNTER-MOVEMENTS

2130. **Beecher, C.** (editor). *Autobiography, Correspondence, etc., of Lyman Beecher, D.D.* 2 vols. New York: Harper, 1866.

2131. **Bushnell, H.** *Christian Nurture.* New York: Scribner's, 1904. 407 pages. (First published, in part, 1847; in its present form, 1860; numerous editions.)

2132. **Cheney, Mary Bushnell.** *Life and Letters of Horace Bushnell.* New York: Scribner's, 1903. xi+601 pages.

2133. **Wright, G. F.** *Charles Grandison Finney.* ("American Religious Leaders.") Boston: Houghton Mifflin, 1893. vi+329 pages.

THE CHURCHES AND THE CIVIL WAR

2134. **Alexander, G.** *A History of the Methodist Episcopal Church, South.* ("American Church History Series," Vol. XI.) (Item 1843.) xii+142 pages.

2135. **Cheshire, J. B.** *The Church in the Confederate States: A History of the Protestant Episcopal Church in the Confederate States.* New York: Longmans, Green, 1912. ix+291 pages.

2136. **Fite, E. D.** *Social and Industrial Conditions in the North during the Civil War.* New York: Macmillan, 1910. vii+318 pages. (Particularly valuable are the chapters on "Education" and "Charity.")

2137. **Johnson, T. C.** *History of the Southern Presbyterian Church.* ("American Church History Series," XI, 313–479.) (Item 1843.)

2138. **Jones, J. W.** *Christ in the Camp: or Religion in Lee's Army.* Richmond. Virginia: B. F. Johnson & Co., 1887. 528 pages.

2139. **McPherson, E.** *The Political History of the United States during the Great Rebellion.* Washington, D.C.: James J. Chapman, 1882. viii+653 pages. (A chapter in the Appendix, "The Church and the Rebellion," pp. 461–554, contains very valuable source materials.)

2140. **Stanton, R. L.** *The Church and the Rebellion a Consideration of the Rebellion Against the Government of the United States; and the Agency of the Church, North and South, in Re-*

lation Thereto. New York: Danby & Miller, 1864. xiv + 562 pages.

2141. **Sweet, W. W.** *The Methodist Episcopal Church and the Civil War.* Cincinnati: The Methodist Book Concern, 1912. 228 pages.

THE CHURCHES AND PROBLEMS OF RECONSTRUCTION

2142. **Douglass, P. H.** *Christian Reconstruction in the South.* Boston: Pilgrim Press, 1909. 407 pages.

2143. **Hodge, C.** *Reunion of the Old School and New School Presbyterian Churches.* New York: Scribner's, 1867. 37 pages.

2144. **Sweet, W. W.** "The Methodist Episcopal Church and Reconstruction," *Journal of the Illinois State Historical Society,* VII, No. 3 (October 1914), 147–65.

THE DEVELOPMENT OF THE NEGRO CHURCHES

2145. **Bragg, G. F., Jr.** *History of the Afro-American Group of the Episcopal Church.* Baltimore: Church Advocate Press, 1922. 319 pages.

2146. **Daniel, W. A.** *Education of Negro Ministers.* New York: Doran, 1925. vii + 13 + 187 pages.

2147. **Du Bois, W. E. B.** (editor). *The Negro Church: Report of a Social Study.* ("Atlanta University Studies.") Atlanta: Atlanta University Press, 1903. viii + 212 pages.

2148. **Hood, J. W.** *History of the African Methodist Episcopal Zion Church.* Charlotte, North Carolina: A.M.E. Zion Publication House, n.d. 318 pages.

2149. **Jenifer, J. T.** *History of the African Methodist Episcopal Church.* Nashville, Tennessee: published for A.M.E. church, n.d. x + 454 pages.

2150. **Phillips, C. H.** *History of the Colored Methodist Episcopal Church.* 2 (1) vols. Jackson, Tennessee: Publishing House C.M.E. Church, 1925. 623 pages.

2151. **Woodson, C. G.** *The History of the Negro Church.* 2d ed. Washington: The Associated Publishers, 1921. x + 330 pages.

THE CHURCHES AND MODERN REFORM MOVEMENTS
TEMPERANCE

2152. **Cherrington, E. H.** *The Evolution of Prohibition in the United States of America; a Chronological History of the*

Liquor Problem and the Temperance Reform in the United States from the Earliest Settlements to the Consummation of National Prohibition. Westerville, Ohio: American Issue Press, 1920. ix+10+384 pages.

2153. **Colvin, D. L.** *Prohibition in the United States; a History of the Prohibition Party and of the Prohibition Movement.* New York: Doran, 1926. x+13+678 pages.

2154. **Kraut, J. A.** *The Origins of Prohibition.* New York: Knopf, 1925. 5+339 pages.

THE RISE OF THE SOCIAL GOSPEL

2155. **Barker, J. M.** *The Social Gospel and the New Era.* New York: Macmillan, 1919. ix+232 pages.

2156. **Ellwood, C. A.** *The Reconstruction in Religion: A Sociological View.* New York: Macmillan, 1922. xv+(2)+323 pages.

2157. **Mathews, S.** *The Church and the Changing Order.* New York: Macmillan, 1907; 2d ed., 1913. viii+225 pages.

2158. **Peabody, F. G.** *Jesus Christ and the Social Question.* New York: Macmillan, 1900; 2d ed., 1915. vii+374 pages.

2159. **Rauschenbusch, W.** *Christianity and the Social Crisis.* New York: Macmillan, 1907; 2d ed., 1912. xv+429 pages.

2160. **Ryan, J. A.** *Industrial Democracy from a Catholic's Viewpoint.* Washington: Rossi-Bryn Co., 1925. 12 pages.

REVIVALISM SINCE THE CIVIL WAR

2161. **Bradford, G.** *D. L. Moody: A Worker in Souls.* New York: Doubleday, Doran, 1927. xi+15+320 pages.

2162. **Ellis, W. T.** *Billy Sunday: The Man and His Message.* Philadelphia: Winston Co., 1914. 342 pages.

2163. **Loud, G.** *Evangelized America.* New York: Dial Press, 1928. xvi+373 pages. (A journalistic presentation of American Revivalism—overdrawn.)

2164. **Moody, W. R.** *The Life of Dwight L. Moody.* New York: Revell, 1900. 590 pages. (Illustrated.)

CHRISTIAN SCIENCE AND OTHER MODERN RELIGIOUS CULTS

2165. **Atkins, G. G.** *Modern Religious Cults and Movements.* New York: Revell Co., 1923. 359 pages.

2166. **Dakin, E. F.** *Mrs. Eddy: The Biography of a Virginal Mind.* New York: Scribner's, 1929. x+(1)+553 pages.

2167. **Kennedy, H. A. S.** *Christian Science and Organized Religion. A Plea for an Impartial Consideration and the Examination of a New Point of View.* San Francisco: Farallon Press. xii+(4)+335 pages.

2168. **Powell, L. P.** *Mary Baker Eddy, a Life Size Portrait.* New York: Macmillan, 1930. xii+364 pages.

THE CHURCHES AND THE WORLD WAR

2169. **Brown, W. A.** *The Church in America; a Study of the Present Conditions and Future Prospects of American Protestantism.* New York: Macmillan, 1922. xv+378 pages. (The best book dealing with the relation of the churches to the war; Dr. Brown was chairman of the Committee on the War and the Religious Outlook and secretary of the War-Time Commission of the Churches.)

IN THE LAST DECADE
MODERN CATHOLICISM IN AMERICA

2170. **Garrison, W. E.** *Catholicism and the American Mind.* Chicago: Willett, Clark & Colby, 1928. 3+267 pages. (A fair-minded presentation of the present situation.)

2171. **Marshall, C. C.** *The Roman Catholic Church in the Modern State.* 2d ed. New York: Dodd, Mead, 1928. xxvi+350 pages. (Written by a fair-minded Protestant.)

2172. **Tyan, J. S., and Moorhouse, F. X. M.** *The State and the Church.* New York: Macmillan, 1922. xiii+331 pages. (Written [edited] for the Department of Social Action of the National Catholic Welfare Council.)

2173. **Williams, M.** *Catholicism and the Modern Mind.* New York: Dial Press, 1928. 348 pages. (By a Trappist monk.)

THE CHURCH AND WORLD-PEACE

2174. **Allen, Devere.** *The Fight for Peace.* New York: Macmillan, 1930. 740 pages.

2175. **Gulick, S. L.** *The Christian Crusade for Warless World.* New York: Federal Council of the Churches of Christ in America, 1923. xiv+197 pages. (Bibliography.)

THE MODERNIST-FUNDAMENTALIST CONTROVERSY

2176. **Cole, S. G.** *History of Fundamentalism.* New York: R. R. Smith, 1931. 360 pages.

2177. **Johnson, J. W.** *Fundamentalism versus Modernism.* New York: Century, 1925. 3+52 pages.

2178. **Machen, J. G.** *Christianity and Liberalism.* New York: Macmillan, 1923. 5+189 pages.

2179. **Smith, W. H.** *Modernism, Fundamentalism and Catholicism.* Milwaukee: Moorehouse, 1925. x+152 pages.

CHURCH UNION

2180. **Briggs, C. A.** *Church Unity: Studies of Its Most Important Problems.* New York: Scribner's, 1909. xii+459 pages.

2181. *Christian Unity: Its Principles and Possibilities.* Prepared under the direction of the Committee on the War and the Religious Outlook. New York: Association Press, 1921. xiv+386 pages.

2182. **Sanford, E. B.** *Origin and History of the Federal Council of the Churches of Christ in America.* Hartford, Connecticut: S. S. Scranton Co., 1917. xii+528 pages.

2183. **Slosser, G. J.** *Christian Unity: Its History and Challenge in All Communions, in All Lands.* London: Kegan, Paul, Trench, Trübner & Co., 1929; New York: Dutton. xx+425 pages.

HISPANIC AMERICA

To understand the development of Christianity in Hispanic America it is necessary to have a knowledge of the Spanish and Portuguese background as well as a general knowledge of the history of the Hispanic-American peoples. The Roman Catholic church was highly developed in Hispanic America during the Colonial period, and an exhaustive bibliography would require many pages. The titles here suggested are the most useful, as well as the most comprehensive, works. Less attention has been given by historians to the Roman Catholic church since independence, and no single comprehensive work can be cited. Since independence, the problem of the relation of church and state has arisen in several of the republics, and some attention must be given to this subject. Also the work of the Protestant churches must be recognized.

EUROPEAN BACKGROUND (SEE ITEMS 680, 682, 1107–8)

2184. **Chapman, C. E.** *History of Spain.* New York: Macmillan, 1918. 4 vols. Barcelona, 1909–14. (Based upon the valuable work of Rafael Altamira y Crevea, *Historia de España y de la civilización española.*)

2185. **Hale, E. E. and Susan.** *Spain.* ("Story of the Nation Series.") New York: Putnam's, 1899. xx+407 pages.

2186. **Lane-Poole, S.** *The Moors in Spain.* ("Story of the Nation Series.") New York: Putnam's, 1893. xx+285 pages. (Other editions under the title, *The Story of the Moors in Spain.*)

2187. **Lea, H. C.** *A History of the Spanish Inquisition.* (Item 1115.) (Gives the best account of the religious background of Spanish colonization.)

2188. **Merriman, R. B.** *Rise of the Spanish Empire in the Old World and in the New.* 3 vols. New York: Macmillan, 1918–25. (A work of great merit.)

2189. **Stephens, H. M.** *The Story of Portugal.* ("The Story of the Nation Series.") New York: Putnam's, 1903. xxiv+448 pages. (There is no good history of Portugal in English; this volume is the best.)

2190. **Watts, E.** *The Christian Recovery of Spain.* (Item 689.)

GENERAL HISTORIES

2191. **Calderon, F. G.** *Latin America: Its Rise and Progress.* translated by Bernard Miall. New York: Scribner's, 1915. 400 pages. (Brilliant interpretation by a South American.)

2192. **Robertson, W. S.** *History of the Latin-American Nations.* New York: Appleton, 1925. xxiii+633 pages.

2193. **Sweet, W. W.** *A History of Latin America.* New York: Abingdon, 1929. 404 pages.

2194. **Williams, Mary W.** *The People and Politics of Latin America.* Boston: Ginn & Co., 1930. vii+845 pages.

COLONIAL PERIOD: GENERAL WORKS

2195. **Bourne, E. G.** *Spain in America.* ("American Nation Series," Vol. II.) New York: Harper, 1904. xx+350 pages. (An excellent introduction to an understanding of Spanish colonization.)

2196. **Helps, Sir A.** *Spanish Conquest of America.* 4 vols. London and New York: J. Lane, 1900. (First published, London, 1836–61.)

2197. **Prescott, W. H.** *The Conquest of Mexico.* 3 vols. New York: Harper, 1852 and numerous other editions. (Exceptionally useful for description of Aztec culture and religion.)

2198. ———. *The Conquest of Peru.* 2 vols. New York: Lippincott, 1873. (Numerous editions. Valuable for the account of Inca culture and religion.)

2199. **Watson, R. G.** *Spanish and Portuguese South America during the Colonial Period.* 2 vols. London: Trübner & Co., 1884.

THE CHURCH IN THE COLONIAL PERIOD
(SEE ITEMS 1124, 1125, 1127)

2200. **Ayarragaray, L.** *La Iglesia en América y la Dominación Española: Estudio de la epoca Colonial.* Buenos Aires: J. Lajouane & Cia editores, 1920. 321 pages. (A brief survey of the church during the Colonial period.)

2201. **Braden, C. S.** *Religious Aspects of the Conquest of Mexico.* Durham, North Carolina: Duke University Press, 1930. xv+344 pages.

2202. **Bravo, F. J.** *Colección de documentos relativos a la expulsion de los Jesuitos de la Republica Argentina y del Paraguay en el reinado do Carlos III.* Madrid: J. M. Perez, 1872; later ed., 1897. xci+404 pages.

2203. **Carbia, R. D.** *Historia ecclesiastica del Rio de la Plata, 1536–1810.* 2 vols. Buenos Aires: Casa Editoria Alfa y Omega, 1914.

2204. **Cleven, N. A. N.** *Readings in Hispanic American History.* Boston: Ginn, 1927. xx+791 pages. (Documents relating to the ecclesiastical affairs of the Indies are found on pages 248–86.)

2205. **Cuevas, P. M.** *Historia de la iglesia en Mexico.* 5 vols. El Paso, Texas: "Revista catolica," 1928. (Contains bibliographies.)

2206. **Englehardt, Fr. Z.** *Missions and Missionaries of California.* 4 vols. 1st ed. Chicago: Franciscan Herald Press, 1912–15. Vol. I, *Lower California*, new ed., 1929. Vols. II–IV, *Upper California.* (The most exhaustive work on the subject.)

2207. **Helps, A.** *The Life of Las Casas "the Apostle of the Indians."* 2d ed. London: Bell & Daldy, 1868. xxi+292 pages.

2208. **Lea, H. C.** *Inquisition in the Spanish Dependencies.* New York: Macmillan, 1908. vii+xvi+564 pages. (Based on the investigations of José Toribio Medina, the great Chilean historian, and is the best work in English on the subject.)

2209. **Lizana, E.** *Collección de documentos históricos, recopilados del archivo del arzobispado de Santiago.* Vol. I, *Cartos de los obispos al Rey, 1564-1814.* Vol. II, *Cedulario, 1548-1649.* Santiago: Publicados par La Revista católica, Impr. de San José, 1919.

2210. *Recopilacion de Leyes de los reinos de las Indias. . . . .* 5th ed. 4 vols. Madrid, 1841. (Numerous editions. Vol. I, Book I, contains the laws concerning the church, tribunals of the Inquisition, universities, books, etc.)

2211. **Velez, S. D.** *Relaccones del estado con la iglesia en la Antigua America Española.* Buenos Aires: Impr. de la Tribuna, 1871. 11+156 pages. (Excellent though brief.)

THE CHURCH SINCE HISPANIC AMERICAN INDEPENDENCE

2212. **Browning, W. E.** *Roman Christianity in Latin America.* New York: Revell, 1924. 96 pages. (A brief summary of the present status of Roman Catholicism in Hispanic America as seen by a Protestant missionary.)

2213. **Butler, W.** *Mexico in Transition from the Power of Political Romanism to Civil and Religious Liberty.* 4th ed. New York: Methodist Book Concern, 1893. xix+324 pages.

2214. **Callcott, W. H.** *Church and State in Mexico 1822-1857.* Durham, North Carolina: Duke University Press, 1926. 357 pages.

2215. **Delany, F. X., S.J.** *A History of the Catholic Church in Jamaica B.W.I. 1494 to 1929.* New York: Jesuit Mission Press, 1930. xi+292 pages. (Largely devoted to the years since 1792.)

2216. **Detweiler, C. S.** *The Waiting Isles: Baptist Missions in the Caribbean.* Philadelphia: Judson Press, 1930. 167 pages.

2217. **Galarza, E.** *The Roman Catholic Church as a Political Factor in the Political and Social History of Mexico.* Sacramento, California: Capital Press, 1928. 188 pages.

2218. **Inman, S. G.** *Evangelicals at Havana.* New York: Committee on Co-operation in Latin America, 1929. 174 pages. (An account of the Evangelical Congress, at Havana, Cuba.)

2219. **Marma, Paolo.** Translated by J. F. McClinchey, *The Conversion of the Pagan World:* a treatise upon Catholic Foreign Missions. Boston: Society for the propagation of the Faith, 1921. xv+303 pages. (Presents the missionary problem from the standpoint of the Roman Catholic.)

2220. **Sanders, F. K.** (editor). *Christian Work in South America.* 2 vols. New York: Revell, 1925. (Official report of the Congress on Christian Work in South America, at Montevideo, Uruguay, April, 1925. Volume I contains reports on "Unoccupied Fields," "Indians," "Education," "Evangelism," "Social Movements," "Health Ministry." Volume II contains reports on "Church and the Community," "Religious Education," "Literature," "Relations between Foreign and National Workers," "Special Religious Problems," "Co-operation and Unity.")

2221. **Speer, R. E.** *South American Problems.* New York: Student Volunteer Movement, 1912. xi+270 pages.

2222. **Wheeler, W. R., and Browning, W. E.** *Modern Missions of the Spanish Main. Impressions of Protestant Work in Colombia and Venezuela.* Philadelphia: Westminster Press, 1925. xii+334 pages.

2223. **Wheeler, W. R.; McGregor, R. G.; Gillmore, Maria M.; Reid, Ann R.; and Speer, R. E.** *Modern Missions in Chile and Brazil.* Philadelphia: Westminster Press, 1926. xviii+434 pages. (Deals largely with Presbyterian missions.)

CHAPTER IX

CHRISTIANITY IN NEWER FIELDS

The history of Christianity as an indigenous movement in large areas of Africa, in India and China and Japan, and in the islands of the Southern Pacific, has not yet been written. Perhaps the religious situation in these territories is too fluid, and the status of Christianity too tentative, or too inadequately determined, to make practicable the writing of formal church histories. Consequently the student must seek information from less direct sources. This will be found most extensively in the literature of the now highly developed missionary enterprises of the various home churches. As sources for a study of their history this literature is indispensable; but at the same time missionary periodicals, reports of societies, conferences and special commissions may usually be studied with much profit by one primarily concerned to gain an acquaintance with the history of the younger churches in the foreign fields. Their social, cultural, and religious environments can also be known from current books on the history of the non-Christian religions and other works called forth by a lively modern interest in international affairs in general. Nevertheless, the student of Christianity's history in the newer fields of its establishment will still, and may for some time to come, feel the lack of standardized collections of first-hand sources representative of the Christian churches themselves in these newer areas of growth. For this section of Christian history collections like *ANF* (Item 313), *CSEL* (Item 217), *GCS* (Item 321), *MPG* (Item 325), *MPL* (Item 326) and the like, remain to be assembled by future scholars.

GENERAL SOURCES OF INFORMATION
PERIODICALS ON MISSIONS

2224. *Asia.* New York, 627 Lexington Avenue, 1898———. (Journal of the American Asiatic Association; valuable for background. See also *Asiatic Review* [London: Westminster Chambers, 1886———.].)

2225. *Chinese Recorder: Journal of the Christian Movement in China.* Shanghai: Presbyterian Missions Press, 1868———.

2226. *Church Overseas: An Anglican Review of Missionary Thought and Work.* Westminster: Press and Publications Board, 1928———. (Incorporating *East and West* and the *Church Missionary Review.*)

2227. *Church Union—News and Views.* Madras: Christian Literature Society, (July) 1930———.

2228. *Home and Foreign Mission Fields: The Missionary Journal of the Southern Baptist Convention.* Nashville, Tennessee, 1916———.

2229. *Indian Christian Review.* Bombay: Kunkar, 1923———. (Published under the auspices of the Indian Christian Ministers' Union.)

2230. *International Review of Missions.* London: Edinburgh House, 1912———. (Published by the International Missionary Council.) (*IRM*)

2231. *Japan Christian Quarterly.* Tokyo: Federation of Christian Missions, 1926———. (Formerly the *Japan Evangelist.*)

2232. *Journal des Missions Évangéliques.* Paris: Société des Missions Évangéliques, 1914———.

2233. *Journal of the Christian Medical Association of India.* Poona: Scottish Mission Industries, (March) 1926———. (Formerly *Medical Missions of India.*)

2234. *Missionary Review of the World.* New Series. New York: 156 Fifth Avenue, 1888———.

2235. *Missions: A Baptist Monthly Magazine.* Boston: American Baptist Foreign Missionary Society, 1910——.

2236. *Missions Catholiques.* Lyons, 1868——.

2237. *Moslem World.* London: Christian Literature Society, 1911——. (A quarterly review of current events, literature, and thought among Mohammedans and the progress of Christian missions in Moslem lands.)

2238. *National Christian Council Review.* Mysore City: Wesleyan Mission Press, 1924——. (Formerly the *Harvest Field.*)

2239. *Neue allgemeine Missionszeitschrift.* Gütersloh: Bertelsmann, 1924——. (Continuing the *Allgemeine Missionszeitschrift* begun in 1874.)

2240. *New China Review.* Hong Kong: Kelley & Walsh, 1919——.

2241. *Revue de l'Aucam.* Louvain, (November) 1929——. (The official organ of L'Association Universitaire catholique pour l'aide aux Missions. Successor to *Les Carnets de l'Aucam.*)

2242. *Revue d'Histoire des Missions.* Paris: Les Amis des Missions, 52 Avenue de Breteuil, 1924——. (Roman Catholic.) (*RHM*)

2243. *Revue de l'Orient chrétien.* Paris: Picard, 1896——.

2244. *Revue Missionnaire.* Lausanne: Mission Suisse Romande, 1924——. (Swiss Protestant.)

2245. *Spirit of Missions: A Missionary Magazine.* New York: 281 Fourth Avenue, 1886——. (Published monthly by the National Council of the Protestant Episcopal Church in the United States of America.)

2246. *Svensk Missionstidskrift.* Uppsala: Sveriges Kristliga Student-rörelses förlag, 1917——.

2247. *Transvaal and Southern Rhodesia Missions Quarterly Magazine.* London: Church House, 1927——.

2248. *United Church Review.* Edited by E. M. Ewing. Ludhiana, 1930——. (Replacing the *Indian Standard* as the official organ of the United Church of North India.)

2249. *World Dominion: A Quarterly Review of Missionary Progress.* London: Livingstone Press, 1923——.

2250. *Zeitschrift für Missionskunde und Religionswissenschaft.* Berlin, 1886——. (Organ of the Allgemeiner evangelisch-protestantischer Missionsverein.)

2251. *Zeitschrift für Missionswissenschaft und Religionswissenschaft.* Münster: Aschendorff, 1911——. (Roman Catholic.)

ATLASES AND BIBLIOGRAPHIES

2252. *Bibliography for Missionary Students.* Edited by H. U. W. Stanton. London: Edinburgh House, 1913. 141 pages.

2253. *Catholic World Atlas.* New and revised edition of *Atlas Hierarchicus.* New York: Society for the Propagation of Faith, 1930. 189 pages and 39 maps.

2254. **Clayton, G. A.** *A Classified Index to the Chinese Literature of the Protestant Churches in China.* Hankow: China Christian Publishers' Association, 1918. xiii+260 pages.

2255. *A List of Books on Education: For Missionaries Engaged in Educational Work.* Supplementary List No. 3. New York: Committee of Reference and Counsel, 1929. 130 pages.

2256. **Murray, J. L.** *Selected Bibliography of Missionary Literature.* New York: Student Volunteer Movement, 1920. 58 pages.

2257. **Probsthain, A.** *Encyclopedia of Books on China.* London: Probsthain, 1927. 283 pages. (Over 4,000 titles, classified in forty-three sections, with annotations; includes books on Tibet, Indo-China, Siam, Korea, and Formosa; an indispensable aid.)

2258. **Rowling, F., and Wilson, C. E.** *Bibliography of African Christian Literature.* London: 2 Eaton Gate, 1923. xvi+135 pages. (Conference of missionary societies of Great Britain and Ireland.)

2259. **Streit, R.** *Bibliotheca missionum.* Münster: Aschendorff, 1916——. (Vol. IV, *Asiatische Missionsliteratur 1245–1599.* Aachen: Missionsdruckerei, 1928. xxiv+626 pages.)

2260. *Ten Years' Selected International Missionary Bibliography, 1912–1922.* IRM (Item 2230), XI (1922), 143–92.

2261. **Work, M. N.** *Bibliography of the Negro in Africa and America.* New York: Wilson, 1928. xxii+698 pages. (Upward of 17,000 titles covering publications in various languages before 1928.)

2262. *World Missionary Atlas.* Edited by H. P. Beach and C. H. Fahs. New York: Institute of Social and Religious Research, 1925. 251 pages and 29 double plates of maps. (Indispensable for the serious student; a vast storehouse of tabulated statistics.)

HISTORIES OF MISSIONS AND MISSIONARIES (SEE ITEMS 295–301, 365, 543, 615–17, 623–29, 947–54, 1222, 1259)

2263. **Barnes, L. C.** *Two Thousand Years of Missions before Carey.* Chicago: Christian Culture Press, 1900. xvii+504 pages.

2264. **Bishop, J. G.** *The Christians and the Great Commission: A Brief History of the Home and Foreign Missionary Work of the Christian Church.* Dayton, Ohio: Christian Publishing Association, 1914. 303 pages.

2265. **Broomhall, M.** *Robert Morrison: A Master-Builder.* London: Student Christian Movement, 1927. xvi+238 pages. (In the "Modern Series of Missionary Biographies"; earlier volumes in the series are on Henry Martyn, Alexander Duff, F. Coillard, Robert Moffat, William Carey, and George Grenfell.)

2266. **Burckhardt, G. E., and Grundmann, R.** *Les missions évangéliques depuis leurs origines jusqu'à nos jours.* 4 vols. Laussane: Bridel, 1884–87. (A translation and revision of G. E. Burkhardt's *Kleine Missions-Bibliothek.* 4 vols. Beilefeld: Velhagen, 1858–62.)

2267. **Burt, E. W.** *Fifty Years in China; The Story of the Baptist Mission in Shantung, Shansi and Shensi, 1875–1925.* London: Carey Press, 1925. 127 pages.

2268. **Campbell, R. J.** *Livingstone.* London: Benn, 1929. 370 pages.

2269. **Carey, S. P.** *William Carey.* London: Hodder & Stoughton, 1923. xvi+428 pages.

2270. **Clough, J. E.** *Social Christianity in the Orient: The Story of a Man, a Mission, and a Movement.* New York: Macmillan, 1914. xiv+409 pages. (Autobiography of a missionary among the Telugus.)

2271. *A Crusader in Kashmir: Being the Life of Dr. Arthur Neve, with an Account of the Medical Missionary Work of Two Brothers and Its Later Development down to the Present Day.* London: Seeley, Service, 1928. 218 pages.

2272. **Debenham, M. H.** *Knights of Healing: A Study Book on Some of the Principles and Methods of Medical Mission Work.* London: Society for Propagation of the Gospel, 1922. 63 pages.

2273. *Die deutsche evangelische ärtztliche Mission.* Nach dem Stande des Jahres 1928. Stuttgart: Evangelischer Missionsverlag, 1928. 243 pages.

2274. **Drach, G.** (editor). *Our Church Abroad: The Foreign Missions of the Lutheran Church in America.* Philadelphia: United Lutheran Publication House, 1926. 277 pages.

2275. *Fifty Years of Foreign Missions of the Reformed Church in the United States, 1877–1927.* Compiled by a committee. Philadelphia: Board of Foreign Missions, 1927. viii+244 pages.

2276. **Glover, R. H.** *The Progress of World-Wide Missions.* New York: Doran, 1924. 416 pages. (Survey of Protestant missionary history for the last century and a half.)

2277. **Greene, E. B.** *A New-Englandér in Japan: Daniel Crosby Green.* Boston: Houghton Mifflin, 1927. xiii+374 pages.

2278. **Hayes, E.** *David Jones, Dauntless Pioneer: An Epic Story of Heroic Endeavor in Madagascar.* London: Livingstone Press, 1923. 127 pages.

2279. **Henrion, Le baron.** *Histoire générale des missions catholiques depuis le XIIIᵉ siècle jusqu'à nos jours.* 2 vols. Paris: Migne, 1846–47.

2280. **Hutton, J. E.** *A History of Moravian Missions.* London: Moravian Publication Office, 1923. 550 pages.

2281. **James, A. T. S.** *Twenty-five Years of the London Missionary Society 1895–1920.* London: London Missionary Society, 1923. 176 pages. (For the earlier period see Item 1549; see also Item 2322.)

2282. **Keyte, J. C.** *Andrew Young of Shensi.* London: Carey Press, 1924. xiii+314 pages.

2283. *Kirk on the Zambesi: A Chapter of African History.* Oxford: Clarendon Press, 1928. viii+286 pages.

2284. **Mason, A. De W., and Barny, F. J.** *History of the Arabian Mission.* New York: Board of Foreign Missions, Reformed

Church in America, 1926. 256 pages. (Statistics to 1924; good Bibliography.)

2285. **McLean, A.** *History of the Foreign Christian Missionary Society.* New York: Revell, 1919. 444 pages.

2286. *Missiones catholicae.* Vatican City: Vatican Press, 1930. xii + 534 pages.

2287. *Les missions catholiques et l'œuvre de civilisation: Conférences données à l'Institut Catholique de Paris, 1927-28.* Paris: Bloud, 1929. 252 pages.

2288. "Les missions catholiques françaises en 1900 et 1928," *RHM* (Item 2242), IV (1928), 481–505.

2289. **Moorshead, R. F.** *The Way of the Doctor: A Study in Medical Missions.* London: Carey Press, 1926. xiii+242 pages.

2290. **Neely, T. B.** *The Methodist Episcopal Church and Its Foreign Missions.* New York: Methodist Book Concern, 1923. 332 pages.

2291. *Nos champs de mission.* 3d ed. Société des Missions Évangéliques, 1922. xxxvi+181 pages. (Bibliography.)

2292. **Paton, J.** (editor). *John G. Paton, D.D., Missionary to the New Hebrides: An Autobiography.* London: Hodder & Stoughton, 1920. 477 pages.

2293. **Paton, W.** *Alexander Duff: Pioneer of Missionary Education.* London: Student Christian Movement, 1923. 240 pages.

2294. *Petite histoire des missions chrétiennes.* Par un laïque. Paris: Société des Missions Évangéliques, 1923. 288 pages.

2295. **Richter, J.** *Geschichte der Berliner Missionsgesellschaft 1824–1924.* Berlin: Missionsgesellschaft, 1924. 740 pages.

2296. **Richter, P.** *Bannerträger des Evangeliums in der Heidenwelt.* 4 (2) vols. Stuttgart: Steinkopf, 1905–8. (Ziegenbalg, Zinzendorf, Egede, Zeisberger, Carey, J. Williams, Grossner, Livingstone, Mackay, Crowther, Posselt, Ziemann, Ramabai, Schwartz, Judson, Hebich, R. Moffat, Coillard, Morrison, Paton, A. Gardiner, J. Evans, Hahn, Imad ed din, Chalmers, Riedel, and others.)

2297. **Schlunk, M.** *Die Weltmission des Christentums: Ein Gang durch neunzehn Jahrhunderte.* Hamburg: Rauhes Haus, 1925. 250 pages.

2298. **Schmidlin, J.** *Das gegenwärtige Heidenapostolat im fernen Osten.* Vol. I, *Ostasien* (Japan, China). Vol. II, *Die Indischen Missionen.* Münster: Aschendorff, 1929–30. (192 and 160 pages; Roman Catholic.)

2299. **Schurhammer, G.** *St. Francis Xavier: The Apostle of India and Japan.* Adapted from the German published in 1926. St. Louis, Missouri: Herder, 1928. viii+321 pages. (A brief reliable account by a Jesuit.)

2300. **Shelton, Flora B.** *Shelton of Tibet.* New York: Doran, 1923. xv+319 pages.

2301. *Un siècle en Afrique et en Océanie, 1822–1922: Revue de nos champs de mission en Afrique et en Océanie.* Paris: Société des Missions Évangéliques, 1923. 182 pages. (Lessouto, Zambèze, Senegal, Gabon, Cameroun, Tahiti, Nouvelle Calédonie.)

2302. **Soothill, W. E.** *Timothy Richard of China.* London: Seely, Service, 1924. 330 pages.

2303. **Streit, R.** *Die Weltmission der katholischen Kirche.* Hünfeld: Oblaten Verlag, 1928. xv+200 pages. (Already published in Italian, Spanish, and French.)

REPORTS OF SOCIETIES, COMMISSIONS, CONFERENCES, ETC.

2304. *American Baptist Foreign Missionary Society, 1930.* The one hundred and sixteenth annual report. New York: Foreign Mission Headquarters, 152 Madison Avenue, 1930. 313 pages.

2305. *American Bible Society.* The one hundred and fourteenth annual report. New York: American Bible Society, 1930. 399 pages.

2306. *American Missionary Association.* The eighty-second annual report. New York: American Missionary Association, 287 Fourth Avenue, 1928. 80 pages.

2307. *Annual Report of the Board of Foreign Missions of the Presbyterian Church in the United States of America.* Ninety-first report in 1928. New York: Presbyterian Building, 1928. xxvii+344 pages.

2308. **Arens, B.** *Die katholischen Missionsvereine.* Freiburg: Herder, 1922. 363 pages.

2309. *British and Foreign Bible Society, for the Year Ending 1929.* The one hundred and twenty-fifth report. London: Bible House, 1929. xxiv+274+99 pages.

2310. *Call to West and East: the Sixth and Final Report of the World Call Series.* London: Church House, Westminster, 1928. xii+182 pages. (Earlier volumes relate to Africa, India, the Moslem World, the Far East, and Our Own People Overseas; the present volume deals with the Jewish world, the West Indies, and the southern Pacific Islands.)

2311. *The Chinese Church as Revealed in the National Christian Conference Held in Shanghai, 1922.* xi+726 pages. (A report rich in information but inadequately edited.)

2312. *The Christian Occupation of Africa: The Proceedings of a Conference of Mission Boards Engaged in Work in the Continent of Africa, Held in New York City, November 1917.* New York: Foreign Missions Conference, 1917. 185 pages.

2313. *The Christian Occupation of China: A Report of the General Missionary Survey Made by the Committee on Survey and Occupation of the China Continuation Committee.* Shanghai: Missions Book Co., 1922.

2314. *Congo Missionary Conference, 1924: A Report on the Ninth "Conférence générale des missionnaires protestants du Congo."* Leopoldville-Est, Congo Belge: Congo Protestant Council, 1925.

2315. *Directory of Christian Missions in India, Burma and Ceylon, 1924–1925.* Compiled by A. McLeish. 14th ed. Ajmer: Scottish Mission Industries, 1924. xxix+394 pages.

2316. *Foreign Missions Conference in North America.* Report of the 37th annual meeting in 1930. Edited by L. B. Moss. New York: Foreign Missions Conference, 1930. viii+484 pages.

2317. **Freytag, W.** *Die deutsche evangelische Heidenmission. Jahrbuch 1929 der vereinigten deutschen Missionskonferenzen.* Berlin: Missions-Gesellschaft, 1929. 112 pages.

2318. **Gerber, W.** *Lutherisches Missions-Jahrbuch für das Jahr 1930.* Leipzig: Wallmann, 1930. 171 pages. (Continuing, since 1922, the *Jahrbuch der sächischen Missionskonferenz.*)

2319. *India in Conflict: Being Impressions of some Members of the Mission of Help.* London: Society for Promoting Christian Knowledge, 1923. ix+179 pages.

2320. *Jerusalem Meeting of the International Missionary Conference,* March 24—April 8, 1928. 8 vols. New York: International Missionary Council, 419 Fourth Avenue, 1928.

2321. *Katholische missionsärztliche Fürsorge: Jahrbuch 1928 des katholischen Vereins des missionsärztlichen Instituts.* 5. Jahrg. Aachen: Missionsdruckerei, 1928. 133 pages.

2322. *London Missionary Society: A Critical Review of Its Work Abroad.* Report of the Survey Committee, 1930. London: London Missionary Society, 1930. 76 pages. (See Item 2281.)

2323. **MacBeath, J.** *The Conquest of Kingdoms: The Story of the Baptist Missionary Society.* London: Carey Press, 1924. 102 pages.

2324. **Mott, J. R.** *The Continuation Committee Conferences in Asia, 1912–13.* New York: Foreign Missions Conference, 1913. 488 pages.

2325. *The National Christian Council: A Five Years' Review, 1922–1927.* Shanghai: 23 Yuen Ming Yuen Road, 1927. 424 pages.

2326. *Ostasien-Jahrbuch 1929.* Edited by J. Witte. Berlin: Allgemeiner evangelischer protestantischer Missionsverein, 1929. 120 pages. (See also the issues for previous years.)

2327. *Report on India and Persia of the Deputation Sent by the Board of Foreign Missions of the Presbyterian Church in the United States of America To Visit These Fields in 1921–22.* Presented by R. E. Speer and R. Carter. New York: Board of Foreign Missions of the Presbyterian Church in the United States of America, 1922. 694 pages.

2328. *Report of the Tenth Quadrennial Convention of the Student Volunteer Movement for Foreign Missions.* Edited by G. Poteat. New York: Student Volunteer Movement, 1928. xii+350 pages. (And earlier volumes.)

2329. *Stockholm Conference, 1925.* The official report of the Universal Christian Conference on Life and Work held in Stockholm, August 19–30, 1925. Edited by G. K. A. Bell. London: Oxford University Press, 1926. 791 pages.

2330. *World Missionary Conference, Edinburgh, 1910.* 9 volumes, containing reports of various commissions. New York: Revell, 1910.

GENERAL HISTORICAL AND SOCIAL BACKGROUND

2331. **Andrews, C. F.** *Mahatma Gandhi's Ideas.* London: Allen & Unwin, 1929. 382 pages.

2332. **Anstey, Vera.** *The Economic Development of India.* London: Longmans, 1930. x+581 pages.

2333. **Brown, A. J.** *Japan in the World of Today.* New York: Revell, 1928. 322 pages.

2334. **Burns, A. C.** *History of Nigeria.* London: Allen & Unwin, 1929. 360 pages.

2335. *The Cambridge History of India.* 6 vols. Vol. V, *British India, 1497–1858.* Edited by H. H. Dodwell. Cambridge: University Press, 1929. xxii+683 pages. (Only three volumes have yet appeared.)

2336. **Clement, E. W.** *A Short History of Japan.* New rev. ed. London: Kegan Paul, 1926. 212 pages.

2337. **Codrington, H. W.** *A Short History of Ceylon.* London: Macmillan, 1927. xxi+202 pages. (Up to the year 1914.)

2338. **Forbes, W. C.** *The Philippine Islands.* 2 vols. Boston: Houghton Mifflin, 1929. (From the beginning of the American occupation.)

2339. **Gait, E.** *History of Assam.* New ed. Calcutta: Thacker, 1927. xv+388 pages.

2340. **Grousset, R.** *Histoire de l'extrême orient.* 2 vols. Paris: Geuthner, 1929. (India, China, Tibet, Indo-China, Sumatra, Java. Japan to come in another volume; also illustrations and a 60-page Bibliography.)

2341. **Harada, S.** *Labor Conditions in Japan.* New York: Columbia University Press, 1928. 293 pages.

2342. **Harris, N. D.** *Europe and the East.* Boston: Houghton Mifflin, 1926. xvi+677 pages.

2343. **Holcombe, A. N.** *The Chinese Revolution: A Phase in the Regeneration of a World Power.* Cambridge: Harvard University Press, 1930. xiv+400 pages.

2344. **Ireland, A.** *The New Korea.* New York: Dutton, 1926. xiv +352 pages.

2345. **Hoskins, H. L.** *European Imperialism in Africa.* New York: Holt, 1930. x+118 pages.

2346. **Leang-li, T'Ang.** *The Inner History of the Chinese Revolution.* London: Routledge, 1930. 392 pages.

2347. **Mayhew, A..** *Christianity and the Government of India.* London: Faber & Gwyer, 1929. xi+260 pages. (Bibliography, pp. 252-55.)

2348. **Morse, H. B., and MacNair, H. F.** *Far Eastern International Relations.* Shanghai: Commercial Press, 1928. xv+1128 pages.

2349. **Ogilvie, J. N.** *Our Empire's Debt to Missions: The Duff Missionary Lecture, 1923.* London: Houghton Mifflin, 1924. xii+276 pages.

2350. *Problems of the Pacific, 1929.* Edited by J. B. Condliffe. Chicago: University of Chicago Press, 1930. xv+697 pages. (Also earlier volumes reporting the proceedings of the Conference of the Institute of Pacific Relations.)

2351. **Scott, J. G.** *Burma from the Earliest Times to the Present Day.* London: Fisher Unwin, 1924. xii+372 pages.

2352. **Thompson, E.** *The Reconstruction of India.* London: Faber & Faber, 1930. 320 pages.

2353. **Toynbee, A. J.** *Survey of International Affairs, 1927.* London: Oxford University Press, 1929. 613 pages. (A volume a year has been appearing, the first being the survey for the year 1925, published in 1927.)

2354. **Williams, E. T.** *A Short History of China.* New York: Harper, 1929. xviii+670 pages.

2355. **Young, C. W.** *The International Relations of Manchuria.* Chicago: University of Chicago Press, 1929. xxx+307 pages.

THE NON-CHRISTIAN RELIGIONS

GENERAL WORKS (SEE ITEMS 117, 120, 127, 133, 136, 425-41)

2356. **Allier, R.** *The Mind of the Savage.* Translated from French. London: Bell, 1929. xiv+301 pages.

2357. *Archiv für Religionswissenschaft.* Leipzig: Teubner, 1898——.

2358. **Bertholet, A., and Lehmann, E.** *Lehrbuch der Religionsgeschichte.* 2 vols. Tübingen: Mohr, 1925.

2359. *Bilderatlas zur Religionsgeschichte.* Edited by H. Haas. Leipzig: Deichert, 1923——. (In progress; excellent illustrative reproductions, with explanatory comments, by various authors.) (*BAR*)

2360. **Cave, S.** *An Introduction to the Study of Some Living Religions of the East.* London: Duckworth, 1921. 275 pages.

2361. **Hare, W. L.** *Mysticism of East and West: Studies in Mystical and Moral Philosophy.* London: Cape, 1923. 356 pages.

2362. —— (editor). *Religions of the Empire.* A conference on "Some Living Religions within the Empire." Held at the Imperial Institute, London, September 22—October 3, 1924, under the auspices of the School of Oriental Studies (University of London) and the Sociological Society. New York: Macmillan, 1925. 519 pages.

2363. **Haydon, A. E.** "Twenty-five Years of History of Religions," *JR* (Item 150), VI (1926), 17–40.

2364. **Hopkins, E. W.** *The History of Religions.* New York: Macmillan, 1918. 624 pages. (Bibliography after each of the twenty-four chapters). Also *Origin and Evolution of Religion.* New Haven: Yale University Press, 1924. 370 pages.

2365. **Huby, J., and Others.** *Christus: Manuel d'histoire des religions.* Paris: Beauchesne, 1913. xx+1036 pages. (Represents standard Roman Catholic scholarship; bibliographies at close of each chapter.)

2366. **Lévy-Bruhl, L.** *How Natives Think.* Translated from French. London: Allen & Unwin, 1926. 392 pages.

2367. **Lowie, R. H.** *Primitive Religion.* New York: Boni & Liveright, 1924. 346 pages. Also *Primitive Society.* Same publisher, 1920. viii+463 pages.

2368. **Moore, G. F.** *History of Religions.* 2 vols. New York: Scribner's, 1913–19. Also *The Birth and Growth of Religion.* Same publisher, 1924. viii+178 pages.

2369. *Mythology of All Races.* Edited by L. H. Gray. Boston: Marshall Jones, 1916——. (Thirteen volumes to 1930.)

2370. *Revue de l'histoire des religions.* Paris: Leroux, 1880——.

2371. **Robinson, T. H.** *An Outline Introduction to the History of Religions.* London: Oxford University Press, 1926. ix+ 244 pages.

2372. *Sacred Books of the East.* Edited by F. Max Müller. 50 vols., including Index. Oxford: Clarendon Press, 1879–1910. (English translations by various scholars.)

2373. **Schmidt, M.** *The Primitive Races of Mankind: A Study in Ethnology.* Translated from German. London: Harrap, 1926. 360 pages.

2374. *Textbuch zur Religionsgeschichte.* Edited by E. Lehmann and H. Haas. 2d ed. Leipzig: Deichert, 1922. 396 pages.

ISLAM

2375. **Bell, R.** *The Origin of Islam in Its Christian Environment.* London: Macmillan, 1926. 232 pages.

2376. **Broomhall, M.** *Islam in China: A Neglected Problem.* London: Morgan & Scott, 1920. xx+332 pages.

2377. *Christian Literature in Moslem Lands: A Study of the Activities of the Moslem and Christian Press in All Mohammedan Countries.* Prepared by a committee. New York: Doran, 1923. xii+306 pages.

2378. **Dale, G.** *Islam and Africa: An Introduction to the Study of Islam for African Christians.* London: Society for Promoting Christian Knowledge, 1925. viii+141 pages.

2379. *Encyclopedia of Islam: A Dictionary of the Geography, Ethnography and Biography of the Muhammadan Peoples.* Edited by M. T. Houtsma and others. London: Luzac, 1916——. (To "Tripoli" in 1930.)

2380. *The Expansion of Islam: An Arab Religion in the Non-Arab World.* Preface by D. S. Margoliouth. London: Edinburgh House Press, 1928. xvi+304 pages.

2381. **Hurgronje, C. N.** *Mohammedanism: Lectures on Its Origin, Its Religious and Political Growth and Its Present State.* New York: Putnam's, 1916. xi+184 pages.

2382. **Lammens, H.** *Islam: Beliefs and Institutions.* Translated from French. London: Methuen, 1929. 256 pages.

2383. *The Moslem World of Today.* Edited by J. R. Mott. London: Hodder & Stoughton, 1925. xv+420 pages.

2384. **Sailer, T. H. P.** *The Moslem Faces the Future: An Introduction to the Study of the Moslem World.* New York: Missionary Education Movement, 1926. x+254 pages. (An introductory book; also good bibliography.)

2385. **Titus, M. T.** *Indian Islam: A Religious History of Islam in India.* London: Oxford University Press, 1930. xviii+290 pages.

2386. **Vaux, Carra de.** *Les penseurs de l'Islam.* 5 vols. Paris: Geuthner, 1921–26.

2387. *Die Welt des Islams: Zeitschrift der deutschen Gesellschaft für Islamkunde.* Berlin: Reimer, 1923——.

BUDDHISM

2388. **Aufhauser, J. B.** *Christentum und Buddhismus im Ringen um Fernasien.* Bonn: Schröder, 1922. 401 pages.

2389. **Carpenter, J. E.** *Buddhism and Christianity: A Contrast and a Parallel.* London: Hodder & Stoughton, 1923. 319 pages.

2390. **Davids, Caroline A.** (Mrs. Rhys). *Buddhism: A Study of the Buddhist Norm.* New York: Holt, 1912. 255 pages.

2391. *The Eastern Buddhist.* Edited by D. T. Suzuki. Kyoto: Eastern Buddhist Society, 1921——.

2392. **Hamilton, C. H.** *Buddhism in India, Ceylon, China and Japan: A Reading Guide.* Chicago: University of Chicago Press, 1931. viii+107 pages. (Bibliography, pp. 100–107.)

2393. **McGovern, W. M.** *An Introduction to Mahāyāna Buddhism.* London: Kegan Paul, 1922. iv+233 pages.

2394. **Pratt, J. B.** *The Pilgrimage of Buddhism and a Buddhist Pilgrimage.* New York: Macmillan, 1928. xii+758 pages. (Thoughtful observations made by an American professor of philosophy during an extended visit to the principal centers of present-day Buddhism.)

2395. **Saunders, K. J.** *Epochs in Buddhist History.* ("Haskell Lectures," 1921.) Chicago: University of Chicago Press, 1924. xix+243 pages.

CHRISTIANITY AND ITS RIVALS IN
VARIOUS COUNTRIES

Problems and Outlook

2396. **Addison, J. T.** *Our Expanding Church.* New York: National Council of the Protestant Episcopal Church, 1930. ix+117 pages.

2397. **Allen, R.** *The Spontaneous Expansion of the Church and the Causes Which Hinder It.* London: World Dominion Press, 1927. xxvii+220 pages.

2398. **Brown, A. J.** *Rising Churches in Non-Christian Lands.* New York: Missionary Education Movement, 1915. xiii+236 pages.

2399. **Clark, E. T.** *The Church and the World Parish.* Nashville, Tennessee: Board of Missions, Methodist Episcopal Church (South), 1929. 315 pages.

2400. *Ideals and Policies for the Development of the Younger Churches: Some Official Statements.* Vol. III, No. 2, of "Jerusalem Meeting" (Item 2320).

2401. **McAfee, C. B.** *Changing Foreign Missions: A Revaluation of the Church's Greatest Enterprise.* New York: Revell, 1927. 288 pages.

2402. **McConnell, F. J.** *Human Needs and World Christianity.* New York: Friendship Press, 1929. viii+231 pages.

2403. **Mott, J. R.** *The Present World Situation.* New York: Student Volunteer Movement, 1915. 259 pages.

Africa and the Near East (See Items 2247, 2258, 2261, 2301, 2312, 2314, 2334, 2378)

2404. **Buell, R.** *The Native Problem in Africa.* 2 vols. New York: Macmillan, 1928.

2405. *Christianity and the Natives of South Africa.* Edited by J. D. Taylor. London: Edinburgh House Press, 1928. xii+503 pages. (The first yearbook of South African missions.)

2406. **Franck, H. A.** *The Fringe of the Moslem World.* New York: Century, 1928. xiv+426 pages. (Describes the attitude of the Near East toward the Christian world.)

2407. **Fullerton, W. Y.** *The Christ of the Congo River.* London: Carey Press, 1928. 216 pages. (The story of the Baptist Missionary Society in the Congo for the previous fifty years.)

2408. **Gollancz, H.** *Settlement of the Order of Carmelites in Mesopotamia* (*Bassora*). London: Oxford University Press, 1927.

2409. **Hasluck, F. W.** *Christianity and Islam under the Sultans.* Edited by Margaret M. Hasluck. 2 vols. London: Oxford University Press, 1929.

2410. "Special Double Africa Number," *IRM* (Item 2230), XV (July, 1926), 323–596.

2411. **Lea, A.** *The Native Separatist Church Movement in South Africa.* Johannesburg: Juta, 1927. 84 pages.

2412. *Light and Darkness in East Africa.* London: World Dominion Press, 1927. 206 pages. (A missionary survey of Uganda, Anglo-Egyptian Sudan, Abyssinia, Eritrea and the Three Somalilands.)

2413. **Maxwell, J. L.** *Nigeria: The Land, the People and Christian Progress.* London: World Dominion Press, 1927. 164 pages.

2414. **Plessis, J. du.** *Evangelization of Pagan Africa.* Cape Town, Africa: Juta, 1930. xii+408 pages.

2415. **Richter, J.** *Geschichte der evangelischen Mission in Afrika.* Gütersloh: Bertelsmann, 1912. 813 pages.

2416. **Schweitzer, A.** *On the Edge of the Primeval Forest. Experiences and Observations of a Doctor in Equatorial Africa.* London: Black, 1922. 180 pages.

2417. **Sibree, J.** *Fifty Years in Madagascar: Personal Experiences of Mission Life and Work.* London: Allen & Unwin, 1924. 359 pages. (By a representative of the London Missionary Society.)

2418. **Smith, E. W.** *The Christian Mission in Africa.* Study based on the Work of the International Conference at Le Zoute, Belgium, September 14–21, 1926. New York: 25 Madison Avenue, 1926. 200 pages.

2419. *Ten Years' Review of Missionary Work in Madagascar, 1911–20.* Antananarivo: London Missionary Society Press, 1921. vii+180 pages.

2420. **Walker, F. D.** *The Romance of the Black River: The Story of the Nigeria Mission.* London: Church Missionary Society, 1930. xvi+267 pages.

2421. **Whiteside, J.** *History of the Wesleyan Methodist Church of South Africa.* London: Stock, 1906. viii+479 pages.

INDIA—INCLUDING CEYLON, BURMA, SIAM (SEE ITEMS 2229, 2233, 2248, 2315, 2327, 2331, 2332, 2335, 2337, 2339, 2347, 2351 F., 2385)

2422. **Bowman, A. H.** *Christian Thought and Hindu Philosophy.* 2 vols. London: Religious Tract Society, 1917.

2423. **Cave, S.** *Redemption, Hindu and Christian.* London: Oxford University Press, 1919. xii+263 pages.

2424. **Chatterton, E.** *A History of the Church of England in India since the Early Days of the East India Company.* London: Society for Promoting Christian Knowledge, 1924. xxiv+ 353 pages. (With "Books of Reference" at the beginning of each chapter.)

2425. "Church Union in South India," *IRM* (Item 2230), XIX (1930), 453–56. (A review of eleven recent books.)

2426. "Church Union in South India," *RC* (Item 153), VII (1930), 1–123.

2427. **Fleming, D. J.** *Devolution in Missionary Education.* New York: Revell, 1916. 310 pages. (Based on the history of five American missionary societies in India; Bibliography on pages 281–306.)

2428. **Heiler, F.** *The Gospel of Sādhu Sundar Singh: An Apostle of the East and of the West.* Translated from German. London: Allen & Unwin, 1927. 277 pages.

2429. **Hopkins, E. W.** *Ethics of India.* New Haven: Yale University Press, 1924. xiv+265 pages.

2430. **Macnicol, Nicol.** *India in the Dark Wood.* London: Edinburgh House Press, 1930. 224 pages. (Bibliography, pages 215–18.)

2431. **McGilvary, D.** *A Half Century among the Siamese and the Lāo: An Autobiography.* New York: Revell, 1912. 435 pages.

2432. **McKenzie, J.** (editor). *The Christian Task in India.* By various writers. London: Macmillan, 1929. xvii+297 pages.

2433. **McLeish, A.** *Christian Progress in Burma.* London: World Dominion Press, 1929. 100 pages.

2434. **Mooy, I. J.** *Bouwstoffen voor de Geschiedenis der protes tantsche Kerk in Nederlandsch-Indië.* The Hague: Nijhoff, 1927. 839 pages.

2435. **Otto, R.** *India's Religion of Grace and Christianity Compared.* Translated from German. London: Student Christian Movement, 1930. 144 pages.

2436. **Parekh, M. C.** *The Brahmo Samaj: A Short History.* Rajkot: Oriental Christ House, 1929. xi+287 pages.

2437. **Pratt, J. B.** *India and Its Faiths: A Traveller's Record.* Boston: Houghton Mifflin, 1915. xv+482 pages.

2438. *Proposed Scheme of Union.* Prepared by the Joint Committee of the Church of India, Burma and Ceylon, The South India United Church and The South India Provincial Synod of the Wesleyan Methodist Church. London: Society for Promoting Christian Knowledge, 1929. xiii+59 pages.

2439. **Purser, W. C. B.** *Christian Missions in Burma.* London: Society for the Propagation of the Gospel, 1911. 246 pages.

2440. **Richter, J.** *Indische Missionsgeschichte.* 2d ed. Gütersloh: Bertelsmann, 1924. 570 pages.

2441. **Schermerhorn, W. D.** "Syncretism in the Early Christian Period and in Present-Day India," *JR* (Item 150), IV (1924), 464–91.

2442. **Simpson, W. J. Sparrow.** *South Indian Schemes.* London: Society for Promoting Christian Knowledge, 1930. ix+187 pages.

2443. *Survey of Medical Missions in India.* Prepared by the Christian Medical Association in conjunction with the National Christian Council. Poona: Staveley Road, 1929. 128 pages.

2444. **Thoburn, J. M.** *The Christian Conquest of India.* Boston: American Baptist Missionary Union, 1906. 291 pages. (Prepared for missions study courses; Bibliography, pages 255–64.)

2445. **Vickland, Ellen E.** *With Christ in Assam.* Philadelphia: Judson Press, 1926. 129 pages. (An account of American Baptist missionary work.)

2446. **Waller, E. H. M.** *Church Union in South India: The Story of the Negotiations.* London: Society for Promoting Christian Knowledge, 1929. 96 pages.

CHINA AND ADJACENT TERRITORIES (SEE ITEMS 2225, 2240, 2254, 2257, 2267, 2311, 2313, 2343, 2354 F., 2376)

2447. **Broomhall, M.** (editor). *The Chinese Empire: A General and Missionary Survey.* London: Morgan & Scott, 1907. (A wide survey by writers having first-hand acquaintance with various sections of the field.)

2448. *A Century of Protestant Missions in China (1807–1907): Being the Centenary Conference Historical Volume.* Edited by D. MacGillivray. Shanghai: Presbyterian Mission Press, 1907. vii+677+xl+52 pages.

2449. *China Christian Year Book, 1929.* Shanghai: Christian Literature Society, 1929. xiv+563 pages. (Sixteenth issue; called *China Missions Year Book* until 1926.)

2450. *Christian Education in China.* The Report of the Educational Commission of 1921–22, conducted by E. D. Burton. Shanghai: Commercial Press, 1922. iv+390 pages.

2451. **Dvořak, R.** *Chinas Religionen.* 2 vols. Münster: Aschendorff, 1895–1903. (The first volume deals with Confucius and the second with Lao-tse.)

2452. **Elia, P. M. d'.** *Catholic Native Episcopacy in China. An Outline of the Formation and Growth of the Chinese Catholic Clergy, 1300–1926.* Shanghai: T'usewei Press, 1927. v+107 pages.

2453. **Ellam, J. R.** *The Religion of Tibet: A Study of Lamaism.* ("Wisdom of the East Series.") London: Murray, 1927. 127 pages.

2454. **Groot, J. J. M. de.** *Religion in China. Universism: a Key to the Study of Taoism and Confucianism.* New York: Putnam's, 1912. xv+327 pages.

2455. **Hodous, L.** "The Chinese Church of the Five Religions," *J R* (Item 150), IV (1924), 71–76. Also "The Anti-Christian Movement in China," *ibid.*, X (1930), 487–94.

2456. **Latourette, K. S.** *A History of Christian Missions in China.* New York: Macmillan, 1929. xii+930 pages. (The standard work; extensive, but unclassified; Bibliography, pages 845–99.)

2457. **Lew, T. T., and Others.** *China Today through Christian Eyes.* London: Student Christian Movement, 1922. 144 pages. Also second series, same publisher, viii+151 pages.

2458. **MacKenzie, A. R.** *Church and Missions in Manchuria.* London: World Dominion Press, 1928. 64 pages.

2459. **McGovern, W. M.** *An Introduction to Mahāyāna Buddhism, with Special Reference to Chinese and Japanese Phases.* London: Kegan Paul, 1921. v+233 pages.

2460. **Moule, A. C.** *Christians in China before the Year 1550.* London: Society for Promoting Christian Knowledge, 1920. xvi+293 pages.

2461. **Oehler, W.** *China und die christliche Mission in Geschichte und Gegenwart.* Stuttgart: Evangelischer Missionsverlag, 1925. 282 pages.

2462. **Porter, L. C.** *China's Challenge to Christianity.* New York: Missionary Education Movement, 1924. vii+248 pages.

2463. **Rawlinson, F.** *Naturalization of Christianity in China: A Study of the Relation of Chinese Idealism and Life.* Shanghai: Presbyterian Mission Press, 1927. viii+216 pages.

2464. **Richardson, D. W.** *The Church in China.* Richmond, Virginia: Presbyterian Committee of Publication, 1929. 224 pages. (Reliable popular treatment.)

2465. **Richter, J.** *Das Werden der christlichen Kirche in China.* ("Allgemeine evangelische Missionsgeschichte," Vol. IV.) Gütersloh: Bertelsmann, 1928. xvi+584 pages.

2466. **Wieger, L.** *A History of the Religious Beliefs and Philosophical Opinions in China.* Translated from the 2d French edition of 1923. Shanghai: Hsien-hsien Press, 1927. 774 pages.

JAPAN—INCLUDING KOREA AND FORMOSA (SEE ITEMS
2231, 2333, 2336, 2341, 2344, 2346)

2467. **Anesaki, M.** *History of Japanese Religion.* London: Kegan Paul, 1930. 423 pages.

2468. ———. *Nichiren, the Buddhist Prophet.* Cambridge: Harvard University Press, 1916. xi+160 pages.

2469. **Aston, W. G.** *Shinto (The Way of the Gods).* London: Longmans, 1905. 390 pages.

2470. **Cary, O.** *A History of Christianity in Japan: Protestant Missions.* New York: Revell, 1909. 367 pages.

2471. **Clark, C. A.** *The Korean Church and the Nevius Methods.* New York: Revell, 1930. 278 pages.

2472. **Coates, H. H., and Ishizuka, R.** *Honen the Buddhist Saint.* Tokyo: Kyo Bun Kwan, 1925. 955 pages. (Important for a knowledge of the Jodo sect, in contrast to orthodox Buddhism.)

2473. **Drake, H. B.** *Korea of the Japanese.* London: Lane, 1930. 226 pages.

2474. **Fisher, G. M.** *Creative Forces in Japan.* New York: Missionary Education Movement, 1923. 248 pages.

2475. **Fisher, J. E.** *Democracy and Mission Education in Korea.* New York: Teachers College, Columbia University, 1928. xiv+187 pages.

2476. **Harada, T.** *The Faith of Japan.* New York: Macmillan, 1914. ix+190 pages.

2477. **Holtom, D. C.** *The Political Philosophy of Modern Shinto.* Tokyo: Z. P. Maruya, 1922. 325 pages. (*Transactions of the Asiatic Society of Japan,* Vol. XLIX, Part II.)

2478. ———. *The Japanese Enthronement Ceremonies: With an Account of the Imperial Regalia.* Tokyo: Kyo Bun Kwan, 1928. x+146 pages.

2479. ———. "A New Interpretation of Japanese Mythology and Its Bearing on the Ancestral Theory of Shinto," and "The State Cult of Modern Japan," *JR* (Item 150), VI (1926), 58–77, and VII (1927), 419–46.

2480. *Japan Mission Year Book, 1930.* Tokyo: Kyo Bun Kwan, 1930. ix+391 pages. (Twenty-eighth issue; formerly *The*

Christian Movement in Japan and Formosa; first issued in 1903.)

2481. **Kato, G.** *A Study of Shinto: The Religion of the Japanese Nation.* Tokyo: Meiji Japan Society, 1926. ix+255 pages.

2482. *Korea Missions Year Book.* Seoul: Christian Literature Society, 1928. 9+x+239 pages. (First issue; formerly included in the yearbook for Japan.)

2483. **Moody, C. N.** *The Saints of Formosa: Life and Worship in a Chinese Church.* Edinburgh: Oliphant, 1912. 251 pages.

2484. **Murao, M. S., and Walton, W. H. M.** *Japan and Christ.* London: Church Missionary Society, 1928. viii+184 pages.

2485. **Paik, L. G.** *History of Christian Missions in Korea.* New York: Stechert, 1929. ix+438 pages.

2486. **Ryang, J. S.** (editor). *Southern Methodism in Korea.* Seoul: Methodist Episcopal Church (South) Board of Missions, 1930. 186+lxviii+302 pages.

2487. **Stauffer, M.** (editor). *Japan Speaks for Herself.* New York: Student Volunteer Movement, 1927. xviii+149 pages.

2488. **Tsuchida, K.** *Contemporary Thought of Japan and China.* London: Williams & Norgate, 1927. 240 pages.

ISLANDS OF THE PACIFIC (SEE ITEM 2301)

PHILIPPINES (SEE ITEM 2338)

2489. **Hibbard, D. S.** *Making a Nation: The Changing Philippines.* New York: Board of Foreign Missions of the Presbyterian Church in the United States, 1926. 128 pages. (Surveys progress since 1898.)

2490. **Higdon, E. K.** "The Nationalist Spirit in the Philippines in Relation to Protestant Christianity," *IRM* (Item 2230), XVIII (1929), 208–15.

2491. **Laubach, F. C.** *The People of the Philippines: Their Religious Progress and Preparation for Spiritual Leadership in the Far East.* New York: Doran, 1925. 515 pages.

AUSTRALIA

2492. *The Australian Encyclopedia.* Edited by A. W. Joel and H. J. Carter. 2 vols. Sydney: Angus & Robertson, 1925. (Several articles on individual churches.)

2493. *The Australian Methodist Missionary Review.* Sydney: Methodist Church of Australia, 1891–1908. (Since 1914 called *Australian Board of Missions Review.*)

2494. **Cameron, J., and Walker, J.** *History of the Presbyterian Church in New South Wales.* 2 vols. Sydney: Angus & Robertson, 1905.

2495. **Carruthers, J. E.** *Lights in the Southern Sky.* London: Epworth Press, 1924. 160 pages. (Australian Methodist biography.) Also *Memoirs of an Australian Ministry, 1868–1921.* Same publisher, 1922. 339 pages.

2496. **Colwell, J.** *The Illustrated History of Methodism. Australia, 1812–1855. New South Wales and Polynesia, 1856–1902.* Sydney: Brooks, 1904. 669 pages.

2497. **Giles, R. A.** *The Constitutional History of the Australian Church.* London: Sheffington, 1929. 320 pages. (Anglican church; contains Bibliography.)

2498. **Goodman, G.** *The Church in Victoria during the Episcopate of Charles Perry (1847–72).* London: Seeley, Service, 1892. xxiv+476 pages. (Has opening chapter on early history.)

2499. **Gribble, E. R.** *Forty Years with the Aborigines.* Sydney: Angus & Robertson, 1930. 228 pages. (Anglican missions.)

2500. **Heaton, J. H.** *The Australian Dictionary of Dates and Men of the Time, 1542–1879.* Sydney: Robertson, 1879. 317 pages.

2501. **The Islander.** Sydney: Gordon, 1912——. (Presbyterian periodical.)

2502. *Morpeth Review.* Sydney: St. Johns College Press, 1928——. (Anglican church.)

New Zealand

2503. **Creighton, Louise.** *G. A. Selwyn, D.D., Bishop of New Zealand and Lichfield.* London: Longmans, 1923. xi+180 pages.

2504. **Dickson, J.** *History of the Presbyterian Church in New Zealand.* Dunedin, 1899.

2505. *Grace, Thomas S.: Being Letters and Journals of a Pioneer Missionary among the Maoris, 1850–79.* Edited by S. J. Brittan and A. V. Grose. Palmerston North: Bennett, 1928.

2506. **Harrop, A. J.** *England in New Zealand.* London: Methuen, 1926. xxiv+326 pages.

2507. **Jacobs, H.** *New Zealand.* ("Colonial Church Histories Series.") London: Society for Promoting Christian Knowledge, 1880.

Other Regions

2508. **Brown, J. M.** *Peoples and Problems of the Pacific.* 2 vols. London: Fisher Unwin, 1927.

2509. **Dixon, R. B.** *Oceanic Mythology.* (Vol. IX of Item 2369.)

2510. **Emerson, O. P.** *Pioneer Days in Hawaii.* Garden City, New York: Doubleday, 1928. xiv+257 pages. (Missionary work of J. S. Emerson.)

2511. **Evans, I. H. N.** *Studies in Religion, Folk Lore, and Custom in British North Borneo and the Malay Peninsula.* Cambridge: University Press, 1923. x+300 pages.

2512. **Young, W. A.** *Christianity and Civilization in the South Pacific.* London: Oxford University Press, 1922. 135 pages.

INDEX

NOTE.—Numbers refer to marginal items, not to pages.